Non-Governmental Human Rights Organizations in
International Relations

Non-Governmental Human Rights Organizations in International Relations

Peter R. Baehr
Honorary Professor of Human Rights, Utrecht University, The Netherlands

First published 2009 by
PALGRAVE MACMILLAN

Palgrave Macmillan in the UK is an imprint of Macmillan Publishers Limited, registered in England, company number 785998, of Houndmills, Basingstoke, Hampshire RG21 6XS.

Palgrave Macmillan in the US is a division of St Martin's Press LLC, 175 Fifth Avenue, New York, NY 10010.

Palgrave Macmillan is the global academic imprint of the above companies and has companies and representatives throughout the world.

Palgrave® and Macmillan® are registered trademarks in the United States, the United Kingdom, Europe and other countries.

ISBN-13: 978–0–230–20134–7 hardback
ISBN-10: 0–230–20134–2   hardback

This book is printed on paper suitable for recycling and made from fully managed and sustained forest sources. Logging, pulping and manufacturing processes are expected to conform to the environmental regulations of the country of origin.

A catalogue record for this book is available from the British Library.

A catalogue record for this book is available from the Library of Congress.

10   9   8   7   6   5   4   3   2   1
18 17 16 15 14 13 12 11 10 09

Printed and bound in Great Britain by
CPI Antony Rowe, Chippenham and Eastbourne

Contents

Preface

Non-governmental organizations play a crucial role in the struggle for the promotion and protection of human rights in the world. That is a basic assumption on which this book is based. The main reason why this book was written is to shed light on their place and activities in international relations.

The book is a reflection of some 40 years of experience with non-governmental organizations working in the field of human rights (HRNGOs). It is based on (1) personal experience as a member of the boards of Amnesty International (1987–1991) and Article XIX (1994–2000), (2) extensive reading on many other HRNGOs, and (3) some recent interviews with practitioners in the field. Some of the material covered in the book is taken from earlier publications as indicated. It is limited to those NGOs that are active in the international field. The reason for not extending this study to domestic NGOs is purely a matter of personal knowledge and expertise.

The period that is covered runs roughly from about 1970 to the present. The examples given in the book are all taken from that period. Because of my personal experience the role of one major human rights organization, Amnesty International, may be somewhat over-emphasized at the expense of other HRNGOs. This does not mean that everything Amnesty does or wants is free from criticism. I have tried to be as objective as possible with Amnesty as with other HRNGOs.

The sources listed are in English and Dutch, the literature I happen to be most familiar with.

I am extremely grateful to the following persons who generously made their time available: Kees Bleichrodt, Ineke Boerefijn, Reed Brody, Cees Flinterman, Lilian Gonçalves, Thomas Hammarberg, Farah Karimi, Gerd Leipold, Eduard Nazarski, Dick Oosting, Hilde Reiding, Bart Stapert and Dirk Steen. Special thanks go to my trusted friend and long-time colleague Leon Gordenker, who read and commented on the entire manuscript. Needless to say that full responsibility for all faults and mistakes rests with the author.

The text of the manuscript was concluded in November 2008.

Peter R. Baehr
Heemstede, the Netherlands, November 2008

List of Abbreviations

AI	Amnesty International
CAT	Convention for the Abolition of Torture and Other Cruel, Inhuman or Degrading Treatment or Punishment
CEDAW	Committee on the Elimination of Discrimination Against Women
CIA	Central Intelligence Agency
CSW	Committee on the Status of Women
DCI	Defence for Children International
ECHR	European Convention for the Protection of Human Rights and Fundamental Freedoms
ECOSOC	Economic and Social Council
ELN	National Liberation Army (of Colombia)
ESC	Economic, Social and Cultural (Rights)
ETA	Euskadi Te Askatasuna
FARC	Revolutionary Armed Forces of Colombia
FARDC	Armed Forces of the Democratic Republic of the Congo
FDLR	Forces for the Liberation of Rwanda
FEDEFAM	Federation of Relatives of Disappeared Persons
FIAN	FoodFirst International and Action Network
GONGO	Government Organized Non-Governmental Organization
HRDN	Human Rights and Democracy Network
HRNGO	Human Rights Non-Governmental Organization
HRW	Human Rights Watch
ICC	International Criminal Court
ICJ	International Commission of Jurists
ICRC	International Committee of the Red Cross
ICTJ	International Center for Transitional Justice
IFI	International Financial Institution
IGO	Intergovernmental Organization
ILGA	International Lesbian and Gay Association
ISAF	International Security Assistance Force (in Afghanistan)
IWRAW	International Women's Rights Action Watch
MNC	Multinational Corporation

NATO	North Atlantic Treaty Organization
NGE	Non-Governmental Entity
NGO	Non-Governmental Organization
NIOD	Netherlands Institute for War Documentation
NJCM	Nederlands Juristen Comité voor de Mensenrechten
NLC	NGO Liaison Committee
ODA	Official Development Assistance
OEF	Operation Enduring Freedom (in Afghanistan)
OSCE	Organization for Security and Cooperation in Europe
TFG	Transitional Federal Government (of Somalia)
UN	United Nations
UNDP	United Nations Development Programme
UNHCR	United Nations High Commissioner for Refugees
UPR	Universal Periodic Review
WTO	World Trade Organization

1
Introduction

It is now more than 60 years ago that, on 10 December 1948, the Universal Declaration of Human Rights was adopted by the General Assembly of the United Nations. It was and is still generally considered the basic document listing the major international standards of human rights. Much has happened since then. All states in the world pay at least lip service to these standards – although many of them also violate them in their daily practice. Human rights have become a regular item of international relations.

What are human rights? They are international standards governing the ways in which governments should treat their own citizens – and non-citizens as well. Governments must not order or permit torture. They must allow freedom of expression and freedom of religion. They must not put people to death without due process of law. They must provide food and clothing and the necessary health services. These civil and political as well as economic, social and cultural rights are contained in the aforementioned Universal Declaration of Human Rights and in the manifold international treaties, covenants and conventions that have followed it both at the global and at the sub-global, regional level.

Much has been achieved. A great many of such binding conventions exist.[1] The human rights glass would seem to be half full. Or is it half empty? Since 1948, in all parts of the world many of these very same standards have been violated. Violations in the Soviet Union, in the People's Republic of China, Apartheid in South Africa, killings in Cambodia (1975–1979), genocide in Rwanda (1991–1994), "ethnic cleansings" in the former Yugoslavia, "disappearances" in Argentina, in Chile, in Guatemala, Sierra Leone, West Darfur in Sudan – the list is nearly endless. How do we know?

We know all of this thanks to accounts in the news media, reports of organs of the United Nations (UN) and regional international bodies and, last but certainly not least, reports by non-governmental human rights organizations – the subject of this book.

Non-governmental organizations, or NGOs as they are commonly named, are a curious phenomenon. Their very title indicates what they are *not*. They are not governments. But what are they? No one definition is generally accepted.[2] Attempts – in the framework of the United Nations – to define the concept on the basis of a catalogue (aims, members, structure, officers, finance, autonomy, activities) or minimum criteria of "transnationality" have failed in light of the diversity of bodies.[3] Anybody can sit down behind a personal computer to devise a letterhead with the title "Organization for the Promotion and Protection of All Human Rights" (to give a general example) or "Society for the Promotion and Protection of the Right to Sleep until 10 o'clock in the Morning" (to give a more specific and perhaps somewhat unlikely example). Such a title is not open to legal challenge, unless somebody had happened to think of the same before. That is the general rule.

For more specific purposes criteria may be devised. For example, many countries require some kind of registration before a newly established NGO can go into actual operation. Such registration procedures may be used by a government to restrict the activities of NGOs that it considers unwelcome, as we will see in Chapter 2. Also at the intergovernmental level similar criteria may exist. In 1996, the Economic and Social Council of the United Nations adopted new "Arrangements for Consultation with Non-Governmental Organizations".[4] One of the principles to be applied to establishing consultative status for an NGO is that the organization should have "a representative structure and possess appropriate mechanisms of accountability to its members, who shall exercise effective control over its policies and actions through the exercise of voting rights or other appropriate democratic and transparent decision-making processes."[5] Criteria for judging such representativeness have, however, not been spelled out. The notion of consultative status grows out of a basic constitutional power in the United Nations structure. It allows NGOs to "request that items be placed on the agenda of the relevant body, attend meetings, submit written statements, and make oral presentations in meetings."[6]

The Economic and Social Council (ECOSOC) is authorized by the Charter of the United Nations to make "suitable arrangements" for consultation with non-governmental organizations.[7] It has established a Committee on Non-Governmental Organizations (NGO-Committee) to make such arrangements and decide which organizations are granted consultative status with the United Nations. The number of organizations with such consultative status has steadily risen from 40 (in 1948) to 3052 (in 2007).[8] What the ECOSOC in fact did was to continue a practice that existed during the League of Nations that consulted on occasion with interested non-governmental organizations concerned with pertinent economic and social activities.[9]

Non-governmental human rights organizations – whether connected with the UN or not – exist in all sizes and shapes. They may run from a letterhead "organization" basically consisting of one individual with or without expert knowledge of the subject, to large organizations with thousands of members. The only matter these phenomena have in common is that they are, or claim to be, "non-governmental". The addition of "claim to be" is needed, to cover the so-called "GONGOs", "QUANGOs" and "DONGOs", which look like HRNGOs, but are not truly non-governmental.[10] It is not always easy to distinguish in practice these government-supported organizations from the real thing. The Panel of Eminent Persons on United Nations-Civil Society relations established by the UN Secretary-General in 2004 (the "Cardozo committee") has also warned against this phenomenon: "Not independent, these 'government sponsored NGOs' reflect their Government's position. The speaking opportunities they use in United Nations forums would be better used by others – in keeping with the original principle of accreditations."[11] Apparently, governments find it useful to hide some of their activities under the guise of being "non-governmental", presumably because that title adds to their credibility. Other NGOs are usually in the best position to tell whether any group, old or newly established, should be considered a true member of the club.

International NGOs dealing with the environment, economic development and human rights nowadays more and more tend to stress a certain commonality in their objectives. Their common aims find expression in terms such as striving for "hope", "equality", "justice" and "human dignity". On a certain level of abstraction, organizations such as Oxfam, Greenpeace and Amnesty International (AI) would seem to have a great deal in common.[12] The directors of some of these international NGOs meet twice a year to discuss common problems, for example in regard to management and their relations to governments. There may even come a time when it will be difficult to distinguish such organizations from each other. However, that time has not yet arrived. Therefore, this book deals only with organizations that specialize in human rights.

A useful definition was developed by the Canadian human rights expert Laurie Wiseberg: "...a private organization which devotes significant resources to the promotion and protection of human rights, which is independent of both governmental and political groups that seek direct political power, and which itself do not seek such power."[13] She thus clearly distinguishes NGOs from political parties that are also private associations but do seek to achieve political power. NGOs are, as Gordenker and Weiss have succinctly put it, "private in their form, but public in their purpose."[14] This definition covers HRNGOs of many different types and sizes, large and small, well endowed and poor, professional and less professional.[15]

A general definition of NGOs, not necessarily working in the field of human rights, proposed by the Secretary-General of the United Nations refers only to one particular group of NGOs:

> An NGO is a non-profit entity whose members are citizens or associations of citizens of one or more countries and whose activities are determined by the collective will of its members in response to the needs of the members or of one or more countries and whose activities are determined by the collective will of its members in response to the needs of the members or of one or more communities with which the NGO cooperates.[16]

This definition is restricted to *membership organizations*. While these are indeed important, not all relevant human rights NGOs belong to that category. The existence of organizations such as Human Rights Watch (HRW) in the United States and the International Commission of Jurists (IJV) in Geneva may remind us that certain human rights NGOs can be very important indeed, although they do not command a membership of their own. In other fields of activity, Greenpeace International and *Médecins sans Frontières* are examples of important NGOs that do not fully meet the Secretary-General's definition.

The non-profit aspect is clearly very important in the Secretary-General's definition. The NGOs that are the subject of this volume, pursue aims of a non-material nature. For these purposes, they do need financial means, which they generate through public fund-raising, membership fees, the sale of publications and occasionally support from government sources. Governmental assistance may, however, put the independence and impartiality of such NGOs into question. That is the reason why many NGOs, though definitely not all of them, refuse to accept such assistance. Refusal of government money is a way of showing to the outside world that a particular NGO is indeed independent, which may add to its credibility. It is not enough to *be* independent, the organization should also *be seen* as such.[17]

HRNGOs themselves need a modicum of human rights, such as freedom of expression and freedom of assembly to operate. The absence of independent human rights organizations in a country may be an indication that such human rights are insufficiently respected in that country.[18]

At the UN World Conference on Human Rights in 1993, differences of view arose between large, well-organized NGOs, usually based in Western countries, on the one hand, and relatively poor, less well-organized organizations often from "Southern" countries, on the other. The latter showed some irritation that the former assumed that they could speak on behalf of *all* NGOs. The claim of different "cultural" approaches, as well as different interests, does not seem to be limited to governments alone.[19] The difficulty of reaching a more or less permanent form of cooperation among HRNGOs may be partly caused by this lack of agreement. However, little study has been devoted so far to North-South tensions among HRNGOs. The human rights expert Makau Mutua has called attention to the fact that mainly Western NGOs worked for the adoption by the UN Commission on Human Rights of the Declaration on Human Rights Defenders: "There is a distinction between those who need norms and those who are able to lobby effectively for their formulation."[20] Yet, he also mentions that in the last decade human rights NGOs in the South have increasingly forced their concerns on the movement's agenda.[21]

Many NGOs carry an image of altruism, of working for the common good, while governments are often seen as consisting of self-serving politicians.[22] While this may be true of many human rights NGOs, it should be emphasized that there is a constant moving back and forth of personnel from NGOs to governmental service and *vice versa*. The same people may be dealing with the subject of human rights, from a different perspective at different times. Often former government employees may end up on the governing boards of HRNGOs after their retirement from government service.

HRNGOs have the advantage over governments of single-mindedness in their pursuit of human rights. Governments cannot afford to do so, as they have always other issues to pursue, such as the protection of national security, the economic well-being of their citizens and, more in general, the maintenance of friendly relations with other governments. Governments that claim to have only the pursuit of human rights at heart are either not doing their jobs properly or are not telling the truth. Moreover, HRNGOs are able to concentrate on universal and timeless values, while governments must always keep an eye on day-to-day events.[23] This may create the dangerous situation that HRNGOs become as it were holy cows that can do no wrong. They become too successful and too comfortable. That is the reason why they should always "review their methods and objectives to ensure that they are true to the spirit which inspired their original founders".[24]

The number of international non-governmental organisations (NGOs) has grown during the twentieth century from 1,083 in 1914 to more than 37,000 in 2000. Around one quarter of today's international NGOs were formed after 1990.[25] Yet, transnational advocacy networks have been active for over a hundred years. Keck and Sikkink mention:

- international pressures for the abolition of slavery in the United States (1833–65);
- the international movement for woman suffrage;
- the campaign against female circumcision in Kenya (1923–41);
- the campaign against foot-binding in China (1874–1911).[26]

According to Theo van Boven, a former director of the then UN Human Rights Centre, NGOs provided 85% of the information provided to the Centre. He has pointed out that the contributions of NGOs rest on two premises: their expertise and their representative character.[27]

One of their main functions is to remind governments of the international obligations these have voluntarily accepted.[28] They point out alleged violations of such obligations with the help of reliable information that they have gathered. This information is more important than the views and comments they express, as these are usually already widely known anyway. It is information that is trustworthy, eagerly sought by all concerned – governments, intergovernmental organizations, as well as other NGOs.

More than 300 organizations can be listed as international human rights organizations.[29] Some 63% of NGOs that operate across national borders are based in Western Europe and North America.[30] This refers to their permanent secretariats but also to their membership, if any. For example, more than 90% of the membership of Amnesty International is located in Western Europe and North America.[31] This creates the inevitable image of "Western organizations" supposedly serving "Western" interests. This image is stimulated and encouraged by governments in the Third World that are criticized by those very NGOs. The cited survey shows a difference between "Northern" (i.e. those based in industrialized countries) and "Southern" (from the Global South) NGOs: the latter are more likely to report than the former that they frequently work to promote the right to development and to promote social, economic, and cultural rights.[32] As was to be expected, the "Northern" NGOs have on the average a larger budget than the "Southern" NGOs.[33]

Given this background, the main objective of this book is to deal with, and find answers to, a number of questions that crop up regularly, both at the academic and the political level. These questions are the following:

- What are currently the *major debates*, both politically and academically, in the field of human rights? What is the *role* that HRNGOs play in those debates? To what extent does the existence of so-called "GONGOs" help or hinder the activities of HRNGOs? (Chapter 1)
- What is the *legitimacy* of HRNGOs? What do they base their actions on? To whom and in what way are they accountable? What is

their role in the growth of issues of globalization? Are HRNGOs closer to the *"grassroots"* of national societies than governments? If so, why? (Chapter 2)

- What is the *impact* of HRNGOs? Under what conditions do they realize their aims? Are membership organizations, using volunteer members, more or less effective than professional organizations, using mainly professional experts? How important are the notions of impartiality and independence? What is the relationship between "Northern" and "Southern" HRNGOs? What about the issue of "Asian values"? (Chapters 2 and 3)
- Is a conscious choice being made between actions using *public forums* or rather *"quiet diplomacy"*? (Chapter 3)
- Why do *governments and international organizations* pay attention at all to the activities of HRNGOs? Conditions for success or failure. To what extent is there an interchange of personnel between governments, international organizations and HRNGOs? (Chapters 3 and 4)
- What is the role of HRNGOs in international organizations such as the United Nations? Is there such a thing as an *international community* in which HRNGOs can operate? (Chapter 4)
- How do HRNGOs contribute to the development of *standard setting* in the field of human rights? (Chapter 5)
- What is the role of HRNGOs in the *promotion and protection of human rights*? (Chapter 6)
- How do HRNGOs deal with human rights violations by *other non-governmental entities?* (Chapter 7)
- What is likely to be *the future* of HRNGOs? Will they persist? (Chapter 8)

Lindblom has raised the question whether the international legal system will reach a point where NGOs have a general right to participate in international legal discourse. She suggests that, as of today, they have at least "a legitimate expectation".[34] Not only that. As I will try to demonstrate in the following chapters, they do not only *expect* to participate. They *do* participate at all levels, locally, domestically and internationally. In this book the focus will be on the international level.

2
Legitimacy

Introduction

Who do HRNGOs represent? On whose behalf do they speak? Are
they democratic?

Non-governmental organizations are often referred to as "grass
roots organizations" which suggests that they are closer to ordinary
people than, for instance, government officials. Otto has referred to
what has been coined the "third system": "(...) my interest is in
those non-state entities that are speaking for groups and individuals
who do not believe that states are adequately representing their
interests."[1] The extent to which that picture is correct, depends on
whether an NGO has a membership and how the structure of the
group is organized. Non-membership organizations such as Human
Rights Watch, the International Commission of Jurists and the
International Crisis Group, may on the whole be able to react
quicker and more flexibly in approaches to governments than membership organizations. Yet, the impact of a membership organization may be greater, because governments are aware that the
views expressed by such an NGO are not only those of a small group
of experts, but may also reflect those of a larger constituency. If the
membership is relatively large, as in the case of Amnesty International,[2] politicians may pay extra attention to the NGO's views.
Another advantage of membership organizations is that the leadership is accountable to the rank and file, which may exert some kind
of control over the actions of the leadership. Fowler has referred,
however, to the danger of "grass roots apathy" – NGOs that become

so much involved in participating in international and national debates that they lose sight of their goals of empowerment.[3]

The UN Economic and Social Council, in its 1996 session mentioned in Chapter 1, decided on new "Arrangements for Consultation with Non-Governmental Organizations".[4] One of the principles to be applied in establishing consultative relations with NGOs states that the organization should have "...a representative structure and possess appropriate mechanisms of accountability to its members, who shall exercise effective control over its policies and actions through the exercise of voting rights or other appropriate democratic and transparent decision-making processes."[5] Criteria for judging such representativeness were, however, not spelled out. Kamminga has reviewed the criteria that were adopted by the ECOSOC and rightly observes that the requirement of a democratic internal structure is "remarkable".[6]

Membership

The mere fact that an NGO has a membership does not necessarily mean that the group is democratically organized. They may put great effort into ensuring that members have a say in the direction of the policies adopted.[7] As Gordenker and Weiss have pointed out: "The nature of representation within nongovernmental organizations as well as within their coalitions, and by NGOs within international gatherings, is a source of some perplexity if not ambiguity for analysts."[8] The two authors suggest moreover that NGO leaders may push their own personal agendas rather than those of their constituents.[9] Internationally, the manner of organization of NGOs between "top down" and "bottom up" organizations differs. The former are centrally organized international groups with national sections, while the latter are federations of nationally organized groups. Both kinds may be democratically organized or less so.

The example of Amnesty International illustrates some of the problems that may arise when organizing an international membership NGO on a democratic basis. This organization comprises a worldwide voluntary membership, which consists of sections, structures, international networks, affiliated groups and international members.[10] The authority for the conduct of affairs is vested in the International Council that meets once every two years. Only representatives of national sections have the right to vote. All national sections hold at least one vote in the International Council. However, sections receive additional votes in proportion to the number of Amnesty groups or individual members they hold. Thus the larger sections, which also hold the purse strings within the organization, such as those of the United States, the United Kingdom, Sweden, France, Germany and the Netherlands, are entitled to additional representatives which may add up to as many as six votes per national delegation.[11] In the International Council, the Netherlands, for example, rates as a major power – a striking experience for those Amnesty representatives (like the present author) who are familiar with similar meetings at the governmental level in the UN General Assembly. Smaller sections have repeatedly but unsuccessfully tried to change this system of weighted voting into one on a "one-section-one-vote" basis. Whether the existing system should be seen as democratic is a matter of debate. A system whereby each national delegation is accorded one vote, as in the UN General Assembly, is not necessarily more democratic than a system of weighted voting. In the latter, the individual members or groups are more strongly represented. A side effect is that, within the Amnesty International Council, the larger as well as wealthier sections of the "North" can easily outvote the sections of the "South".

Only a relatively small percentage of the members of Amnesty International are active members. Rather most of them should be seen as (financial) supporters than as active members. That makes the democratic accountability of the organization even more questionable. Moreover, the mere fact that an NGO has members does not necessarily mean that it is a democratic organization. Witness the following rhetorical question: "When was the last time that Greenpeace gave its members the opportunity to pronounce themselves on the policy line of the organization?"[12]

As for effectiveness of a human rights NGO, membership may be a blessing and a curse. The blessing consists in the moral as well as material support that the membership can give. Members can write letters and offer material and moral support to victims of human rights violations. The leadership of the organization derives some of its legitimacy from the consciousness of having its members' support. On the other hand, that same membership will want to see results of the actions of the organization. That may affect both the possibility of using the technique of "quiet diplomacy" and of cooperating with other organizations, with the result that each of these organizations becomes more or less "invisible" to its own membership. "Quiet diplomacy" may sometimes be more effective than public actions, as it prevents the government in question from losing face. It may rather be persuaded to do something on behalf of victims of human rights violations, if such action is not *seen* as the result of NGO pressure. On the other hand, many HRNGOs' representatives lack the diplomatic *finesse* that is needed for quiet diplomacy. This leads to the conclusion that NGOs should do what they are good in: publicly expressing themselves on matters of their concern.

In discussing the desirability of "international participatory democracy" Otto has called for a form of accountability of NGOs to their constituencies in civil society.[13] She rightly points out that international NGOs need to evolve an infrastructure that would assist with such projects. She mentions as two key aims of NGO participatory strategies "...to build in protections against Western domination and to promote the strengthening of transnational identities."[14] However, she fails to acknowledge that the Western dominated NGOs may be among the more effective ones. Building protection against such Western domination may go at the expense of the very NGOs that work on behalf of the weak and downtrodden. It is also by no means an established fact that improving the democratic nature of membership organizations will be to the benefit of those on whose behalf the NGOs are working.

Bendell has reported that a study of 600 NGOs world-wide found that there was virtually no thought given to the issue of their own accountability:

> Their reasoning for this included efficiency, as accountability processes are seen as too expensive, as well as protestations that their power was nothing compared to governments and business, so their accountability was not a serious issue. (...) Thus, initiatives on accountability were viewed with suspicion, which is understandable given the questionable motivation of some lobbyists and government officials for regulating NGOs.[15]

The issue of whom precisely NGOs represent remains unsolved for the time being. In view of all of these difficulties, one may well come to the conclusion that the issues the NGOs take up are more important than their own democratic representativeness. But in the absence of more formal criteria for such representativeness, the claim of many of them of being grass roots movements raises substantial doubts.[16]

Accountability

When challenged by NGOs, governments often raise the question of whom the NGO represent. On whose behalf do they undertake their activities? To whom are they accountable?[17] To what extent are their own activities transparent? The answer is not always easy to give, as many of the NGOs do not necessarily have a democratic structure and do not represent more than their own membership. The Dutch human rights scholar Sophie van Bijsterveld has provided the following answer:

> NGOs present new points of view and attention *that they have defined themselves*. These are points of views and of attention which they consider to be not or not sufficiently being discussed. NGOs should therefore be considered in terms of representation: representation of values and interests, rather than representation of persons.[18]

Indeed, as Hugo Slim has put it: "NGOs and human rights organisations have a particular responsibility to lead by example in this area and shine as beacons of legitimacy and accountability.[19]

Writing in 2004, Jan Aart Scholte doubted the readiness of NGOs to face the problem of their own accountability: "Regrettably, most civil society groups have operated very limited and unimaginative accountability mechanisms in relation to their own activities."[20] However, in more recent years, some changes seem to have taken place. Many of the NGOs tend to discuss their accountability to what they call their "stakeholders". These include, next to the members of the NGOs, the victims of human rights violations, the donors of the NGOs, other human rights defenders as well as the general public as whole.

The major international NGOs have tried to tackle the question of their accountability. In June 2006, 11 NGOs, including Amnesty

International, Greenpeace International, Oxfam International and International Save the Children Alliance, adopted an International Non-Governmental Organizations Accountability Charter.[21] They held a press conference to declare "their adoption of the Charter, galvanize support around the issues of civil society legitimacy, accountability, and transparency; and invited other NGOs to undertake the same commitment in order to promote and garner support for the highest common standards of conduct for NGOs working transnationally."[22] The Charter stated that international NGOs "can complement but not replace the over-arching role and primary responsibility of governments to promote equitable human development and well-being, to uphold human rights and to protect ecosystems." The parties to the Charter "aim to be both politically and financially independent. Our governance, programmes and policies will be non-partisan, independent of specific governments, political parties and the business sector."[23] The NGOs do not reject financial support from some of the larger private foundations:

> [B]ringing in participants from small and/or Southern based INGO unable to pay their own costs have also been covered by small grants from various foundations (Ashoka, Bertelsmann, Hewlett, Ford) and by contributions in kind by larger participating organisations and organisers of the events. In March 2006, the Ford Foundation has approved a small two-year grant to CIVICUS: the World Alliance of Citizen Participation to serve as the Secretariat for the IANGO [i.e. International Advocacy Non-Governmental Organizations] Workshop and the INGO Accountability Charter. Beyond that period, Charter Founding Signatories aim to render the Accountability Charter a financially self-sustaining initiative.[24]

As most of these private foundations enjoy a tax-deductible status, these NGOs receive at least indirectly government support. However, this need not affect their independence.

Reliability

Providing reliable information (to governments, intergovernmental organizations, politicians, the news media, academics as well as the general public) is the most important precondition to be fulfilled by any NGO to have an impact. As Whitney Brown has noted: "One of Human Rights Watch's main goals is to promote changes which increase recognition and protection of human rights. Its main role for achieving these changes is *through reporting facts.*"[25] It is more important than the views and comments that are being expressed, as these are often already known anyway. Information that is trustworthy is eagerly sought by all concerned.[26] The information provided by some NGOs is sometimes unavailable through other means, which makes their input often indispensable to governments.[27]

An expert professional staff fills a clearly felt need in connection with the collection of reliable information. NGOs that command such a staff, can more easily provide such information than organizations that have to rely mostly on volunteers. They may possess the necessary expertise, but often lack a bureaucratic memory of the past. Volunteers come and go and, though mostly highly motivated, they may lack experience. Therefore, the existence of a professional staff, greatly adds to the information-gathering capacity of an NGO. Amnesty International, with a professional staff of more than 300 individuals in its International Secretariat in London, provides an example.

Reliability links closely to credibility. A government that is the target of well-founded information, will do its utmost to discredit the source organization by questioning its motives (e.g. "'political'"), its financial resources ("CIA-supported", "communist umbrella organization", etc.) and also its methods of work. In case such efforts are successful and the credibility of the organization's work has been successfully challenged, it may suffer for many years to come. An example outside the field of human rights is the environmental protection organization Greenpeace, whose credibility suffered from the information it provided on the dismantling of the oil platform "Brent Spar" in 1995, which was proved only partially correct.

"New" kinds of violations of human rights seem to emerge often. Before the 1970s, most people thought that torture lay buried in the past. Human rights organizations have brought out that torture is used in this day and age. The phenomenon of involuntary disappearances was also brought to light by NGOs. In the 1990s, the world was confronted with "ethnic cleansing", a term nobody had heard of before. The hearings before the Yugoslavia Tribunal in The

Hague provide almost daily new material of what harm human beings can do to each other. Reports about the Democratic Republic of the Congo and the province of West Darfur in Sudan provide us with new material of human atrocities. Moreover, NGOs can provide new insights or new perspectives that create public interest for what are in reality ancient problems.

Human rights organizations understand the crucial importance of maintaining high standards of reliability. But even in the most truthful organization mistakes do occur. As soon as such a mistake is discovered, the organization will usually go on record of having been mistaken and present the correct information. An example was the Amnesty International report of December 1990 on Occupied Kuwait which said that more than 300 premature babies were reported to have died after Iraqi soldiers removed them from incubators, which were then looted. The report quoted an unnamed Red Crescent doctor stating that 312 babies died in this way.[28] This story, which shocked many people all over the world at the time, later appeared to be based on false information. The daughter of the Kuwaiti ambassador to the United States was found to be the source of the report. Amnesty International had by that time already distanced itself from the allegations, saying that it had "found no reliable evidence that Iraqi forces had caused the deaths of babies by removing them or ordering their removal from incubators."[29] This relatively isolated incident did not damage the overall reputation of the organization, but if such things happen more frequently, they may have grave negative repercussions for an organization.

Access

All NGOs need access to governments under their observation. This means that an NGO should be able to approach government officials to make them aware of its views. "Access" may mean one of many things. It may mean that the organization can call an official on the telephone to make him or her aware of new information that may then be put to him/her in written form. It may mean having the ability to engage the official in a formal or informal conversation with representatives of the NGO, in order to raise the matter at the ministerial or cabinet level or at intergovernmental meetings. The degree of such access may differ according to the role human rights play on the domestic political scene of the country in question. In politically open societies, such as the Netherlands or Norway, access is easier and more effective than in China or in Indonesia, where it may not exist at all.

In certain countries, former NGO executives hold positions in national governments and NGO representatives are routinely included in official delegations to sessions of the General Assembly of the United Nations and special conferences. For instance, two NGO members were part of the Turkish Government's delegation to the Beijing + 10 meeting, "where they felt that their presence made a difference."[30] Antonio Donini, then himself a sometime senior officer in the Executive Office of the UN Secretary-General, considers this development "a welcome feature".[31] And so it is, if seen from the perspective of gaining maximum access.

Access, however, may lead to undesired repercussions. Maximum access may be gained at the expense of risking one's independence. When, for example, the Netherlands Government invited two NGO members to participate in its official delegation to the Vienna World Conference on Human Rights, these two persons were given maximum access. At the same time, they were expected to share some of the workload with the other members of the delegation, such as writing the daily reports to the ministry in The Hague, which for all practical purposes was hard for them to refuse. Yet, an outside observer may wonder whether when doing this they were not in danger of losing their independent position and becoming more or less "ordinary" members of the delegation.[32]

Australia provides another vivid example. There, members of parliament, including members of the government, participate in an informal group "Parliamentarians for Amnesty International". Without questioning the motives and good intentions of these individuals, one may wonder about the wisdom of this practice.[33] The distinction between what is the government and what is an NGO may thus be blurred. Yet, that distinction remains important, because the government can only seldom go as far as an NGO in embracing human rights. It has by definition other concerns to consider. Therefore, there should always remain a clear distinction between what is government and what is not.[34] If an NGO succeeds in penetrating into the innermost chambers of governmental deliberations, it may end up by having to share some of the government's political responsibilities as well. However, CEDAW-member Cees Flinterman has pointed out: "In the end you work for the same matter: from different responsibilities you work for a further strengthening of the human rights of women."[35]

Herman Burgers, who has served in a senior position within the Dutch Ministry of Foreign Affairs and after his retirement became a member of the governing board of the Dutch section of Amnesty International, relates the activities of an official of the Ministry *who at the same time* worked on behalf of Amnesty International: "In this setting it is remarkable to note that no one seems to object to civil servants, in the capacity of members and chairman of an Amnesty International Committee, criticizing the policy of their own ministry. Dutch NGO's indeed play a peculiar role."[36] In fact, the ministry may be less troubled by such mixing of responsibilities than the NGO that would seem to benefit from the arrangement.

Reiding has observed that there often was an exchange of personnel between Dutch officials involved in policy-making in the field of human rights law and Dutch human rights NGOs. One of the leading persons in the Dutch Amnesty International's lobby for a system of universal jurisdiction was employed by the Ministry a few years later, while the Netherlands representative to the Working Group negotiating the UN Committee against Torture later became a member of the board of the Dutch section of Amnesty International. According to her, there was "no absolute mental distance between governmental and non-governmental organisations."[37]

In another case, in the Netherlands, the chairman (i.e. the present author), of the Advisory Committee on Human Rights and Foreign Policy, which was an advisory body to the Minister of Foreign Affairs, was elected member of the International Executive Committee of Amnesty International, which is the international governing board of that organization. With the approval of the Foreign Ministry, he expected to combine the two positions for a while, but his prospective colleagues in Amnesty International thought otherwise. They themselves did not question the independence of the Advisory Committee but felt that it would be difficult to explain to people in other parts of the world that a person who (1) was appointed by the head of state to (2) a body whose reports were published by the Ministry of Foreign Affairs and (3) whose executive secretary had his office within the Ministry, could be expected to be independent.

Amnesty officials felt that the position of chairman of such an advisory committee might endanger Amnesty's reputation of impartiality.[38]

Some governments make a considerable effort to maintain periodic contacts with NGOs in the field of human rights. For example, the Canadian Ministry of Foreign Affairs until 2005 annually organized a two-day consultation with NGOs. These sessions preceded the principal meetings of the UN Commission on Human Rights. The meetings which included as many as 60 to 80 participants, were addressed by the Foreign Minister or his deputy. This "forum" was useful – especially for those NGOs that were already engaged in the Geneva human rights system – though it has also been described as "a dialogue of the deaf".[39] This procedure provided the NGOs with at least access to the responsible ministry officials, although it did of course not guarantee them that their views would be adopted. NGO representatives sometimes tend to forget that access is a necessary but not a sufficient condition for success.[40] When the Human Rights Commission was replaced by the Human Rights Council, that meets at least three times a year, the Canadian meetings were dissolved.[41]

Of a more incidental nature were the meetings that the Irish Foreign Ministry organized with NGO representatives in the course of a major policy review which took place in 1995. A series of seven public seminars dealing with various aspects of Ireland's foreign policy were held in universities around the country between November 1994 and March 1995. The topic of human rights was one of seven that were covered.[42] Participation in the seminars, which were advertised in the national press, was open to all. Attendance at each of the seminars numbered between 200 and 250 persons. The seminars brought members of the public, representatives of NGOs, public representatives and members of the diplomatic corps into direct dialogue with ministers and civil servants on issues of foreign policy. The meetings were termed by the Foreign Ministry as "a useful and stimulating innovation".[43]

Kerstin Martens, writing about Amnesty International, has made the point that it is often not the entire government or all diplomats of a delegation interacting with AI, but rather an individual delegation member who is having a good relation with a single AI representative.[44]

Gordenker and Weiss have called attention to a less formalized, though perhaps even more effective channel of access, either direct or indirect, which consists of prominent persons, who thanks to their expertise, experience, office or other distinguishing characteristic earn respect or deference.[45] Examples that come to mind are former US President Jimmy Carter, the late Eleanor Roosevelt, the late Willy Brandt, Norwegian Prime Minister Gro Harlem Brundlandt and former Dutch Foreign Minister Peter Kooijmans.[46] No less important than knowledge and expertise may be the personal acquaintances such persons have. As a Dutch saying goes: *"Kennis is macht, maar kennissen geven nog meer macht."*[47]

Access then to the government is of great importance to NGOs. Impact requires access, although it provides no guarantee for success. Too easy access entails risks for NGOs. They may be hedged in by the government and its permanent officials, thus running the risk of being seen by the public as an extension of the government. Seen from the government's perspective, there is little to be lost and much to be gained by such close relations, especially if the NGOs are reliable. It is rather the NGOs that have to maintain a certain degree of caution in these relations.

Cooperation among NGOs

Cooperation among NGOs can be crucial for their impact. Yet, NGOs are also notorious for their wish for independence. Coordinating NGOs is, according to one UN official, "like herding cats".[48] This, it may be added by way of comment, is of course equally true of governments. Amnesty International used to have a reputation of standing for its independence and unwillingness to associate itself with other HRNGOs for fear of endangering its cherished mandate. It was therefore seen by other NGOs as somewhat aloof if not arrogant. This has changed in recent years and Amnesty can be seen as often joining coalitions of HRNGOs for common purposes.

NGOs are well aware of the need to work together to realize common aims. Ritchie has mentioned a great number of examples of successful cooperation between NGOs coalitions and UN agencies: "NGO coalitions are perhaps increasingly essential partners in the advocacy roles that are needed to ensure that governments make decisions in the global political interest and carry out the obligations that result from international conferences and conventions."[49] Two examples of successful coalition building are the International Campaign to Ban

Landmines[50] and the Coalition for the International Criminal Court.[51] Kamminga comments that it would be unlikely that the two treaties would have enjoyed the impact and the large number of ratifications without the continuing support of their respective NGO coalitions.[52]

At the European level there is the "Human Rights and Democracy Network"(HRDN). According to its website,[53] its vision is that ...

> human rights and democracy are placed at the heart of the European Union's internal and external policy agenda. This vision should manifest itself in a European Union that effectively protects human rights at home and is a force for positive change in the world. In pursuit of this vision, the network aims to influence EU and member state human rights policies and the programming of their funding instruments to promote democracy, human rights and sustainable peace.[54]

The network has now 38 members.[55]

In the Cardozo report the importance of NGO aggregation is clearly brought out:

> However well-resourced the United Nations becomes for engaging with civil society, it should resist hand-picking civil society organization actors, especially for deliberative processes. It is clearly in the interest of the United Nations to have fewer, more compelling and more professional presentations by non-State actors in its forums. This indicates the need for effective civil society networks. The United Nations should not organize them or press them to speak with a single voice. But it can define categories of relevant actors, such as the major groups concept used by the Commission for Sustainable Development. The United Nations should therefore *offer incentives for aggregation, without requiring it.* This could be done by publicizing and rewarding good practices, particularly with extra speaking time.[56]

There thus exists considerable pressure, both from the outside and the inside, on HRNGOs to coordinate their efforts. From the outside, in intergovernmental meetings, certain governments try to limit the number of NGO interventions using the argument that it is too time consuming to have to listen to the statements of so many NGOs that basically all have the same message to convey. These same governments have, however, no qualms about similar endless interventions by diplomatic delegates, exercising their "right of reply", etc. Writing as a friendly critic, Gaer has observed that the NGOs should show more self-discipline by grouping their statements.[57]

In principle, the NGOs themselves also see the need for closer cooperation and coordination of their activities in order to mobilize scarce resources and avoid duplication of efforts. However, the diverse nature of the various NGOs with regard to aims to be achieved, their size, financial resources and cultural background, makes it extremely difficult to bring about such cooperation. For example, Amnesty International and Human Rights Watch – whatever their public relations officers may say – continue to see each other as at best friendly competitors, quite eager to steal a march on each other. However, at the level of the researchers there are long-term relationships between quite a few AI and HRW staff.[58]

Moreover, as Hudock has pointed out, the competition for scarce financial resources militates against the formation of networks or coalitions.[59] Writing about the field of international development and referring to the need for "organizational survival", she sees the competition for funds as a zero sum game: whatever one NGO gets, another will not receive. Furthermore, the larger, well-organized NGOs in "the North" have better access, know the correct ways – if not through personal acquaintance – to approach the wealthy foundations most of which are also located in "the North".[60]

Paradoxically, international conferences organized by governments to discuss pressing international problems serve as a catalyst for bringing together non-governmental organizations. Recent examples are the world conferences on environment and development (Rio de Janeiro 1992), human rights (Vienna 1993), population and development (Cairo 1994), women's issues (Beijing 1995) housing problems (Istanbul 1996), and racism (Durban 2001), all of which saw the phenomenon of "parallel" conferences of NGOs.[61] These NGOs might never have met, if not the occasion of the governmental meetings had brought them together. Ritchie even claims that the success of the intergovernmental meeting itself depends to a great extent on the activities of the NGOs: "World conferences and summits need the full-scale input and presence of NGOs and their coalitions to have any hope of achieving their goals."[62]

The United Nations World Conference on Human Rights in 1993 in Vienna witnessed an impressive gathering of more than 1500 NGOs, whose meetings "downstairs" in the Austria Centre were far more colourful and more informative than the somewhat dull meetings of government representatives "upstairs".[63] Prior to the World Conference, from 10 to 12 June, human rights NGOs met in order to discuss the accomplishments and shortcomings of the UN human rights programme and to formulate common recommendations to be considered by the governments at the official conference. The NGO Forum was addressed by a number of well-known keynote speakers.[64] Many of the organizations represented in Vienna, such as representatives of Kurdish, Palestinian, Basque, *Sendero Luminoso* and other armed opposition groups, all of whom clearly aim for political power, were not *human rights* NGOs in the sense of Wiseberg's definition quoted in Chapter 1. That was also true of the representatives of the Christian Democratic and Liberal International, both of whom have close ties with political parties of the same name. Clearly, not very strict rules for admission had been applied. In view of the diverse nature of the various NGOs attending the conference, it is hardly surprising that "... clashes ensued between the new, national NGOs and traditional international NGOs."[65]

According to Gaer, NGO ideas and priorities were well represented on two central questions – universality of human rights and the establishment of a High Commissioner for Human Rights: "NGO presence and proposals heavily influenced the outcome."[66] On both issues, she seems, however, somewhat to overstate her case. It is true that NGOs "... expressed impatience with arguments about particularities advanced by the very governments committing atrocious abuses." But it goes too far to claim that "... [u]ltimately, the NGOs succeeded in conveying the validity and importance of their message when the World Conference on Human Rights itself reaffirmed universality."[67] The text of the Final Declaration of the Vienna Conference reads on this point as follows:

> All human rights are universal, indivisible and interdependent and interrelated. The international community must treat human rights globally in a fair and equal manner, on the same footing,

and with the same emphasis. *While the significance of national and regional particularities and various historical, cultural and religious backgrounds must be borne in mind,* it is the duty of States, regardless of their political, economic and cultural systems, to promote and protect all human rights and fundamental freedoms.[68]

That text falls short of the kind of full victory by NGOs claimed by Gaer.

On the issue of the High Commissioner for Human Rights, Gaer acknowledges that his mandate "… is less specific and less activist than the proposals of NGOs or supportive governments."[69] This conclusion is confirmed, if one compares the original proposal of Amnesty International with the resolution that finally emerged from the UN General Assembly.[70] On the other hand, it can be deemed a success, if looked at from the perspective that finally an idea that had lain more or less dormant since 1947 was now adopted against all odds under the prodding of NGOs, Amnesty International in particular. To an outsider, it is not quite clear how and why the World Conference in the final end decided to adopt the proposal to urge the General Assembly to consider the establishment of a High Commissioner. On this point, Gaer limits herself to the observation that … [h]ard and often creative negotiating was needed."[71] Clapham has noted that the final result at the World Conference rested on a compromise, which refers to the negotiations about the final text, but he does not make clear why the considerable group of opponents, especially among Asian governments, in the end permitted to have the idea as such to be accepted.[72]

After the Vienna Conference, cooperation among HRNGOs was expected henceforth to be coordinated by an NGO Liaison Committee (NLC), which was elected on the last day of the NGO Forum.[73] Although the NLC was to have a permanent character, this did not work out. The committee was formally disbanded in 1995. The reason was that the regional networks – in Asia, Africa and Latin-America – asserted that it was more important to work at the regional level than to try and work internationally.[74]

Both from the outside and the inside considerable pressure is exerted on HRNGOs to coordinate their efforts. NGOs should show more self-discipline by grouping their statements.[75] The Principles for Consultation with Non-Governmental Organizations, adopted by the ECOSOC, contain a similar suggestion: "Where there exist a number of organizations with similar objectives, interests and basic views in a given field, they may, for the purposes of consultation with the Council, form a joint committee or other body authorized to carry on such consultation for the group as a whole."[76]

In principle, the NGOs themselves also see the need for closer cooperation and coordination of their activities, in order to mobilize scarce resources and avoid duplication of efforts. However, in view of the diverse nature of the various NGOs, with regard to aims to be achieved, their size, financial resources, and cultural background, it has so far proved extremely difficult to bring about such cooperation. The independent *International Service for Human Rights*, a shoestring operation in Geneva, is doing its best to supply information – e.g. on procedures at the UN, schedules of meetings, nature of the issues under discussion, etc. – to all human rights organizations. This type of effort clearly deserves to be expanded. As soon as the provision of facilities in conference centres and the right to take the floor at intergovernmental gatherings, let alone the provision of financial aid, are at stake, NGOs ostensibly working for similar aims, may become fierce competitors. In this respect, they resemble competing governments who also are reluctant to give up their sovereign rights for the sake of mutual cooperation. One thing is clear, however: it should be left to the NGOs themselves, to find the proper channels for cooperation. It is NGOs that should find the ways to organize their own international cooperation.

Conclusions

In this chapter emphasis has been put on the role of international human rights NGOs. It must be noted that, in addition there are other important roles for NGOs such as awareness raising through human rights education, standard setting, extension of supervisory mechanisms and the necessary follow-up. Human rights NGOs play a role of some significance in international relations. That in itself remains a remarkable feat that calls for explanation. They criticize governments for violating human rights or for allowing or condoning such acts. Why should national governments pay attention at all to what HRNGOs have to say? The NGOs have no power; they rely on a relatively limited membership, if at all. They pose no economic or military threat. Yet, they are given the floor at meetings of intergovernmental organizations and at international conferences. Their representatives are received in national capitals and their views are paid at least lip service to. Governments even go as far as setting up or sponsoring fake NGOs to counter the activities of the real ones. Why? The only answer to this question,[77] which is the same that is offered by the NGOs themselves, is the often cited "mobilization of shame". This refers to the circumstance that all governments like to be known as civilized and as observing the international human rights standards that they themselves have helped to devise. No government will easily admit that it allows violations of those standards to take place. Yet, most governments in the world at some time or other violate them. This discrepancy between norm and practice creates the space in which HRNGOs can operate. Starting from the point of agreement as to how governments ought to behave, they draw attention to violations of these standards. Basically, governments have two ways of reacting to such allegations: admittance or denial. In view of their above-cited adherence to international human rights standards, admittance of violations of such standards logically means that something will be done about it. In such cases, one can say that the NGOs' activities are successful.

Many human rights NGOs are criticized for their lack of transparency and accountability. Whom do they represent? The view expressed in this volume is that the quality of the information that they generate is of far greater importance than their accountability. Yet, in view of the expressed criticisms, the formulation of the Accountability Charter may be of some help. The question remains of course whether that Charter is mainly of a symbolic character, having little importance for the actual behaviour of NGO representatives.

If, as often happens, the government in question denies the allegation, the reputation of the NGO for reliability is at stake. In the absence of other elements of power, reliability is the only source of strength HRNGOs can dispose of. By continuous truthful reporting an organization can build up a reputation of reliability, which must be jealously guarded. It can be threatened from two sides. First, of course by an offending government which may try either to discredit the HRNGO by questioning its motives or methods of work and by disseminating disinformation. But there is also a danger from the opposite direction. Political opponents of the government in question may try to use HRNGOs for purposes of their own by feeding the HRNGO with news about alleged atrocities on the part of the government that may actually never have taken place.

Conditions for reliable reporting are a well-trained professional staff, access to information and of course the necessary financial resources. The latter are needed for paying the staff, building up a database, financing on-site inspections and to pay for the publications of the organization.

Reliability is a precondition, but not a guarantee of success. That depends also on the degree of access to government officials and the help of the media. As has been pointed out in this chapter, access to government officials is tremendously important to HRNGOs, yet should not be gained at the risk of losing independence. Access is a two way process. It allows HRNGOs to put their views to government officials, but these officials in turn will also use the opportunity to try to influence the NGOs. There is admittedly a thin line between having access and guarding the independent position of an NGO, in order to show that it is not working to advance a particular government's interests. By their nature, NGOs can afford to be more single minded in pressing human rights issues than governments. A government has other matters of concern as well. That is why it is to be recommended that there always should remain some distance between the two.

Again, access alone is no guarantee for success, either. A HRNGO that commands a membership, can use that membership for various purposes, such as letter-writing to cabinet ministers, government officials and members of parliament of its own or of foreign countries. The membership – if sufficiently large – may also serve as an electoral threat. It comes close to what may be seen as an element of public opinion in the field of human rights. However that may be, the issue of representativeness of HRNGOs remains in the end an unsolved matter. There is no way of setting rules in this regard. In the end, it is left to the HRNGOs themselves to decide on their own representativeness.

Coordination at least, and mutual cooperation if possible, are helpful for HRNGOs. They may decide to channel their efforts and thus be more effective. Yet, such coordination and cooperation must not be the result only of government prodding. Governments may find NGOs troublesome and try to limit their activities by calling for "restraint" and "self-discipline", however reluctant they may be to display such restraint and self-discipline themselves. NGOs should opt for coordination and cooperation only if they find that helpful to carry out their activities. Such cooperation may be found in the realm of exchange of information and pooling of efforts. On the other hand, the existence of some form of healthy competition among NGOs is not necessarily a bad thing. It may actually be helpful to the cause of human rights and to the plight of victims of human rights violations.

All of the factors discussed in this chapter contribute to the effectiveness of HRNGOs. All of them are necessary, yet none of them on its own will be sufficient. In the end it all depends on the "conscience of mankind" that was mentioned in the Universal Declaration of Human Rights. The mobilization of this conscience – in addition to shaming governments into respecting human rights – remains the only and most effective weapon of non-governmental organizations working in the field of human rights.

3
Independence

Introduction

Independence is an important precondition for NGOs to have any form of impact – independence that is of governments. That provides them with greater room for criticizing governments that allegedly violate human rights. Naturally, most governments do not appreciate such activities. They will try to question the independence of such NGOs. During the Cold War, the Soviet Union tried, for example, to discredit Amnesty International that had questioned the lack of human rights such as freedom of expression and freedom of religion in the USSR. It suggested that Amnesty was financed from "unknown sources", such as the CIA.[1] The Shah of Iran, who had also been the subject of criticisms by Amnesty, suggested at one time that the organization was a Zionist as well as communist organization, financed by the CIA![2]

For their part, governments that have been criticized by NGOs, will try to discredit the veracity of such statements. Thus the Soviet Union used to accuse Amnesty International of being financed by imperialist secret services; it alleged that members of the staff and the board of Amnesty maintained contacts with British and American intelligence services and that it was partisan in its anti-Soviet reports. The Chinese government has made similar allegations against Amnesty International and Asia Watch, calling their reports on rights abuses biased and politically motivated.[3] Such accusations are not limited to the (former) communist world. During the regional meeting for Asia in preparation of the World Conference on Human Rights, in April 1993, former Thai Foreign Minister Thanat Khoman criticized self-appointed private sources and their accusations of violations as made for "selfish political or economic gain"; he said that private organizations that arrogate to themselves the right to denounce violations, should themselves be investigated. Later, outside the conference he said that he had only been referring to Amnesty International and Asia Watch as biased for not reporting on human rights violations in Western countries. He accused Amnesty of drawing from Western governments and having links with the CIA.[4] Many of the countries of the Global South question the legitimacy of the actions and credibility of the information submitted by NGOs that are not from their respective countries or region.[5]

Some governments exert pressure to have the consultative status of the more critical NGOs with the ECOSOC suspended. Examples include successful complaints brought by the United States against the International Lesbian and Gay Organisation (1994), by Sudan against Christian Solidarity International (1999) and by Cuba against the International Council for the Associations for Peace in the Continents (2000). In 2003, ECOSOC suspended the consultative status of Reporters Without Borders, because members of that organization had protested against the election by the Commission of Human Rights of a Libyan representative to be its chairperson. In 2004, the Indian movement Tupal Amaru had its consultative status suspended for having staged an anti-American demonstration at a session of the Commission on Human Rights.[6]

The UN Committee on NGOs has been criticized for conferring consultative status upon too many organizations, thereby endangering a substantive collaboration between the UN and NGOs in very practical terms. On the other hand, it was accused of too often rejecting organizations that deal with human rights under the pretext of "misbehaviour", thereby muzzling critical voices at the UN.[7] On this point expert opinions would seem to differ. Peter Willetts, who is an acknowledged expert on NGO activities, has strongly rejected the suggestion by NGO activists that significant numbers of NGOs are rejected for political reasons.[8]

In many states, NGOs must register, before they can begin their operations. Such registration may be of a purely technical character, but it can also be used by the authorities to prevent activities by NGOs that they consider undesirable. Kamminga has made the point that the recognition process by which an NGO can acquire legal personality is often called "registration": "Registration (...) is a powerful "tool by which states may prevent the operation of NGOs of which they disapprove."[9]

In January 2006, Russian President Vladimir Putin signed amendments to the Russian law on associations that significantly tightened registration requirements for international NGOs. The authorities received wide-ranging powers to close the offices of any foreign NGO implementing a project that did not have the aim of "defending the constitutional system, morals, public health, rights and lawful interests of other people, guaranteeing the defence capacity and security of the state". The amendments were later withdrawn and subjected to further consideration by the Russian Government. However, in early 2008, Human Rights Watch issued a report charging the Russian Government with using new rules to hinder the work of NGOs. Its executive director was denied a visa to travel to Moscow.[10]

Financial independence

One way of showing its independence is to decline government funding. Finance is the most sensitive question.[11] Certain organizations draw legitimacy from their refusal to take money from political or corporate bodies. Many of the larger NGOs pay considerable attention to the issue of financial transparency, have their annual reports and accounts audited by certified accountants, and make records of sizable donations publicly available.[12]

Organizations with many (relatively wealthy) individual members, such as Amnesty International, can afford to refuse virtually all kinds of governmental support. This may raise other questions, as most of its members happen to be citizens of Western countries, but it at least avoids the suspicion that it receives financial as well as political directives from governments. For example, another human rights NGO, the International Commission of Jurists, began as an organization sponsored and financed by the CIA: "The ICJ did not begin as a citizen-initiated transnational movement that challenged state sovereignty. The United States created the lawyers' organization to counter subversion of Western European democracies and to help destabilize communist states behind the Iran Curtain."[13] Only later it evolved into a truly, politically as well financially independent NGO.

Smaller NGOs may not be able to survive without some kind of governmental support. For example, the London-based organization for freedom of expression, Article XIX, does accept government money, but only from "nice" governments such as the Netherlands, Norway, Denmark and Sweden that are not expected to try to influence its work or its choice of operations. The International Center for Transitional Justice (ICTJ) lists no less than 23 governmental agencies among its supporters.[14] Among these is the office of the European Commission in Bogotà, Colombia. This means that the European Commission has earmarked certain funds for activities by the ICTJ in Colombia, thus in a subtle but unmistaken way influencing its freedom of policy making, the more so as the ICTJ undoubtedly must report to the European Commission on the successes and failures of its activities in Colombia.

Hopgood relates that Amnesty's founder Peter Benenson had at one point arranged British government's funding for Amnesty's work in Rhodesia, beyond the knowledge of the International Executive Committee, Amnesty's governing body.[15]

A government may seek to determine the nature of the projects that are undertaken, which may also affect the attitude of the NGO in question to it. The old saying "who pays the piper, calls the tune" has not lost any of its significance. Some governments respond to criticism by claiming that the NGO involved lacks independence and supports the interests of another state. Moreover, the image of the NGO in question may be damaged in the public's eye. It is not enough *to be* independent; the organization should also *be seen* as independent (or "impartial", the term used by Amnesty International).[16]

Scholte has rightly warned against the risks NGOs run in financial dependency: "Indeed, eagerness to obtain funds has led some civil society associations to compromise their autonomy. These co-opted organisations became voices – rather than watchdogs over – official agencies, political parties and powerful individuals in global governance."[17]

When Thomas Hammarberg resigned as secretary-general of Amnesty International in 1986, he gave a moving "farewell address", that warned against any form of corruption:

> My final recommendation (...) is about the spirit inside the move-
> ment. We are growing, we are getting more money, we make many

more travels than before, we are more important than ever. This is fine. But let us not be carried away by that, and let's not be corrupted by it. Corruption is not a big nasty beast, sleeping outside the air-lock here. Something that you can easily identify and you could protect yourself against—keep outside. Corruption is invisible, corruption is creepy, corruption is very contagious. It often starts with friendship relationships but it spreads very easily. Money of course is one aspect but only one aspect. We work on money that people have given us on trust, those who give Amnesty International money, who finance our work, our salaries here, they give it because they believe that that very power is going to be the business of the release of prisoners. That means that we must maintain a moral here to be careful of money (...) But there are other things than money, I don't think we should go to unnecessary conferences and mingle too much with the false diplomatic world. I don't think that we should allow ourselves to begin to personalize our work, because we are only representatives. We should stay amateurs, that's what it is about.[18]

What Hammarberg clearly had in mind was to throw up a dam against over-professionalization and to return to what Hopgood calls the "keepers of the flame": "They are the guardians of the Amnesty ethos, found in its purest form in researchers at the I[nternational] S[ecretariat] but also in many parts of the membership of Amnesty sections worldwide, especially volunteers who coordinate work in sections on individual countries and who possess a deep attachment to those countries and a long-standing relationship with IS researchers."[19] That would mean to forgo certain funds and certain activities, as when Amnesty refused funds from the Ford Foundation because of its alleged links with the CIA.[20]

Some NGOs may, in certain phases of their existence, be very dependent on government subsidies. Hilde Reiding has noted that the organization Defence for Children International (DCI) received grants of between 25,000 and 50,000 Dutch guilders from the Dutch Ministry of Foreign Affairs:

The grant was crucial during the attempt to launch the organisation; not only was DCI's founder [Nigel] Cantwell at the point of giving up, it also set a precedent for subsequent support from other governmental donors. Hence without this grant, DCI would probably not have been able to take a next step and to take the lead in the creation and functioning of the NGO Ad Hoc Group [that prepared a draft of the Children's' Convention].[21]

Another dilemma facing NGOs, particularly in the forum of the United Nations, is whether to maintain its principled attitude to the very end, with the risk of not achieving anything, or whether to accept a compromise, for example when working together with other NGOs; accepting too many compromises may bring an NGO too close to government(s), risking its independence. Furthermore, it may be more effective to resort to "quiet diplomacy" behind the screens, rather than opting for public campaigning. Helena Cook, a former legal adviser of Amnesty International, has asserted: "What is most important for Amnesty *is always to maintain its independence* and never to compromise its capacity to criticise and to insist on the highest standards of human rights protection at the UN."[22]

Even though the major international NGOs may not seek or accept governments' funds, their headquarters and membership, if any, are usually located in Western (or from the perspective of the Global South) Northern countries.[23] Such organizations engage mainly Northern, urban, elite, English-speaking civil society professionals.[24] That often raises suspicions among governments in the Global South that these NGOs represent mainly Northern (or Western) values – or they will claim that this is the case, when challenged on their human rights performance. Amnesty International receives 91% of its income from the eleven largest national sections, all located in Western countries.[25]

Human Rights NGOs also distribute aid to relatively poor countries from the global South, which gives rise to another source of tension.[26] On the one hand, NGOs need to set clear mandates and do their best to secure successful outcomes. On the other hand, human rights aid is most effective, if grantees play an important role in articulating and pursuing what they perceive to be the most pressing problems in their local communities.[27]

Only very few governments in the world – such as that of the Netherlands – are as a matter of principle – willing to help to support financially NGO campaigns that are critical towards the official government policy.[28] But even in the Netherlands, it led in 1973 to the forced resignation of the late Prince Claus, the Crown Princess' husband, as chairman of the National Commission for Development Strategy that used government development funding to support the actions of the Angola Committee, that were not fully in accordance with the government's policies.

Cultural relativism

A great deal of discussion took place during the 1990s about what was called "cultural relativism", the notion that universal human rights reflected mainly view held in Western countries, which supposedly differed from for instance "Asian values". The governments of countries such as China, Indonesia, Malaysia and Singapore were often cited as critics of the universality of human rights.[29] These debates culminated in the famous, often cited formula adopted at the 1993 World Conference on Human Rights: "All human rights are universal, indivisible and interdependent and interrelated. The significance of national and regional particularities and various historical, cultural and religious backgrounds must be borne in mind."[30] The precise meaning and significance of that formula has never been adequately clarified. The wording was no more than a diplomatic compromise.

At the level of non-governmental organizations, however, the universalism of human rights was "universally" accepted. The conference of Asian governments in Bangkok was preceded by a meeting of Asian non-governmental organizations (25–28 March 1993), That meeting resulted in a non-governmental Bangkok Declaration on Human Rights which left no doubt about the universal character of human rights:

> Universal human rights standards are rooted in many cultures. We affirm the basis of universality of human rights which afford protection to all of humanity. Including special groups such as women, children, minorities and indigenous peoples, workers, refugees and displaced persons, the disabled and the elderly. *While advocating cultural pluralism, those cultural practices which derogate from universally accepted human rights including women's rights, must not be tolerated.* **As human rights are of universal concern**

and are universal in value, the advocacy of human rights cannot be considered to be an encroachment upon national sovereignty.[31]

These NGOs did not hide behind a notion of cultural relativism, defending violations of international human rights standards with an appeal to alleged "other" culturally determined values. On the contrary, they demanded that where cultural practices deviate from international human rights standards, the latter ought to prevail.

Since then, more human rights NGOs have originated in the global South, especially in relation to women's human rights. One of the best known and most effective is the International Women's Rights Action Watch Asia Pacific (IWRAW). This organization emerged in 1993 as an autonomous organization in Malaysia, connecting national women's NGOs, in particular from developing countries, to the review process of state parties' reports to the CEDAW committee, by training them to provide shadow reports to the Committee and bringing them to the Committee's sessions. "It thus crucially aided women's empowerment as rights holders at the grass roots levels."[32]

The emergence of more human rights NGOs in the Global South will undoubtedly help to stress the universal character of human rights to the detriment of notions of "cultural relativism".

Supplying information to governments

"The primary purpose of consultations with NGOs is to enable governments to take advantage of the vast array of expertise that can be provided by these groups."[33] That was not always the case. A group of Dutch researchers has noted that until the end of the 1980s the use of NGO information by government delegates was considered controversial.[34]

Members of UN supervisory committees and "special procedures" make use of information supplied to them by NGOs for the purpose of the examination of state reports and the human rights situation in states. In the early years, the use of such "unofficial information" was frowned upon. For instance, especially Eastern European members of the UN Human Rights Committee opposed the use of such information.[35] Members of the Committee would surreptitiously glance at documents submitted to them by NGOs, hiding them under their desks. Nowadays, the use of this type of information is no longer subject to debate within the Committee.[36] Indeed, members of this as well as other UN expert committees eagerly look for NGO materials before a country examination, because it helps make their questioning more precise, factual and less abstract.[37] The thematic mechanisms of the UN rely almost exclusively upon NGO information.

A special feature of NGO participation in international conferences is, as Lindblom has observed, that some states appoint NGO experts to take part in or even form the governmental delegation.[38]

John Sankey has drawn attention to a serious threat to the impact of NGOs by what he has called "compassion fatigue": "NGOs will have to work even harder to explain what has already been achieved and how much more needs to be done to meet future challenges."[39] He concludes as follows:

> [T]he human rights NGOs have to be the conscience of the world, as one government will often be reluctant to make accusations against another because of political alliances, commercial interests or fear of the 'pot calling the kettle black'(...) NGOs have to be tough, resolute, well-briefed and adequately funded if they are to be able to pursue a particular cause or crusade through the labyrinthine procedures of the United Nations for so many years.[40]

Media attention

HRNGOs would be hard put to have any impact, if the media would not pay attention to their activities. The voluminous Yearbooks of Amnesty International and other human rights organizations may be reliable and trustworthy, but they are rarely read by government officials or the general public in their entirety. Their message is normally conveyed by accounts in the newspapers, radio and television. According to Nowak and Schwarz, NGO activities at the Vienna World Conference were given more space in the media than the official conference.[41]

The need for publicity may lead NGOs to what Ritchie has called "dramatic postures" for the sake of gaining publicity.[42] Such stunts may include pop music performances by well-known entertainers, television shows, on occasion sponsored by commercial firms, or imitations of human rights violations such as torture or isolated imprisonment. The limits of what is acceptable in this sphere and the ethics of accepting company money for such purposes are often hotly debated within the organizations.

There is always a danger that the message the human rights organization wants to convey may be lost in the glare of publicity, that, as it were, "the show takes over". For instance, many members of the audiences attending the pop concerts in a world tour by such artists as Bruce Springsteen, Peter Gabriel and Sting, in the "Human Rights Now!" event in 1988 may not have been aware that they were taking part in an *awareness event*.[43] The tour was underwritten by a commercial enterprise.[44] Internally, within Amnesty there was initially a great deal of discussion over the wisdom of having such an arrangement. In the event, the commercial enterprise was given a relatively low profile during the concerts, thanks to which fears that Amnesty might be associated with the selling of one particular brand of sports wear, did not materialize.

The "mobilization of shame" is greatly dependent on media exposure. Politicians in general and governments in particular are more likely to be persuaded to act on behalf of human rights, in the face of media attention or the threat of it. Even if HRNGOs make use of "quiet diplomacy", when approaching governments, for instance to bring about the release of a particular political prisoner or to end cases of torture, around the corner there is always the threat of media exposure. What remains in the last resort, is publicity in order to try to change a government's attitude and behaviour by public pressure. Chances of success are greater if the country concerned traditionally pays attention to expressions of public opinion, but there are no governments – ranging from full-fledged democracies to dictatorships – that can afford to ignore fully their public relations.

Timing

Timing is essential for impact. An action that comes too early may be as ineffective as one that comes too late. Therefore it is of crucial importance that an NGO is well-informed about the precise nature and the stages of the decision-making process, both as far as governmental and intergovernmental agencies are concerned. Agendas may be set or changed at the last moment. Informal consultations may take place that are crucial to the decision-making process. International meetings are always short of time, which may lead to last minute decisions. At international conferences, the preparatory process may be as important as, or even more important than the actual conference itself, which may last only for one or two weeks.[45] The late Johan Kaufmann, an experienced Dutch diplomat, has given a vivid account of the time problem at such international meetings:

> A one week conference is in fact a five day conference, or at most six days. There is bound to be irritation when at the end of the fourth day it becomes clear that the conference is hopelessly short of time. A conference scheduled to last for a fairly long period, say three or four weeks, suffers from a phenomenon that might be called 'conference myopia': attention is focused on the immediately following days; the weeks beyond appear far off and plenty of time seems to be available to deal with the agenda. Suddenly the last week has arrived, time is running out and tempers get correspondingly short. Like students preparing for an examination, delegates must make careful use of the time available to prepare for the moment of truth, the last days of the conference when the principal decisions must be taken.[46]

Representatives of HRNGOs must be always well aware of such factors and be prepared to strike when the iron is hot.

National governments may also be engaged in the manipulation of time. Faced with a dilemma-type of situation where all available choices have negative repercussions, a government may opt for postponing the decision, hoping for a change of circumstances. Gaining time may be akin to victory. The government may also suggest that nothing has been decided yet, leaving open when exactly a definitive decision will be taken.[47]

For the purpose of being well aware of the timing process, it is helpful to have permanent representations in national capitals and at the headquarters of intergovernmental organizations. Amnesty International, for example, maintains permanent missions at the

United Nations in New York and Geneva and with the European Union in Brussels.

Treaty-making

Seeking independence from governments may have far-reaching consequences. For instance, in treaty making, Helena Cook, a former legal adviser of Amnesty International, reports that as a matter of policy the organization refrains both from supporting specific draft texts and from putting forward its own drafts: "Instead, it concentrates on promoting and lobbying for the essential principles and issues that it considers ought to be included in the text. This enables it to maintain a certain distance from the process of governmental negotiation that is involved in reaching final agreement in a text, a process which often results in weakening compromises."[48]

Other human rights NGOs are not so strict in refusing to submit texts. In the case of the Convention of the Rights of the Child, numerous joint proposals were drafted by NGOs. By submitting detailed proposals to governmental delegations, they were able to exert considerable influence on the ongoing negotiating process.[49] A similar coalition of NGOs worked on drafting what was to become the Optional Protocol to the Convention on the Abolition of Torture. Kamminga observes: "It is no exaggeration to suggest that some of the most important legal instruments of recent years would not have seen the light without the input of NGOs. This role may range from a mere stimulating role to the participation in drafting exercises as full participants with the right to make proposals on an equal footing with States."[50]

Foreign policy

NGOs, unlike governments, can single-mindedly pursue their aims. Governments must always be prepared to accept compromises, either in their negotiations with other governments, or in their pursuit of other worthwhile policy goals.

In foreign policy practice, situations may be faced in which different policy objectives may not turn out to be compatible. Incompatible policy aims may demand a choice among alternatives. Having to make difficult choices and setting priorities is part of *all* policy-making, but even more so in the field of human rights than in other areas.

First, a human rights policy may impinge on the maintenance of friendly relations with foreign governments, especially if the foreign government in question is responsible for gross human rights violations. That will call for a response by those governments that emphasize human rights in their foreign policy. Their embassies will be instructed to report on the human rights situation, if necessary on the basis of some specific fact-finding, which may involve asking questions that will be perceived as unfriendly by the offending government. The latter may see this as endangering mutual friendly relations. Obviously, these relations will be perceived as even further endangered, if the questions are followed up by criticism, the more so if such criticism is publicly expressed.

In addition, a human rights policy often implies that a government deals with matters that other governments consider part and parcel of their domestic affairs. Criticism induces the defence of traditional sovereignty on the part of the suspected government. For many years, the government of the Republic of South Africa claimed that apartheid was a purely domestic matter with which on the basis of article 2, paragraph 7 of the Charter of the United Nations, the outside world, and the United Nations in particular, had no business.[51] Eventually, the Security Council acted on the basis that the situation in South Africa, if unchanged, might endanger international peace and security. South Africa is of course not the only state that has tried to hide its violations of human rights behind the domestic jurisdiction provision of the Charter.[52]

Governments prefer to keep their human rights violations secret, or, if such efforts are unsuccessful, claim that they are no business of outsiders, or of what is often grandly called the "international community".[53] That "international community" for its part, will appeal to the seriousness of the violations in question as the reason why they should be considered, disregarding the domestic jurisdiction argument. Resolutions of UN-bodies and other international organizations are often cited in support of this argument. Thus it is argued, for instance, that the right to life is of such a fundamental nature that it should be considered more important than national sovereignty. This can be seen as an important argument in support of interference by international organizations such as the United Nations.

Government, for their part, may interfere with the freedom of operation of NGOs. In Central Asia, the governments of Uzbekistan, Turkmenistan and Kazakhstan have moved to regulate NGOs for fear of their influence in political discourse.[54] The International Center for Not-for-Profit Law has been regularly reporting growing government interference with NGOs in the name of terrorism prevention.[55]

Anna-Karin Lindblom has interviewed a number of diplomats that were involved in the preparation of the Statute of the International Criminal Court in Rome, 1998.[56] She observes that the more NGOs kept to the kind of role that governments expected from them, the more they were welcome. If they "overstepped" that role, they risked not being welcome anymore. All state representatives agreed that whenever wide access was granted to NGOs, the "real" negotiations tended to move elsewhere. "[W]hen particular NGOs delivered very critical statements during or after the completion of difficult negotiations, this produced a bad atmosphere and a negative reaction towards NGOs among government delegations."[57] This situation creates a real dilemma for NGO representatives. While on the one hand they will want to make their points as they see them (which is also what their supporters expect from them), at the same time, in order to gain the maximum of effectiveness, they may be forced to accept compromises and to soften their tone, in order to retain the attention of the state representatives who are in the position to make the real decisions. Indeed, also for NGOs holds true what Edmund Burke once said about governments: "All government, indeed every human benefit and enjoyment, every virtue and every prudent act, is founded on compromise and barter."[58]

According to Lindblom's findings knowledge and expertise particularly gained NGOs a positive reputation among government representatives: "[I]t created a negative attitude towards NGOs when they were unrealistic and 'too critical' of governmental positions and compromises."[59] This finding does not make it any easier for NGOs to strike the "right" attitude. What will be quite realistic to them, may sound unrealistic to diplomats. Should one consider the Burmese human rights activist Aung San Su Kyi "unrealistic" when she keeps insisting on freedom of expression and freedom of assembly, which the Burmese military junta undoubtedly considers as "too critical" of its performance? Obviously not, if one wants to take human rights seriously, as she does. Moreover, the victims of human rights violations will appreciate such "unrealistic" demands, which as time goes by eventually may become "realistic". In other words, it calls for a rather sophisticated consideration of opportunities and possibilities to adopt an approach that will be the most effective to reach the result that is desired. Long-time personal experience will help NGO representatives to find that most effective approach.

Cases from recent Dutch foreign policy

A study of human rights in the foreign policy of the Netherlands had dealt with eight cases, covering the period of the 1980s and 1990s.[60] Pressure was exerted on the Dutch government by domestic groups that were concerned over the human rights situation in the countries in question. They provided information to members of parliament and to government officials as well to the news media, asking for action. This pressure was strongest in the case of apartheid in *South Africa*, over which two cabinets were close to being forced to resign.[61] The domestic groups urged the government to impose an oil embargo on South Africa, which it refused to do. The struggle against apartheid was relatively easy to understand, easy to explain to the general public and therefore also relatively easy to "score" on for the parliamentary and extra-parliamentary opposition: apartheid was plainly wrong and should be opposed by all available means.

Also in the case of *Chile*, the Dutch labour movement, which had close links with the defeated government of President Salvador Allende, pressured the Dutch government to castigate human rights violations by the military government of President Augusto Pinochet.[62] Predominant was the political will to react strongly to the gross human rights violations that occurred in the country, a policy that was generally supported by public opinion in the Netherlands.

While the human rights situation in *Argentina* was not much better than that in Chile, members of the Dutch parliament were remarkably unsuccessful in influencing foreign and trade policy with that country.[63] The Dutch government continued to stimulate and subsidize exports, including the export of arms to Argentina. This may reflect the fact that Dutch economic interests in Argentina exceeded those in Chile. This made the Dutch government more reluctant to insist on stressing the human rights concerns in Argentina. Also in the case of Chile, there were close ideological ties between President Allende and the Dutch Labour Party, which were non-existent in the case of Argentina. Furthermore, the Dutch government seems to have chosen to balance its strong insistence on human rights in Chile with a more reserved attitude in the Argentinean case. Another reason was the open character of repression in Chile as compared to the politically far more chaotic situation in the Argentina of Isabel Peron.

The domestic human rights organizations dealing with Argentina were also less well organized and less effective than their counterparts that dealt with Chile. This meant less pressure on members of parliament, who therefore seem to have been less motivated to insist on boycott actions against Argentina. In its absence, the Dutch government remained free to follow its own course.

In the case of *Turkey*, Amnesty International and other human rights organizations repeatedly asked the Netherlands government to have recourse to the "Vienna mechanism" of the Organization for Security and Cooperation in Europe (OSCE) – which it refused, however, to do.[64]

In the case of the *Soviet Union*, there was a great deal of activity both by NGOs and by members of parliament, especially with regard to the fate of individual dissidents as well on behalf of "refuseniks".[65] *Ad hoc* committees dealt with the cases of individual dissidents. Many of those committees had ties with similar organizations abroad with which they exchanged information. While the NGOs tried to generate as much publicity as possible, they had their greatest effect through the help of members of parliament.

Quite outspoken were the NGOs with reference to *Indonesia*, where strong ties existed with Indonesian NGOs at the local scene.[66] Dutch NGOs such as the Indonesia Committee, the Dutch sections of Amnesty International and the International Commission of Jurists (NJCM) continually bombarded members of parliament, the government, and the news media with new information about human rights violations in the country, urging them to do something about it. These actions did not meet with great enthusiasm on the part of the business circles that wanted to resume the former close economic ties between the two countries and who saw their plans for economic investments in Indonesia thwarted by the human rights situation and the actions that were related to it. This situation created a dilemma for the Dutch government which it found hard to resolve. On the one hand, in order to accommodate domestic human rights NGOs and out of genuine concern, it wanted to express its views about the human rights situation – preferably confidentially, but if necessary, in public. On the other hand, there were serious doubts whether raising the issue, especially by the former colonial ruler, would help to improve matters, while at the same time it clearly damaged the chances of improving bilateral economic relations.

In the case of *South Africa*, pressure by Dutch NGOs had little result.[67] Although the Dutch government continued to condemn apartheid verbally, it refused to give in to more drastic demands by NGOs, such as initiating an oil embargo or even breaking off trade relations with South Africa altogether. Such actions were considered as too great an interference in South Africa's domestic relations or as disproportionately hurting Dutch economic interests. Moreover, it was felt that if the Netherlands took such actions on its own, this would hardly be effective. Efforts to involve other Western governments in such drastic actions failed however.

Conclusions

Independence (or "impartiality" as Amnesty International prefers to call it) is an important source of strength for NGOs. This means that the NGOs should not receive instructions from governments, not receive any substantial financial support from governments and not work in close cooperation with government representatives. If the opposite is true, it will greatly damage an NGO's effectiveness. Independence from governments is a crucial element for the effectiveness of an NGO.

The nature of their independence may affect the consultative status of NGOs under ECOSOC rules. Governments that have come in for criticism by an NGO for their human rights record, may retaliate by objecting to awarding consultative status to that particular NGO or trying to remove such status. Individuals working for a government will always be seen as representatives of that government, no matter what their personal views or affiliations are. Thus when the delegate of Libya was a candidate to become chairperson of the UN Commission on Human Rights in 2003, this was a controversial matter, in view of Libya's dismal human rights record at the time.[68]

The requirement of formal registration may be a purely technical matter, but can also be used by a government to muzzle the voice of an independent NGO.

Financial independence is of great importance, certainly as far as the overall program activities of an NGO is concerned. Nevertheless, many NGOs are prepared to accept government support for particular projects, implying that this will not negatively affect their independence. However, accepting such funds may free funds for other projects, governments may in this way manage to direct an NGO's program of work. From the point of view of independence, refusal to accept any government funds would be the wisest policy. However, there are only few NGOs able or willing to follow such a "pure" course of action. The activities of the major human rights NGOs cost a great deal of money for travelling, maintaining a professional staff, and research work. The question always remains: how and where to obtain that money?

Major human rights NGOs risk the danger of "overprofessionalization". That may strengthen their position *vis-à-vis* governments but carries the risk of creating too great a distance with the rank and file. The grassroots may not feel comfortable with a highly sophisticated approach to human rights problems.

The fact that most human rights NGOs are located in Western countries does not mean that they only present "Western" views of human rights (though that accusation is often heard). The views will be based on universal standards, but presented by Western-based organizations. That detracts from the impact of the NGOs. It would be far better, if more human rights NGOs would be based in non-Western countries. Their views should be presented by non-Western individuals.

Little has to be added to what has already been said in this chapter about the importance of media attention. It is a crucial condition for impact by HRNGOs. Without media attention there is no impact. However, NGOs should be careful with pulling stunts just for the sake of media attention. Such stunts are counterproductive if they become an end in themselves. Yet, in the realm of the violation of human rights, always "new" things seem to occur. Before the 1970s, most people would have thought that torture was a matter of the past. HRNGOs made clear that it was not. Later, it was the matter of involuntary disappearances that was called attention to. In the

1990s, the world saw the phenomenon of "ethnic cleansing" which nobody had heard of before. The hearings before the International Criminal Tribunal on the Former Yugoslavia provide daily evidence of what human beings can do to each other. Reports on Rwanda, Burundi and other places in the world provide sufficient material to keep HRNGOs as well as the communication media occupied. Furthermore, by offering new insights or new perspectives, HRNGOs may draw renewed public attention to what are in fact old problems. Since the terrorist attacks of 9/11 (2001), many governments have taken strong anti-terrorist measures, often at the expense of basic human rights.[69]

Finally, HRNGOs must keep the time factor in mind. Information about the nature of the decision-making process is important to choose the right time for actions. Correct timing can be a decisive factor for achieving maximum impact. Experience with the way governments and intergovernmental agencies operate, can be helpful in this regard. Here, HRNGOs may help each other by exchanging information. Also, former or present government officials may be willing to share their experience and expertise in this field.

The fact that human rights NGOs can afford to be single minded in their pursuit of human rights is a source of strength as well as weakness. Its strength is that they only pay attention to human rights concerns and can put all their efforts in that direction. A weakness is that government representatives may be less impressed by their actions, as they do not fully understand the dilemmas these government representatives face. When expressing their foreign policy goals, these government representatives must be more cautious, as criticism of another government's human rights record will always mean interference in its domestic situation, affecting its national sovereignty. It will always be easier for NGOs than for other governments to speak out on human rights in a particular country.

4
The United Nations

Introduction

In June 2008, the UN Human Rights Council held the second round of its first Universal Periodic Review (UPR).[1] During that meeting NGOs were given the opportunity for an oral presentation lasting two (!) minutes. Several NGOs made use of that opportunity. For example, a Dutch organization, "Aims for Human Rights" spoke on behalf of a number of other Dutch NGOs to comment on the report of the Netherlands government. In November 2007, they had already submitted a rather critical written comment.[2] Although the UPR as such is a new phenomenon, the Human Rights Council continued a practice that had begun under its predecessor, the Commission on Human Rights, whereby NGOs were given the opportunity to attend its meetings and speak from the floor:

> [T]he participation of and consultation with observers, including (…) national human rights institutions, *as well as non-governmental organizations*, shall be based on arrangements including Economic and Social Council. Resolution 1996/31 (…) and practices observed by the Commission on Human Rights, while ensuring the most effective contribution of these entities.[3]

In its first year, 284 NGOs participated in Council sessions, slightly less than in the former Commission.[4] Such participation is not common practice in other UN organs, with the exception of the International Labour Organization with its tripartite setup.

This active participation by NGOs had seen years of preparation. Writing in 2004, Hill stated:

> At the political level, the UN has shifted from an organization in which only governments spoke to themselves, to one that now brings together the political power of governments, the economic power of the corporate sector, and the 'public opinion' power of civil society as principals in the global policy dialogue.[5]

Recent examples of this trend include the hearings of the General Assembly in June 2005 with NGOs, Civil Society and the Private Sector and increasing dialogue between the Security Council and NGOs, especially on the ground in conflict-affected countries.[6] Willetts has referred to an "opening up of the UN" that is welcomed by those who see it as an indication of the UN becoming more pluralistic and serving as an interlocutor between governments, business and NGOs.[7]

Nevertheless, from its very beginning, the United Nations has been involved in the debate on human rights. A principal purpose of the organization is to achieve international cooperation in promoting and encouraging respect for human rights and fundamental freedoms for all without distinction as to race, sex, language or religion.[8] The Charter, moreover, contains numerous other references to the notion of human rights.[9] The Universal Declaration of Human Rights, adopted by the General Assembly in 1948, lists the major standards of human rights. Together with the two legally binding international covenants adopted in 1966[10] and the two Optional Protocols to the International Covenant on Civil and Political Rights (1966 and 1989), it is commonly referred to as the "International Bill of Human Rights".[11]

In a cogently written article Herman Burgers makes clear that the strong language on human rights contained in the UN Charter had started after the First World War and was not so much due to the discovery of the Nazi atrocities after the Second World War, as has often been assumed.[12] He does, however, not dispute that the later efforts that brought about, among other things, the Universal Declaration of Human Rights, were to a great part motivated and strengthened by what had happened in Nazi Germany.[13] By then, the idea that "such matters should never happen again" had taken root. Writing in 2008, one is forced to acknowledge that this idea, as strongly as it may have motivated the fathers and mothers of the Universal Declaration, has by now become outdated. A world that has been confronted with genocide in Cambodia, mass killings in Somalia, ethnic cleansing in the former Yugoslavia, mass killings and collective rape in Sudan, knows that "such matters" have happened again and again – even though they differ in detail.

Such awareness has encouraged non-governmental organizations to continually press the cause of human rights; there are now more non-governmental human rights human rights organizations than ever before in history.[14] Many of their activities are directed at, or take place in, organs of the United Nations, as anticipated by the Charter.[15] These two phenomena, United Nations organs on the one hand and non-governmental organizations on the other, account for a major part of the efforts on behalf of the protection and promotion of human rights in the world. The rest of this chapter takes up these efforts.

The Vienna World Conference on Human Rights

At the 1993 World Conference on Human Rights, held in Vienna, Austria, more than 800 NGOs sent representatives.[16] Their common purpose was the use for the first time to put their views before so broad an international audience. For some of them that was simply enough, while many others wanted explicitly to have an impact on the results of the conference.[17]

No commonly accepted definition covers all the human rights groups that were represented in Vienna. Henry Steiner, reporting on a meeting of human rights activists held in 1989, has written "that self-perception and self-definition by NGOs constitute the only sensible method of identifying human rights organizations."[18] He adds: "An attempt at authoritative definition could block a natural and important growth of the human rights movement, such as its earlier evolution toward economic and social rights, or its present initiatives towards linking human rights concerns with developmental and environmental issues."[19] This conclusion which seems realistic and which would leave everything open has the important disadvantage that it leaves unclear what it means when intergovernmental organizations or conferences recognize the role of non-governmental organizations. The World Con-

ference on Human Rights included in its Final Document the following passage:

> The World Conference on Human Rights recognizes the impor-
> tant role of non-governmental organizations in the promotion
> of all human rights and in humanitarian activities at national,
> regional and international levels. The World Conference on Human
> Rights appreciates their contribution to increasing public aware-
> ness of human rights issues, to the conduct of education, training
> and research in this field, and to the promotion and protection of
> all human rights and fundamental freedoms. While recognizing
> that the primary responsibility for standard-setting lies with
> States, the Conference also appreciates the contribution of non-
> governmental organizations to this process. In this respect, the
> World Conference on Human Rights emphasizes the importance
> of continued dialogue and cooperation between Governments
> and non-governmental organizations. Non-governmental organ-
> izations and their members *genuinely involved in the field of human
> rights* should enjoy the rights and freedoms recognized in the
> Universal Declaration of Human Rights, and the protection of
> the national law. These rights and freedoms may not be exercised
> contrary to the purposes and principles of the United Nations.
> Non-governmental organizations should be free to carry out their
> human rights activities, without interference, *within the frame-
> work of national law* and the Universal Declaration of Human
> Rights.[20]

Although the quoted passage gives credit to the work of non-
governmental organizations, exactly what type of organization is
meant remains undefined. Moreover, the italicized words imply
some kind of qualification or restriction, but it is not clear which
organ should be charged with the interpretation of this clause. In
other words, the precise meaning of the entire passage remains very
vague, which most probably is what was intended. The statement
was after all drawn up by government representatives, and governments and non-governmental organizations – at least those of the
type within Wiseberg's definition mentioned in Chapter 1 – are normally at odds with each other. As Herman Burgers – who as a former
government official and later board member of the Dutch section of

Amnesty International, has been intimately familiar with both sides – has written, the relationship between ministries of foreign affairs and NGOs "is often coloured by mutual distrust".[21] He continues:

> Usually the NGOs are asking for more action than the government is prepared to take. (...) Government officials may regard NGOs as one-sided in insisting on human rights objectives without recognizing the government's wider responsibility. They may perceive some NGO appeals as an inconvenient interference with what they consider reasonable conduct of foreign policy. (...) As to the other side of the relationship, NGOs may suspect the government of not being sincere in its proclaimed human rights policy.[22]

Cooperation with governments and the UN

The inbuilt tension between governments and NGOs in the field of human rights does not preclude close cooperation. The Dutch Government, for instance, when working on the preparation of the International Convention against Torture in 1984, sent one of its top civil servants to the headquarters of Amnesty International in London when that organization expressed reservations with regard to the proposed draft-convention. This illustrates the importance some governments attach to the views of certain non-governmental organizations.[23] The Dutch government also used to send the annual reports of Amnesty International for comment to its diplomatic missions abroad.

In the end, NGOs derive their greatest impact from the degree to which they can provide reliable information about human rights situations that is not (yet) available to governments or inter-governmental organizations. The Human Rights Committee is almost totally dependent upon NGO briefings, documentation and advice.[24] The Committee on Economic, Social and Cultural Rights has listed standards for such information. The NGOs must base themselves on the International Covenant on Economic, Social and Cultural Rights; the information must be of direct relevance to the issues dealt with by the Committee; the information must be reliable and not be subject to abuse.[25] Helena Cook, a former legal adviser of Amnesty International, has warned against the danger of Amnesty's monopoly of information: "Several UN mechanisms would hardly have anything to work with if it were not for Amnesty's materials. *This degree of dependency is undesirable for all concerned* and Amnesty consistently attempts to inform other NGOs, particularly those without ready access to the UN, about the mechanisms, how they work and how to submit information to them in an effort to broaden and strengthen this vital information base."[26]

Theo van Boven, former head of what was then the UN Centre for Human Rights, has stressed his close relations with NGOs on which he relied for detailed information: "It was thanks to them, in fact, that we could carry on our work, because I have always claimed that 85 percent of our information came from NGOs. We did not have the resources or staff to collect information ourselves, so we were dependent. They did a lot of work which we should do at the UN."[27]

The "special procedures" of the Human Rights Council, i.e. the special rapporteurs and working groups, base their activities to a great part on information received from NGOs. By way of example, the Working Group on Enforced and Involuntary Disappearances has reported that its chairman met with NGOs from Asia, and with representatives of Amnesty International, Human Rights Watch and the International Commission of Jurists in order to "(...) discuss specific country situations and the work of the Working Group".[28] It also expressed its concern that "in some regions", non-governmental organizations were not present, or well-funded enough to be able to work effectively on disappearances.[29]

A lack of knowledge and expertise about the United Nations system and its procedures seems to be a common problem among many NGOs. Many NGO spokesmen are very knowledgeable about their own fields of special interest, but less so about UN procedures.[30] When the Convention on the Rights of the Child was drafted, an informal NGO Ad Hoc Group was created that brought together more than twenty NGOs, some of which had expertise on the rights of the child, while others were more generally active in the field of human rights. This Ad Hoc Group is generally believed to have had an important impact in the preparation of the Convention.[31]

Similarly in 1997, International Women's Rights Action Watch Asia Pacific initiated a program called "From Global to Local" to build the capacity of women's groups from countries reporting under the International Convention for the Elimination of Discrimination against

Women. It facilitates their presence during the review process in the Committee, allowing NGOs to observe the presentations, responses and commitments of their governments and enables them to provide alternative information to the Committee and raise pertinent issues not contained in the States Parties' reports; and it allows NGOs to make plans for monitoring State Party compliance with the recommendations of the Committee's concluding reports.[32]

The Cardozo Report

In his report on strengthening the United Nations, UN Secretary-General Kofi Annan devoted considerable attention to the role of non-governmental organizations, more than 2,000 of which held consultative status with the UN. In his report, he noted a number of difficulties that put considerable strain on the relationship between the UN and the NGOs. Therefore he had decided to appoint a panel of eminent persons to study the matter and put forward recommendations.[33] In 2003, the Secretary-General appointed a committee, under the chairmanship of Fernando Henrique Cardozo, a former President of Brazil, to review the relationship between the United Nations and civil society.

The Cardozo panel was asked to review existing guidelines, decisions and practices that affect civil society organizations' access to and participation in the United Nations system and in other international organizations with a view to identifying new and better ways to interact with non-governmental organizations and other civil society organizations; to identify ways of making it easier for civil society actors from developing countries to participate fully in United Nations activities; and to review how the Secretariat is organized to facilitate, manage and evaluate the relationships of the United Nations with civil society and to learn from experience gained in different parts of the system.[34]

The panel came out with a strong plea for a greater role of civil society organizations in the United Nations system: "[T]he panel believes that constructively engaging with civil society is a necessity for the United Nations, not an option."[35] It argued in favour of the United Nations becoming a more outward looking organization than it had been so far and to "connect the local with the global". It stressed the country level as the starting point for engagement in both the operational and deliberative processes. The Panel made 30 recommendations. Among these were the following:

- The United Nations should become a more outward-looking organization; member-states should signal their preparedness to engage other actors [i.e. NGOs] in deliberative processes.
- The United Nations should embrace an array of forums such as:
  - interactive high-level roundtables to survey the framework of issues;
  - global conferences to define norms and targets;
  - multi-stakeholder partnerships to put the new norms and targets into practice;
  - multi-stakeholder hearings to monitor compliance, review experience and revise strategies.
- The existing consultative and accreditation process of NGOs under the Economic and Social Council, which has met with a great deal of criticism,[36] should be replaced by a single overall procedure to be administered by the General Assembly.
- The UN Secretariat should conduct a thorough pre-screening of NGO applications for accreditation, on the basis of clear criteria determined by an intergovernmental body.
- The UN Secretariat should foster "multi-constituency processes" as new conduits for discussion of UN priorities, redirecting resources now used for single-constituency forums covering multiple issues.
- The General Assembly should permit "carefully planned participation" of actors besides central governments in its processes. The Assembly should regularly invite contributions to its committees and special sessions by NGOs.
- The members of the Security Council should strengthen their dialogue with civil society with the support of the Secretary-General, among others by improving the planning and effectiveness of the Arria formula.[37]

The Secretary-General reacted favourably to the Cardozo report: "Expanding and deepening the relationship with non-governmental organizations will further strengthen both the United Nations and the intergovernmental debates on issues of global importance. The Panel makes a compelling case for the United Nations to become a more outward-looking organization."[38] He endorsed most of the recommendations of the report.

The Secretary-General's report notwithstanding, states have been reluctant to adopt the Cardozo panel's recommendations.[39] Most of them tend to see NGOs, especially those dealing with human rights, as their natural adversaries. Governments resist providing such NGOs with a forum at the United Nations to express grievances and criticisms that may apply to themselves.

The Cardozo report stated that the existing mechanisms for accreditation were politicized, too time-consuming and expensive.[40] It proposed that the process should be technical rather than political and recommended speeding up the process and reducing political interference. These recommendations were, however, not followed up. No changes have been introduced into the system since the publication of the report: "Apparently, this was considered too hot a potato to touch."[41]

The Geneva Office

Through the years, human rights have acquired a place of increasing importance at the United Nations. The debates in the Human Rights Council and other UN-bodies have the character of strongly fought contests. Thus for many years the European Union in close cooperation with the United States and other Western governments tried to have the Council pass a resolution condemning human rights practices in China. The Chinese government has always successfully opposed this by introducing a "no action" resolution. Although resolutions carried at the Council do not involve sanctions, they are seen as moral condemnations ("naming and shaming"), which governments do not like.

For a long time, there has been an unwillingness on the part of the member-states to provide the UN with sufficient means to deal seriously with human rights. The Office of the High Commissioner for Human Rights was understaffed and underfinanced, but (former) High Commissioner for Human Rights Louise Arbour succeeded in almost doubling the human rights budget to $100 million.[42]

The location of that Office in Geneva, away from the central decision-making of the UN, is another case in point. In 1974 what was then called the 'Division of Human Rights' was transferred from New York to Geneva, because, as Theo van Boven has written, East European and Arab nations in particular wanted it away from the American Jewish lobby.[43] Another reason was that the Secretary-General wanted this division, "which for all political purposes was considered more of a liability than an asset," removed from the political centre.[44] Van Boven, has argued in favour of either moving the Centre back to New York or strengthening the status of the Centre's Liaison Office in New York.[45] He is right, if the Secretary-General and the member-states would be willing to give human rights the central point of political attention it deserves. It is, however, extremely unlikely that this is going to happen in the near future. The place given to the High Commissioner for Human Rights is a case in point. Her office is located in Geneva with a liaison office in New York. I shall return to the position of the High Commissioner below.

Non-governmental organizations and intergovernmental organizations such as the UN base their human rights activities on international human rights standards such as the Universal Declaration of Human Rights, the two international Covenants of 1966 and numerous other declarations and treaties. International functionaries in the field of human rights should ideally reflect in their actions and behaviour those very standards. Among these functionaries are the Secretary-General of the United Nations, the Chairman of the Human Rights Council, the Special Rapporteurs and Working Groups and, of course, the High Commissioner for Human Rights. Should they also publicly express criticism over human rights violations and mention the names of the countries concerned? Or should they rather, in the tradition of "quiet diplomacy", limit themselves to expressing their views in private? Secretary-General Peréz de Cuellár opted for the latter course, when he refused to renew the contract of the director of the UN human rights division, Theo van Boven, who had expressed himself critically about the human rights situation in a number of countries.[46] The issue received a great deal of attention in a book by the British journalist Iain Guest, which contains a running indictment of efforts on the part of Argentina to cover up serious human rights violations, including involuntary disappearances.[47] He shows how, for many years, a campaign was conducted to undermine Van Boven's position and he leaves no doubt that in his opinion the UN succumbed too easily to political pressure.

In such cases, effectiveness should be the major consideration. There is no reason to assume that silence on the part of UN functionaries always helps to promote human rights. UN personnel can pre-eminently represent the world's conscience, as codified in inter-national instruments. It should be a source of inspiration for human rights advocates and of hope to the victims.

High Commissioner for Human Rights: ideal and reality

The idea of the creation of a High Commissioner for Human Rights was launched in the United Nations more than forty years ago, in 1947.[48] In the early years it met with little positive response. In the 1960s came a new impetus, possibly due to the efforts of John Humphrey, the first director of the Division of Human Rights.[49] Despite the efforts of Costa Rica, Uruguay and other states, it was not adopted. That, it was widely assumed, was the end of the affair. As late as 1987 the Dutch human rights expert, Willem van Genugten, had good reason to name an article about the subject "the slow death of a good idea".[50]

Since then earlier opposition declined. In 1992, in the course of the preparations for the World Conference on Human Rights, the human rights organization Amnesty International re-introduced the idea of what it then called a Special Commissioner for Human Rights.[51] The mandate of that Special Commissioner should cover the full range of rights in the economic, social, cultural, civil and political spheres. His[52] task would be to maintain an overview of all the UN's human rights activities and their relationship to other pro-gramme areas; to take initiatives and coordinate UN action in response to human rights emergencies; to ensure that appropriate attention be given to human rights concerns in any country of the world; to develop programmes in areas which have been neglected or insufficiently developed; to formulate and oversee the human rights components of other UN operations; and to ensure the inte-gration of human rights issues and concerns in the full range of other UN activities and programmes. The new functionary should be given sufficient authority and responsibility to respond to human rights problems on his own initiative to ensure that the UN acts impartially and objectively in all human rights situations deserving of attention in any region of the world, based on his own inde-pendent appraisal rather than only on the specific authorization of a governmental body. He should be given the authority to spur governments to greater cooperation in tackling human rights concerns addressed to them by the UN. Finally, the Special Commissioner should be publicly accountable in all his activities. Amnesty International envisaged that the new functionary should be most appropriately based in New York "to ensure that human rights are taken seriously at the political level to secure his or her close involvement in high-level consultations and discussions on all issues with implications for human rights promotion and protection and to facilitate the liaison and coordination between the New York headquarters and the Geneva-based human rights bodies and mechanisms." If based in Geneva he should have a high-level representation in New York.

Amnesty's proposal received initially a mixed reaction. The first regional preparatory meeting for the World Conference in Tunis in November 1992, did not even mention the proposal in its Final Declaration.[53]

When the World Conference in Vienna began, many delegations were still very sceptical about the proposal, either because they were afraid that the new official would become too powerful, or because his function would be at the detriment of existing UN human rights organs such as the Centre for Human Rights and the Special Rapporteurs and Working Groups in the field of human rights. Thus – at least to outside observers – it came as somewhat of a surprise that the Final Declaration of the Vienna Conference did contain a reference to a High Commissioner: "The World Conference on Human Rights recommends to the General Assembly that when examining the report of the Conference at its forty-eighth session, it begins, as a matter of priority, consideration of the question of the establishment of a High Commissioner for Human Rights for the promotion and protection of all human rights."[54]

What Amnesty International clearly had in mind was the appointment of an official with the authority to initiate action, if need be urgently, in the field of human rights. The General Assembly opted for an official under the directorate of the Secretary-General with a far more limited mandate.

The "international community"

Manifold references presume that accountability for human rights violations rests with the "international community".[55] Is there such a thing? In his book *Power Politics,* first published in 1941, George Schwarzenberger, basing himself on the writings of the German sociologist Ferdinand Tönnies, introduced the distinction between "international society" that did, and the "international community" that, he argued, did not exist. In his words:

> The criterion by which a society can be distinguished from a community may be formulated in a variety of ways. While a society is the means to an end, a community is an end in itself. Whereas a society is based on interest and fear, a community requires self-sacrifice and love. In the words of Tönnies, the members of a society remain isolated in spite of their association, and those of a community are united in spite of their separate existence.[56]

Clearly, the world has not yet made that much progress, but is still, as in 1941, at the society stage. Nevertheless, politicians, diplomats and journalists alike are keen to suggest otherwise by employing the term "international community". For example, the United Nations Secretary-General's report on the massacre in the Bosnian enclave of Srebrenica in 1995, where some 7,000 Moslems were killed by Bosnian Serb forces, contains many references to this alleged international community, without ever defining the term concretely.[57] At one point the report even refers to the debate "within the international community *and* within the United Nations,[58] implying that the international community is something different from, or beyond, the United Nations.

Non-governmental organizations such as Human Rights Watch and Amnesty International too have referred in their reports about the conflict in the former Yugoslavia on many occasions to the activities or lack of activities of the "international community". Thus Human Rights Watch, in its report on Srebrenica, stated that "the international community has failed to fulfil its moral and legal duty to prevent genocide and to insist that those [who] commit acts of genocide (...) be brought to justice."[59] Amnesty International devoted even an entire report to "The International Community's Responsibility to Ensure Human Rights."[60] In October 1995, it presented a 10-point program for the international community to implement human rights in Bosnia and Herzegovina, which included: the international community should provide adequate, secure long term funding for human rights implementation; and the international community must resolve cases of "disappeared" and "missing" persons as a matter of urgency to bring those responsible to justice and determine the fate of those persons. However, neither Human Rights Watch nor Amnesty International ever made clear to whom exactly they were addressing their recommendations.

A report by the Netherlands Institute for War Documentation (NIOD) also referred in a number of places to the international community.[61] However, in its epilogue the authors of the Report show their awareness of the difficulties in using the term:

> The decision-making processes within what we sometimes rather presumptuously refer to as 'the international community' are, almost by definition, slow and faltering. The governments and international organizations concerned have a marked tendency to 'wait and see', postponing any actual decision as they carefully weigh up their own interests and determine their own positions. Intervention is therefore almost always reactive rather than proactive. Preventive action taken before major disruptions occur is largely unheard of.[62]

The term "international community", if not defined, is then a vague concept that is used for all kinds of objectives. For instance, the international community was supposed finally and decisively to defeat the Taliban in Afghanistan. In 1999, on behalf of the international community, Americans and British (as well as the Dutch), acting within the framework of the NATO alliance, intervened in Kosovo in order to defeat the oppressive regime of Slobodan Milosevič. This was done without authorization by the UN Security Council. And finally, in August 2008, "the international community" was supposedly unable to intervene in the conflict between the Russian Federation and Georgia (presumably neither of whom was as of that moment a member of that "international community"). The term begs to be banned from academic as well as political, discourse.

Conclusions

Human rights are very much the subject of activities of both intergovernmental and non-governmental organizations. The non-governmental organizations see it as their task to spur inter-governmental organizations, such as the United Nations, into action. Secretary-General Boutros-Ghali may have been overoptimistic when he mentioned the protection of individual human rights one of the "great practical and intellectual achievements of the international community". "The concept of an 'International Community' contains as much aspiration as reality."[63] Many governments still see these NGOs as troublesome interferers with their legitimate domestic affairs. Yet, they cannot afford to ignore them completely, among other reasons because of the force of domestic and world public opinion. Some governments even try to enter the fold of the non-governmental world themselves through the device of government-supported GONGOs.

Governments have on the whole different aims than non-governmental organizations. While the latter may concentrate all their efforts on the improvement of the respect of international human rights, the former have different interests to pursue as well. Such interests include the preservation of law and order, the continuation of its own regime, the protection of national and international security and the development of the national economy. There exists thus an inbuilt discrepancy between governments and non-governmental organizations. This discrepancy surfaces in the debates and decision-makings of the United Nations.

The proposal for a High Commissioner for Human Rights originated from a non-governmental organization. Although – against all odds – the proposal was eventually adopted by the General Assembly, the way it was dealt with and the contents of the final decision provide a vivid illustration of the gap between the two worlds in which human rights are debated: the governmental and the non-governmental one.

The history of the establishment of the High Commissioner for Human Rights illustrates that governments and non-governmental organizations have different interests to pursue. The High Commissioner, as originally conceived, is a potential threat to many governments. He may push human rights concerns more than is to their liking. Therefore it is in their interest to keep his powers at a minimum. The Secretary-General of the United Nations cannot and will not do more than whatever a majority of the member states will allow him to do. That is one of the reasons why human rights manifestly are not at the top of his political agenda.

The discrepancy does not rule out cooperation. Governments are often in need of the reliable information that is gathered by non-governmental organizations. Through their expertise non-governmental organizations may provide material that governments can use in their negotiations. The UN Human Rights Council and the Advisory Commission, where NGOs have access to the floor, provide a useful meeting place for the two. For their part, NGOs make use of their contacts with friendly governments and with functionaries of international organizations to push their areas of concern. They may submit draft texts for new international human rights treaties. They submit information to UN Special Rapporteurs or working groups, which may end up in the reports of these units. NGOs also make use of intergovernmental gatherings to meet among each other. The phenomenon of "parallel conferences of non-governmental organizations" such as have taken place at the international women's conferences is a useful spin-off of international governmental gatherings. Some of the more than 800 NGOs represented in Vienna, agreed to meet again in the future. It remains to be seen, however, whether they will be able to mount the organizational and financial means to set up such a meeting on their own.

Even if the precise definition of what constitutes a non-governmental organization remains unclear, their activities may be less impeded. It becomes a problem, as soon as issues such as providing facilities in conference centres and the right to take the floor at intergovernmental gatherings, let alone the provision of financial aid, are at stake. Then non-governmental organizations working for similar aims may become fierce competitors. One thing is clear: it should not be left to governments to make the selection as to which NGO should be recognized and which not. In the end it should be left to the non-governmental organizations to organize themselves.

5
The Promotion of Human Rights: Standard-Setting

Introduction

NGOs have an important role in standard-setting. They base their activities on existing standards but may also work at devising new standards. The human rights provisions in the Charter of the United Nations were products of NGO determination and persistent lobbying, in which, according to William Korey, the American Jewish Committee played a leading role.[1] John Humphrey, the first director of the United Nations Division of Human Rights, relates that "these people, aided by the delegations of some of the smaller countries, conducted a lobby in favour of human rights for which there is no parallel in the history of international relations, and which was largely responsible for the human rights provisions of the Charter."[2] Similarly, various provisions of the Universal Declaration of Human Rights "were the handiwork of NGOs."[3]

Amnesty International explicitly refers to the Universal Declaration of Human Rights as the basis of its activities: "Amnesty International's vision is of a world in which every person enjoys all of the human rights enshrined in the Universal Declaration of Human Rights and other international human rights instruments."[4] On the basis of the Universal Declaration, Amnesty and other NGOs have been active in further developing international standards of human rights. In the beginning, standard-setting was the primary preoccupation of NGOs. One of the oldest NGOs, the Anti-Slavery Society, had been preoccupied since the eighteenth century with lobbying for the establishment of standards to outlaw one of the oldest human rights abuses.[5]

Basing herself on interviews with staff members of Amnesty International, Kerstin Martens observes that Amnesty International is nowadays involved in numerous drafting processes: "AI today contributes to more drafting processes than other NGOs and usually participates during the whole process, whereas other NGOs neither have the sources nor the means to do that."[6] Helena Cook, former legal adviser of Amnesty International, has made the point that its criticisms of particular governments practice and its recommendations for improvement "carry far greater weight when they are based on norms set by the UN."[7] In other words, Amnesty devises new standards for adoption by the UN, fully aware that their adoption may contribute to greater impact of its own actions.

To illustrate how NGOs camp to set standards, the rest of this chapter will take up five issues: torture, involuntary disappearances, women's rights, children's rights and homosexual persons. These issues do not represent all the issues of standard-setting by human rights NGOs. But they may provide an insight into the activities of NGOs in this field.

The prohibition of torture

Until the early 1970s torture was regarded as an abuse of the distant past. Yet, from classical times throughout the Middle Ages torture was practised on a wide scale all over Europe.[8] By the end of the 18th century, *de jure torture* had been abolished in most countries.[9] The practice of torture by the Nazis led to the inclusion in the Universal Declaration of Human Rights of article 5: "Nobody shall be subjected to torture or to cruel, inhuman or degrading treatment or punishment." However, only some twenty-five years after the adoption of the Universal Declaration, due to the efforts and information mainly gathered by NGOs, the realization gradually gained ground that torture had again become a matter of this day and age.

In 1973, Amnesty International published its first report on torture. It contained practices of torture in no less than sixty countries, including Algeria (by the French armed forces, 1954–1962), Greece (during the military junta, 1967–1974), the Portuguese colonies in Africa, and the United Kingdom and Northern Ireland. Additional reports followed in 1984 and 2000.[10] A conference on the abolition of torture was convened in Paris by Amnesty International.[11] The conference recommended that codes of ethics and conduct be formulated for all those whose professional skills might be used in the service of torture: doctors, lawyers, prison officers, military personnel and the police.[12] In 1975, the General Assembly of the United Nations adopted a Declaration on the Protection of All Persons from Being Subjected to Torture and Other Cruel, Inhuman or Degrading Treatment or Punishment.[13]

NGOs were active in devising such professional codes. In 1975, the World Medical Association adopted a declaration concerning guidelines for medical doctors concerning torture. It stated that doctors should not countenance, condone or participate in torture practices. Furthermore, Amnesty International drafted, together with the International Commission of Jurists a code for lawyers on torture.[14] The recommendations of a seminar on an international code of police ethics, convened by Amnesty International in 1975, were circulated by the government of the Netherlands among the delegations attending the Fifth UN Congress on the Prevention of Crime and the Treatment of Offenders. That resulted eventually in a Code of Conduct for Law Enforcement Officials adopted by the UN General Assembly in 1979.[15]

None of these documents was legally binding. That higher standard was reached only when the General Assembly, prodded by NGOs, adopted in 1984 the International Convention for the Abolition of Torture and other Cruel and Inhuman or Degrading Treatment or Punishment (CAT).[16] Amnesty International participated actively in the preparation of the Convention. Amnesty focused on issues regarding the obligation on states to extradite or try alleged torturers; universality of jurisdiction in respect of torturers; an effective implementation mechanism; extending all relevant provisions to ill-treatment as well as torture; rehabilitation of victims; and ensuring that only punishment considered lawful under international law would be excluded from the definition of torture.[17]

Other prominent NGOs joined the combat against torture. In 1974 in France "Actions of Christians for the Abolition of Torture" was founded, to be followed by the establishment of similar groups in other countries. In 1977, in Switzerland, the Swiss Committee against Torture (later to be renamed the Association for the Prevention of Torture) was founded; it was to play an important role in the preparation of CAT.[18] With Amnesty International, it initiated an effort to devise an Optional Protocol to CAT, that would establish an international inspection system, as had already been set up under the European Convention against Torture, by independent experts of all places of detention in a state party. The Optional Protocol was eventually adopted by the UN General Assembly in 2002.[19]

In addition to the work at the global level, regional instruments were concluded by the Organization of American States (1985) and by the Council of Europe (1987). Also in those cases, NGOs played a role of importance.

Involuntary disappearances

The Nazi regime was probably the first to practice "forced disappearances"[20] of persons to eliminate its victims without a trace. In the 1960 and 1970s, in a number of Latin American countries the phenomenon of "disappearances" manifested itself. Dissidents, opponents of the military regime in such countries as Guatemala, Argentina, Chile and Uruguay[21] suddenly disappeared. When the concerned relatives asked the authorities for information, they were told that nothing was known about the case. Officials would suggest that the person in question had perhaps gone to visit his girlfriend, that he was in financial debt or had gone away for other reasons of a personal nature. As the cases usually concerned political opponents of the regime, the relatives did not easily accept such "explanations" and continued to ask to be informed of the whereabouts of their loved ones. Very often it later turned out that the person in question had been put to death, often after having been tortured.

Starting in 1977, in Buenos Aires, weekly public meetings took place of women, who soon got the name of "Mothers of the Plaza de Mayo" after the central square where they assembled to hold weekly meetings to dramatize their horror at the "disappearances" of their children and other relatives. They aimed to shake their fellow-Argentineans from their apathy and hoped to find out what had happened to their children or other relatives.[22] The peaceful demonstrations of the "Crazy Mothers" drew international attention to the disappearances. A Latin American Federation of Relatives of Disappeared Persons (FEDEFAM) was established to coordinate the activities of the separate national organizations. Amnesty International started in 1980 a campaign against "disappearances".[23] Outside Latin America, citizen committees were established for Chile, Argentina, Guatemala and other states, which pressured their own governments to do something about violations of human rights in Latin America in general and disappearances in particular.

FEDEFAM played a key role in the 1980s to develop international standards on involuntary disappearances. Several groups such as the Human Rights Institute of the Paris Bar Association, the Permanent Assembly for Human Rights of Argentina and another Argentinean group, the Initiative Group for an International Convention against Forced Disappearance, prepared draft declarations and conventions on forced disappearance.[24]

In 1992, the General Assembly adopted a Declaration on the Protection of All Persons from Enforced Disappearance.[25] The International Commission of Jurists took the lead on advancing the text through the Assembly, and Amnesty International was closely involved in the drafting and in lobbying for its adoption.[26] According to the Declaration, disappearance constitutes a violation of the rules of international law guaranteeing *inter alia* the right to recognition as a person before the law, the right to liberty and security of the person, and the right not to be subjected to torture and other cruel, inhuman or degrading treatment or punishment. Disappearance also constitutes a grave threat to the right to life. In 1994, an Inter-American Convention on Forced Disappearances was adopted.

In 2006, the General Assembly adopted an International Convention for the Protection of All Persons from Enforced Disappearance.[27] Under that Convention "enforced disappearance" is described as the arrest, detention, abduction or any other form of deprivation of liberty by agents of the state or by persons or groups of persons acting with the authorization, support or acquiescence of the state, followed by a refusal to acknowledge the deprivation of liberty or by concealment of the fate or whereabouts of the disappeared person, which places such a person outside the protection of the law. The Convention states that no one shall be subjected to such disappearance and state-parties must report to a Committee on the measures taken to give effect to their obligations under the Convention.

In 2007, an International Coalition against Forced Disappearances was formed. It consisted of a global network of organizations for families of disappeared persons and NGOs working in a non-violent manner against the practice of enforced disappearances at the local, national and international level. In August 2008, the coalition sent an appeal letter to all heads of state, asking them to sign and ratify that International Convention for the Protection of All Persons from Enforced Disappearances, to refrain from entering reservations incompatible with the object and purpose of the Convention, to recognize the competence of the new Committee on Enforced Disappearances, to receive and consider individual complaints, and to enact domestic legislation necessary to fully implement the Convention. The letter was to arrive on 30 August, the 25th International Day of the Disappeared.[28]

Women's rights

Women's organizations were instrumental in getting a reference to equal rights of men and women inserted in the Universal Declaration of Human Rights.[29] They also helped to obtain the establishment of a separate Commission on the Status of Women (CSW).[30] The United Nations Decade for Women (1975–1985) resulted in the recognition that violence against women was an issue of human rights. "Women's rights are human rights," became a universally accepted standard. By 1979, women's organizations had helped to draft and energetically lobbied for the adoption by the General Assembly of the United Nations of a Convention on the Elimination of All Forms of Discrimination Against Women.[31] The Convention provides for a committee (CEDAW) that considers reports submitted by state parties on the legislative, judicial, administrative or other measures they have adopted to give effect to the provisions of the Convention and on the progress made in this respect. In 1994, this international Convention was followed by the Inter-American Convention on the Prevention, Punishment and Eradication of Violence against Women.[32]

In 1985, the International Women's Rights Action Watch (IWRAW) was established during the NGO forum at the Nairobi Women's conference; it monitored the work of the CEDAW Committee. It provides country specific information to the Committee on a regular basis.[33] In

1991, an international campaign of "16 Days of Action Against Gender Violence" took place. The CEDAW Committee was for a long time reluctant to establish formal relations with NGOs, until in 1997 it decided "that NGO involvement in its work should be welcomed cautiously, but in such a way as to ensure that the independence of [its] experts was not compromised."[34] More recently, the Committee has strengthened its contacts with NGOs.[35]

Women's rights received a great deal of attention at the second World Conference on Human Rights in Vienna in 1993.[36] In the final document of the Vienna Conference, states recognized the human rights of women to be "an inalienable, integral and indivisible part of universal human rights".[37] The Vienna Declaration also led to the appointment of a UN Special Rapporteur on Violence against Women. Yet, women's rights activists also have highlighted the inequalities between the "women's mechanisms" and the so-called "mainstream mechanisms."[38] They have also argued that the human rights system did not sufficiently promote and protect the dignity and human rights of women. They claimed that the monitoring bodies did not address those concerns that are mainly experienced by women and which affect their dignity and human rights.[39] For example, the definition of torture, by focusing only on purposeful torture by public officials, excluded what is seen as the most common severe violence experienced by women – that in their own homes.[40]

At the Fourth World Conference on Women in Beijing in 1995, international women's groups were strongly represented. In that conference great emphasis was placed on removing economic barriers to gender equality, "such as the feminization of poverty, healthcare for women, and access to education and employment."[41] In 1999, this was followed by the adoption of an Optional Protocol to the Convention on the Elimination of Discrimination against Women. The Protocol opens the possibility for individuals to lodge a complaint with the CEDAW Committee in order to seek redress for alleged violations of specific rights mentioned in the Convention It also allows the Committee to undertake inquiries when it receives reliable information about grave or systematic violations of the rights protected in the Convention.

Connors, writing in the 1990s, has observed that international human rights NGOs used to be dominated by men and paid accordingly greater attention to issues of central importance to men: "Thus human rights NGOs have paid little attention to the concerns of women and women's NGOs have developed little interest or expertise in human rights."[42] It was only in 2004 that Amnesty International started a campaign on violence against women. It concerns a further involvement of existing standards, including the following:

- The implementation of existing laws that guarantee access to justice and services for women subjected to violence including rape and other forms of sexual violence;
- New laws to be enacted that will protect women's human rights;
- Putting an end to law that discriminate against women.[43]

Women's organizations must by now be considered among the strongest NGOs in the field of human rights. As Ineke Boerefijn has correctly observed: "Thanks to strong lobbies by women's organisations violence against women has been put on the [international] agenda on a permanent basis."[44]

Children's rights

The roots of the Convention on the Rights of the Child can be traced to an NGO called "Save the Children International Union", that drafted the first declaration of the rights of the child that was adopted by the League of Nations in 1925.[45] It formed the basis of the United Nations Declaration of the Rights of the Child adopted by the UN General Assembly in 1959.[46] The General Assembly designed 1979 as the Year of the Child.[47] The role of NGOs in the preparation of the International Convention on the Rights of the Child has been extensively described and analysed by Cynthia Price Cohen, then Executive Director of the Child Rights International Research Institute.[48]

A Polish proposal was submitted to the Commission on Human Rights, which established a Working Group to draft a Convention on the Rights of the Child.[49] NGOs participated in the Working Group as non-voting observers: "In reality, the distinction between members and observer states was in name only, because all drafting was done on the basis of consensus and an objection from any participant was sufficient to kill a proposed text."[50] The NGOs participated actively in the meetings of the Working Group.[51]

In 1983, about 30 NGOs established the Informal Ad hoc NGO Group on the Convention on the Rights of the Child.[52] The NGO Group established a schedule of two yearly meetings. About 30 NGOs participated in these meetings, with Defence for Children International acting as the secretariat.[53] Decisions in the Group were made by consensus. Price Cohen reports that there was little or no difficulty in getting government sponsors for most NGO Group proposals.

Another striking feature was the informality of the contacts at a weekly "Swedish pea soup party": "This informality and personal warmth created a comradely relationship which diminished possibilities of NGO/government conflicts. The end result was that NGOs were perceived as co-partners in the Convention's drafting, rather than being seen as adversaries."[54] Reiding writes that, "when a text discussed in the Working Group was not generally supported, government delegates would sometimes give a signal to the NGO to write an alternative proposal that could break the deadlock".[55]

Price Cohen reports that, partly through the good atmosphere, there were "more successes than failures" in the NGO activities. Failures had to do with "too little or too late", as when the NGOs failed to insert an article on medical experimentation in the Convention.[56] They failed completely in relation to Article 38 of the Convention, which permits the participation of children aged 15 to 17 years in armed conflicts.[57]

The Convention is unique in that it is the only international human rights treaty that expressly gives NGOs a role in monitoring its implementation. It states in article 45: "The Committee may invite the specialised agencies, the United Nations Children's Fund and *other competent bodies* as it may consider appropriate to provide expert advice on the implementation of the Convention in areas falling within the scope of their respective mandates."[58] After the Convention had been adopted, the NGO Group considered disbanding altogether, but after due deliberations it decided to continue under a new name: the NGO Group for the Convention of the Rights of the Child. This group has a Liaison Unit that supports participation of the NGOs, particularly national coalitions, in the reporting process to the Committee on the Rights of the Child as well as other activities to ensure the implementation of the Convention. One important area is the management of Alternative Reports that are submitted to the Committee.[59]

With the adoption of the Convention the process of standard setting had not yet come to an end. The NGOs cooperated in the drafting of an Optional Protocol to the Convention of the Rights of the Child on Involvement of Children in Armed Conflict.[60] In 1992, the NGO Quaker Peace and Service noted before the Committee on the Rights of the Child that the organization had since 1985 argued for the improvement of existing norms and for the development of norms relating to child soldiers. The NGO formulated recommendations to the Committee as did the representatives of other NGOs.[61] For eight years, the issue of an Optional Protocol was debated until it was adopted by the General Assembly in 2000.[62]

Amnesty International and homosexuality[63]

For many years, members of Amnesty International debated whether the organization should work for the release of persons imprisoned or detained for their homosexual identity or orientation or for homosexual acts committed in private and between consenting adults. This issue even threatened to split the organization along multicultural lines. While members in Western Europe and North America tended to consider it rather obvious that Amnesty should work for such persons, many people in Asian, African as well as some Latin American countries thought otherwise.

Agreement existed only to work for (a) persons imprisoned or detained for advocating equality for homosexuals, (b) persons charged with homosexuality as a pretext, while the real reason for their imprisonment was the expression of their political, religious or other conscientiously held beliefs, (c) persons subjected to medical treatment while in prison with the aim of modifying their homosexual orientation without their agreement.

The issue was hotly debated for a number of years, resulting in various voluminous studies of the matter. The differences of view can be roughly summarized as follows. Those in favour of working for imprisoned homosexuals argued that "(homo)sexual orientation" and "(homo)sexual identity" are attributes similar or subordinate to the category of "sex", which has for many years been in the mandate and that it would only be logical to add this category of persons to the mandate. The opponents felt that in societies where homosexuality is considered a physical ailment or a reflection of socially deviant behaviour, activities on behalf of such individuals would be seen as not related to human rights and make Amnesty look ridiculous;[64] moreover, if Amnesty were to work for imprisoned homosexuals, it would run the risk of having to deal with all sorts of other sexual practices such as paedophilia.

The debate within Amnesty was followed with considerable interest by "gay" groups from outside the organization that saw this as an opportunity to advance their cause. They considered – probably rightly – that a decision in their favour by the major human rights organization in the world would be a major accomplishment and could be used to press the issue elsewhere. They also perceived that Amnesty was vulnerable on this issue, at least in Western societies. In view of this pressure from outside and in view of their own convictions, the West European and North American sections were faced with what was basically a political choice: to press the issue of homosexual equality might risk losing actual as well as potential adherents in Third World countries whose support was considered vital from the point of view of showing that the human rights concerns of the organization were of a truly universal nature; not to press the issue might cause loss of image (as well as members) in their own countries. Many of the African and Asian members of Amnesty International, for their part, tended to deny the existence of homosexuals in their countries and the imprisonment of such persons, while stressing at the same time its taboo character.

The number of cases to be taken up played some role in the debate, when the opponents argued that there were actually only very few cases in the world of persons imprisoned or detained *solely* for their homosexual identity or orientation and that it was therefore a somewhat academic issue. Against this it was argued that in some societies it might actually be dangerous to reveal one's homosexuality and that more cases might come up, if properly researched. Moreover, the proponents argued that the issue should be decided as a matter of principle disregarding numbers.

There was a general assumption at the 1991 International Council that the issue should be decided one way or the other and that no further "studies" were needed. It was also felt by many that already a disproportionate amount of time and energy had been spent on this issue to the detriment of other more important issues. Some of the Western European and North American delegations were under specific instructions from their membership to have the matter solved this time. In the end, after considerable debate and much internal lobbying, those Third World delegations that had hitherto opposed change, gave up their opposition.

The proposals for solving the issue ranged from an amendment of the Statute to simple interpretations of existing texts. The International Council adopted by consensus a simple resolution deciding "to consider for adoption as prisoners of conscience persons who are imprisoned solely because of their homosexuality, including the practice of homosexual acts in private between consenting adults". The resolution expressed the realization that this decision would increase the difficulty of the development of Amnesty in many parts of the world and instructed the International Executive Committee to draft guidelines regarding action on behalf of imprisoned homosexuals, "taking into consideration the cultural background of various areas where we have sections and groups or countries in which AI is proposing development."

Thus ended the major internal debate on the issue of homosexuality. The result had visible features of a political compromise. Thus it was not explicitly decided how the position taken related to the text of the Statute. There is nothing in the Statute, except for a broad interpretation of the word "sex,"[65] which would cover such activities. The issue of whether the decision on homosexuality would indeed open the debate on other sexual practices was never faced. Nor was a fundamental debate held on the issue of whether Amnesty's new stand on homosexuality meant a departure from its emphasis on universal human rights values. Politically, it was also a matter of attracting one constituency (the gay community) at the risk of possibly losing another (potential AI-members in the Third World). There seems no reason to assume that the position taken has negatively affected Amnesty's membership development in Third World countries, as the opponents feared. Amnesty was and remains an organization most of whose members are located in Western countries, but that is probably more for financial reasons and for the emphasis the organization used to put in civil and political rights rather than economic and social rights.

Conclusions

The contributions by NGOs to standard setting in the field of human rights are indispensable. Although treaties are of course concluded by states, the NGOs play an indispensable role in the preparatory phase. The customary procedure, at the global level,[66] is roughly the following:

1) NGOs, often helped or stimulated by academics, and also with the help of United Nations officials, think of the need for a formal standard in the field of human rights. The principles and ideas are informally debated.
2) The ideas resulting from that process are brought to the attention of the representatives of national states.
3) Discussions are started in organs of the United Nations, such as what used to be the Commission on Human Rights and what is now the Human Rights Council, which may result in the establishment of a "working group".
4) Discussions in the working group result in the adoption of a non-binding "declaration", first by the human rights body and later by the General Assembly.
5) After a number of years, NGOs bring up the idea of the adoption of a binding treaty or what is often called a "convention".
6) Discussions will start in the Commission/Council, which may result in the establishment of another "working group".
7) The text of a draft convention will be discussed in the Commission/Council. After its adoption it will be sent to the General Assembly for definitive adoption.
8) The Convention will enter into force after ratification by the required number of states.
9) NGOs will monitor the implementation of the Convention.

The main discussants of such texts are the representatives of NGOs, UN officials and delegates of national governments. It will often depend on the technical expertise of the individuals involved as to who will take the lead in these discussions.[67]

On many issues formal or informal coalitions are built of general human rights organizations such as Amnesty International, Human Rights Watch, the International Commission of Jurists on the one hand, and on the other hand organizations that specialize on the issue under consideration, such as the Association for the Prevention of Torture, the Latin American Federation of Relatives of Disappeared Persons (FEDEFAM), the International Women's Rights Action Group

(IWRAW), Defence for Children International, and the International Lesbian and Gay Association (ILGA). The combination of the expertise of these two kinds of organizations can create a very powerful force. The general human rights organizations know where and when information should be supplied and pressure applied, while the specialized organizations will provide the needed information.

On certain issues, such as torture or involuntary disappearances, there may, certainly in the beginning, exist a clear difference between the NGOs and the governments involved. On other issues, such as the rights of children, the process has more to do with solving technical differences on which governments and NGOs may be working closely together.[68] The governments may want to use the NGOs for their own purposes, which means that the NGOs, in order to guard their independence, should be on guard to prevent themselves from being "hedged in".[69]

On certain issues the main purpose of the NGOs is to develop standards to protect (potential) victims of human rights violations. Victims of torture practices or involuntary disappearances are not in the position to fight for their own rights. They need the help of NGOs. To a certain extent that is also true of children whose rights are being violated. They need the help and efforts of adults to work on their behalf. Women and homosexuals on the other hand can through their organizations work on their own behalf. That carries the danger of possible "ghettoization": women working only for women, homosexuals working for their fellow-homosexuals, etc. Of the 23 members of the CEDAW Committee 22 are women. Over-specialization poses an obvious danger.

On some issues such as the prohibition of torture, women's[70] and children's rights NGOs usually agree with each other. The rights of homosexuals formed a more difficult issue, as members of one and the same organization (Amnesty International) held very different views. It was (and is to a certain extent) an issue on which representatives of western nations may hold different views from many members of nations in Africa and Asia. That makes it far more difficult to develop common standards of behaviour. Closely related is the cultural background of the members in question – an issue that is preferably avoided by the leadership of NGOs. They tend to stress the universality of human rights. That does not mean, however, that everybody will agree on everything.

Torture and involuntary disappearances were hardly known before NGOs raised them. The problems were hardly known before then. Women's rights and children's rights, on the other hand, can be considered "old" issues. In that respect, NGOs took up widely known issues. The role of the NGOs was to bring out and stress new developments. The rights of homosexuals were "new" in the sense that it was a subject that was rarely mentioned.

6
The Protection of Human Rights

Introduction

NGOs put in great efforts to report on violations of human rights. They call attention to specific violations affecting individuals or groups and remind governments of their treaty-bound obligations. Their main weapon is publicity generated by the "mobilization of shame". This makes use of the expectation that all governments prefer to be known as civilized and as observing the international human rights standards that they themselves have helped to devise. No government will easily admit that it allows violations of those standards to take place. Yet, most governments in the world at some time or other violate them. This discrepancy between norm and practice creates the space in which human rights NGOs operate. Starting from the point of agreement as to how governments ought to behave, they draw attention to violations of these standards. Basically, governments have two ways of reacting to such allegations: admittance or denial. In view of their adherence to international human rights standards, admitting violations of such standards implies corrections. In such cases, one can say that the NGO's activities have been successful.

If, as often happens, the government in question denies the allegation, the reputation of the NGO for reliability is at stake. In the absence of other elements of power, reliability is the only source of strength human rights NGOs can apply. By continuous truthful reporting an organization can build up a reputation of reliability, which must be jealously guarded. It can be threatened from two sides. First, an offending government may try either to discredit the NGO by questioning its motives or methods of work and by disseminating disinformation. But there is also a danger from the opposite direction. Political opponents of the government in question may try to use NGOs for purposes of their own by feeding it with news about atrocities that in fact may never have taken place.

Prisoners of conscience

Amnesty International bases its reputation on its reporting of individual cases: named individuals who are suffering from human rights violations or abuses by their government. From its beginnings, the organization has demanded the freeing of "prisoners of conscience": the imprisonment, detention or other physical restrictions imposed on any person by reason of his or her political, religious or other conscientiously held beliefs or by reason of his or her ethnic origin, sex, colour, language, national or social origin, economic status, birth or other status, provided that he or she had not used or advocated violence.[1] For many years, this was the main activity, if not the "moral bedrock" of the organization.[2] One of the best known prisoners of conscience is the Burmese human rights activist, Aung San Suu Kyi, who for many years has been held under house arrest.

As individuals, members of Amnesty International work for the release of prisoners of conscience. Until a few years ago this meant the "adoption" of one or more prisoners of conscience by so-called "adoption groups" (renamed "local groups" in the 1980s). From the International Secretariat these groups received case sheets, containing detailed information about prisoners of conscience. The groups tried to get in touch with the prisoners in question, sent them letters and packages to inform them that they had not been forgotten.[3] The groups also wrote to the authorities to persuade them to release the prisoner(s) of conscience.[4] In order to emphasize Amnesty's political impartiality, until the end of the Cold War, every adoption group was allocated three prisoners of conscience: one in a Western country, one in the communist bloc and one in the Third World, in order to emphasize Amnesty's political impartiality. Researchers could not always meet the demand for case sheets. Some groups got not more than one prisoner to work on.[5]

However, Tomuschat noted that letter writing may risk becoming a blunt instrument and subordinate officials may be entrusted with throwing incoming messages into the wastebasket. Therefore NGOs must constantly search for new and effective instruments of action.[6]

In order to protect the groups and to prevent them from becoming engaged in domestic political conflicts, they were not supposed to adopt prisoners of conscience in their own country. This was sometimes difficult to accept, for example for new Amnesty members in Eastern European countries towards the end of the Cold War. They felt concerned about the human rights situation at home and found it difficult to accept that they had to work for cases in, for example, Argentina or Sierra Leone. This "no work in own country rule" has been relaxed in recent years. The Secretary-General of Amnesty, Irene Khan, related in a recent speech in Amsterdam,[7] that she had paid an official visit to her own country, Bangladesh. That would have been extremely unlikely in the past.

Most of these adoption groups have been abolished, but they are still mentioned in the International Statute.[8] A new development is the notion of "individuals at risk". These are individual victims of human rights violations that are considered exemplary for the human rights situation in the country concerned. The expectation is that working for such an individual will also improve the more general human rights situation in that country. In all individual cases questions are asked such as: What can Amnesty achieve in this case? What will be the long-term effects? What will be the impact of the action on the individual concerned?

Better or worse?[9]

Human rights organizations as a general rule only reluctantly claim success for their actions. The standard answer to questions about the precise impact of their activities is: "We really don't know." Expansion of their activities neither proves that the number of human rights violations covered by their mandates has grown, nor that their effectiveness has increased or decreased. It only shows that the information that is made available has grown.

If a government criticizes another government for its human rights record, it tends to harp controversy. A state is entitled under Article 41 of the International Covenant on Civil and Political Rights to complain to another state that it fails to give effect to its obligations. If the matter is not adjusted to the satisfaction of both states parties

concerned within six months after the receipt of the initial communication, the matter may be referred to the Human Rights Committee.
This provision of the Covenant has *never* been employed. Despite
numerous obvious violations, governments have avoided direct complaints. Given the far-reaching restrictions on the Committee's powers
and on those of the *ad hoc* Conciliation Commission, it is cause for
wonder why the direct complaint procedure was even included in
the treaty.[10] The interstate complaint procedure under Article 33 of the
European Convention on Human Rights is also rarely used. In the
45 years since the ECHR entered into force, only 17 State complaints
have been submitted.

The absence of states' complaints serves to illustrate that the
faits et gestes of governments do not tell us very much about
the state of human rights in the world. Their decisions to act or not
to act *vis-à-vis* violations of human rights are governed by other
considerations than the state of human rights in the world.

Then what about the reports of non-governmental organizations?
Their decisions to issue reports are governed by the availability of
evidence, by financial considerations and personnel matters. For
many years, during the 1970s and 1980s, other human rights organizations criticized Amnesty International for not paying sufficient
attention in its reports to the human rights situation in China.
The human rights organization had virtually no access to China
and therefore little to report. This deficiency has meanwhile been
repaired.[11] On the other hand, if there is anything to report on human
rights violations within Amnesty's mandate in one of the Western
countries, such violations may be somewhat overemphasized.[12]

There are what may be considered some positive developments.[13]
For instance, even states that still practise the death penalty, see it
now as in accordance with human rights standards to be abolished
in due times rather than as a "normal" penalty under criminal law.[14]

In the past, human rights law that was valid in peacetime, was
rather clearly distinguished from humanitarian law applying in
times of war. Many conflict situations now even defy clear class-
ification as wars. Consequently, the old distinction between human
rights law and humanitarian law fails to satisfy. In the Former
Yugoslavia, murders occurred, as well as rape, torture, hijacking,
"ethnic cleansing", and all kinds of other violations of fundamental
human rights in a situation that might be called war, civil war or

acts of armed gangs. Similar situations were found in Sudan, Rwanda, Burundi, Congo, Liberia, and in some Latin American countries. For the victims, it does not make much of a difference whether they are the objects of violations of international human rights law or international humanitarian law.

The mandate of the Permanent International Criminal Court, established by an international conference in Rome in 1998, which was strongly attended by a great number of human rights NGOs, covers four subjects: (a) genocide, (b) crimes against humanity, (c) war crimes and (d) the still undefined crime of aggression. The first two clearly are violations of human rights. Concluding that the creation of the Court is a positive step must await knowing how many states will become party to it. The fact that the United States, China, India and Israel have refused to adhere to the Statute is not a good omen. The US Government first tried to prevent the adoption of the Statute When it was finally adopted the US opposed it wherever possible. The American Service Members' Protection Act authorizes the President "to use all necessary and appropriate means" to free any member of the US armed forces detained by or in connection with the ICC.[15] This act was dubbed by critics "The Hague invasion act" – a term that did not go unnoticed in the Netherlands!

Truth and reconciliation commissions are a relatively new phenomenon. They appear after a change of regime, when those who have been engaged in gross violations of human rights have given up their positions of power and been replaced by another, often democratic, regime. Such commissions mainly aim at uncovering the facts of human rights violations under the previous regime.[16] They explicitly do not undertake adjudication, but rather reconciliation. Especially the truth commissions that were set up in Chile, after the fall of the Pinochet-regime, and the one in South Africa have received a great deal of attention. Similar such commissions have operated for instance in Uganda, Argentina, Chad, El Salvador and one in Guatemala that was called commission of clarification.

The composition of such a commission requires a great deal of care, in order to avoid the impression that it has been established with certain political objectives in mind or in order to whitewash the past. Its members must have the confidence of the public and their independence must be guaranteed. Some of these commissions have considerable powers. The one in South Africa had the authority to compel witnesses to appear and to hear them under oath. It could even offer a perpetrator indemnity ("amnesty") for the human rights violations he discloses, provided he has performed them for political objectives. The Commission must decide whether the violation in question constituted such a political act.

The first and foremost task of such commissions is to present the facts. Often these facts are already well-known among the people involved, but they ask for an official recognition. Hayner has called this "sanctioned fact-finding". The recognition of the facts should help such events from occurring again in the future. For that reason the report of the Argentinian National Committee on Disappeared Persons was given the title *Nunca Más!* (Never Again!).

To establish such a commission, a number of questions must be answered regarding the scope of its mandate, the time period to be covered, the question of whether its activities should be published, and the question whether the names of the culprits should be made public.[17] The question must also be answered whether it should begin its activities as soon as possible after the change of regime or whether it is wiser to have some time elapse. Starting quickly may keep public attention from waning. On the other hand, this may argue for waiting, so that emotions have cooled down and the commission can do its work in an atmosphere suitable for quiet and dispassionate analysis.

The International Center for Transitional Justice, an NGO, advises governments that want to establish a truth commission. It has formulated its mission as follows:

> The International Center for Transitional Justice (ICTJ) assists countries pursuing accountability for past mass atrocity or human rights abuse. The Center works in societies emerging from repressive rule or armed conflict, as well as in established democracies where historical injustices or systemic abuse remain unresolved.

> In order to promote justice, peace, and reconciliation, government officials and nongovernmental advocates are likely to consider a variety of transitional justice approaches including both judicial and nonjudicial responses to human rights crimes. The ICTJ assists in the development of integrated, comprehensive, and localized approaches to transitional justice comprising five

key elements: prosecuting perpetrators, documenting and acknowledging violations through nonjudicial means such as truth commissions, reforming abusive institutions, providing reparations to victims, and facilitating reconciliation processes.

The Center is committed to building local capacity and generally strengthening the emerging field of transitional justice, and works closely with organizations and experts around the world to do so. By working in the field through local languages, the ICTJ provides comparative information, legal and policy analysis, documentation, and strategic research to justice and *truth-seeking institutions*, nongovernmental organizations, governments and others.[18]

Genocide

Some progress has also been made in combating genocide. The term "genocide" was coined in 1944 by the Polish jurist Raphael Lemkin[19] to refer to the coordinated and planned elimination of a national, religious, or racial group by activities directed to undermine the foundations of survival of the group in question. The immediate cause for formulating the term was the Nazi program to destroy the Jews. In 1948, the General Assembly of the United Nations adopted the Convention on the Prevention and Punishment of the Crime of Genocide. Article II of the Convention describes genocide as any of the following acts committed with the intent to destroy, in whole or in part, a national, ethnical, racial or religious group, such as:

(a) Killing members of the group;
(b) Causing serious bodily or mental harm to members of the group;
(c) Deliberately inflicting on the group conditions of life calculated to bring about its physical destruction in whole or in part;
(d) Imposing measures intended to prevent births within the group;
(e) Forcibly transferring children of the group to another group.[20]

Persons charged with genocide, according to the Convention, shall be tried by a competent tribunal of the State in the territory of which the act was committed, or by such international penal tribunal as may have jurisdiction (Article VI). This article has remained until recently a dead letter. States party to the Convention can submit disputes relating to the interpretation, application or fulfillment of the Convention to the International Court of Justice (Article IX). This has happened only once so far, when Bosnia-Herzegovina submitted a complaint against the Federal Republic of Yugoslavia (Serbia and Montenegro).[21] With regard to the mass killings by the *Khmers Rouges* in Cambodia (1975–1979) that resulted in the death of between 1 and 2 million people, non-governmental organizations have urged governments to file a state complaint against Cambodia because of its violation of the Genocide Convention. The (non-governmental) Cambodia Documentation Commission in New York had collected extensive documentation material about genocide in Cambodia, on the basis of which it has urged states to arrive at an international condemnation of the crimes committed by the *Khmers Rouges*. However, no government has been willing to take such an initiative.

The United Nations has always been reluctant to employ the term "genocide", as this might rule out negotiations with the government that has been so accused. But in regard to the situation in the Former Yugoslavia and in Rwanda the term "genocide" has nevertheless been used. In the Former Yugoslavia there were "grave breaches and other violations of international humanitarian law (...) including willful killing, 'ethnic cleansing', mass killings, torture, rape, pillage and destruction of civilian property, destruction of cultural and religious property and arbitrary arrests".[22] The killing of more than 7,000 Moslems in the Bosnian enclave of Srebrenica was termed by an independent observer "Europe's worst massacre since the Second World War."[23] In 1994, more than half a million Tutsis were cruelly killed by members of the Rwandan army, while more than one million Rwandese fled the country.[24] This does not necessarily mean that all these misdeeds were acts of genocide, but the Statute of the International Tribunal on the Former Yugoslavia explicitly mentions genocide as one of the crimes for which it may prosecute persons (Article 4). By way of definition, the terms of the Genocide Convention are used. The same is true for the Rwanda Tribunal.

In June 1996, the Yugoslavia Tribunal took up the cases of the Serbian-Bosnian leader Radovan Karadzič and General Ratko Mladič. Both were indicted for organizing a mass and systematic campaign of genocide and ethnic cleansing resulting in thousands of deaths.

The mandate of the Permanent International Criminal Court explicitly includes acts of genocide. Karadzič was finally arrested in July 2008 and transferred to The Hague, where his trial has begun.

Instruments of supervision have also grown in number as well as in effectiveness. Regional human rights courts now sit in Europe, the Americas and in Africa. The Permanent International Criminal Court has begun its operations. There exists a wide spectrum of national reporting obligations under various international human rights treaties. This is a welcome development, though many states do not, or only at considerable delay, meet their reporting obligations – because they are either unable or unwilling to do so. The UN Commission on Human Rights has established an increasing battery of special rapporteurs, both on thematic and country issues. All of these have been adopted by its successor, the Human Rights Council. The special rapporteurs issue annual reports that in some instances have helped to end certain cases of human rights violations. The coordinating role of the Bureau of the UN High Commissioner for Human Rights has improved. In the field of protection of minorities the High Commissioner on National Minorities of the Organization for Security and Cooperation in Europe (OSCE) has been making some progress in helping to prevent human rights abuses, although cases of failure to do so (Kosovo!) have also come to light.

Manifold non-governmental organizations aid and spur on global and regional instruments of supervision. These NGOs are greatly helped by a critical and independent press, both printed and audiovisual, which sees to it that the NGOs reports receive a wide distribution. This may all sound much better than it is. On the negative side considerable and widespread violations of all human rights continue to face the world. Consultation of the annual reports of Amnesty International and other human rights organizations, but also of organs of the United Nations and the United States Department of State, demonstrate that there is no universal implementation of human rights standards. A great many gross, systematic violations, i.e. violations instrumental to the achievement of governmental policies are perpetrated by the signatories of solemn treaties in such a quantity and in such a manner as to threaten or infringe the rights to life, to personal integrity or to personal liberty of the population as a whole or of one or more sectors of the population.[25] The following violations are among the most important that are at issue: the prohibition of slavery and discrimination, the denial of the right to life, torture and cruel, inhuman or degrading treatment or punishment, genocide, disappearances and "ethnic cleansing".

The problem of refugees and displaced persons in the world remains far from solved. Millions of men, women and children whose human rights – either civil and political or economic, social and cultural – have been violated are forced to leave their homes; in places, such as Congo, Rwanda, Eritrea, Ethiopia, Kosovo, to name just a few. The receiving countries, especially those in Western Europe, have given up their former policies of "hospitable admission" and now try to limit the number of refugees that are accepted, as much as possible. The UN High Commissioner for Refugees finds it increasingly difficult to take care of the needs of these people who are living in often miserable circumstances.

Such basic rights as the right of everyone to an adequate standard of living, including adequate food, clothing and housing are not fulfilled in greater parts of the world. Countless people lack access to basic education and do not enjoy the right to the enjoyment of the highest attainable standards of physical and mental health. According to the 2008 UNDP report, some 1.2 billion people around the world live on less than a dollar a day, while almost 850 million go hungry every night. Lack of access to essential resources goes beyond financial hardship to affect people's health, education, security and opportunities for political participation. Of the 4.4 billion people in developing countries, nearly three-fifths lack basic sanitation.[26]

The bottle is clearly neither empty nor full. How one wants to describe the situation remains very much a matter of personal taste and preference. This author tends to describe the human rights situation in the world rather as a bottle that is half full than as a half empty one. The half full bottle can be filled, so as to make it full. One thing is clear: however full the bottle, great efforts on behalf of human rights remain as necessary as ever. While it is praiseworthy that human rights are accepted in principle, this is by far not enough.

Shadow reports

Many NGOs write "shadow reports" in reaction to governments' reports to international monitoring committees. These reports are not necessarily more truthful or more factual than those submitted by governments. They do pose challenges and raise issues that may be left out or ignored by governments. That makes these "shadow reports" highly useful to the treaty committees.

The same is true, *mutatis mutandis*, for the findings of the treaty committees. They do not have a monopoly on wisdom, either. But they consist (mainly) of independent international experts, who may raise matters and ask questions that a government may preferably avoid. For instance, Boerefijn c.s. have reported that it was thanks to information provided by NGOs that the Committee on the Prohibition of Torture started an investigation into torture practices in Turkey, Egypt and Peru.[27]

All of the committees have now made it their habit to publish "concluding observations" after the discussion with the government in question has ended. These observations usually contain an evaluation of the state report and of the dialogue with representatives of the state party; they refer to positive developments, bottlenecks, matters of concern to the Committee and end with a number of suggestions and recommendations. These recommendations may serve as point of departure when the next periodic report of the state party is being considered. The committees seem on the whole to have become more daring in their pronouncements.

An NGO's shadow report on the Netherlands[28]

This section contains an example of one Dutch NGO with regard to the government's report to the Committee on Economic, Social and Cultural Rights. The Netherlands Jurists Committee of Human Rights NJCM, the Dutch section of the International Commission of Jurists, provides independent and systematic comment on the periodic reports by the Netherlands to the UN treaty committees.

The Netherlands seems to have met most of its human rights obligations in the field of ESC rights.[29] Most of the remaining issues relate to specific categories of persons. NJCM has noted this, for instance, with regard to the issue of health care:

> Over the years, a number of reports have been produced concerning disparities in the Dutch health care system in terms of accessibility, availability, and the quality of care. (...) According to these reports, groups such as women, the elderly, and members

of ethnic minorities experience, on an average, considerably more problems in obtaining the care they need than other groups.[30]

In the Netherlands, aspects of discrimination against women at work inspire complaints.[31] One may not necessarily agree with the CEDAW Committee, which seems to consider part-time work activities as inferior to full-time work. Yet, judgment on this question will be determined by the extent to which the choice of part-time work is a free one or forced upon women by prevailing circumstances. Neither the Government reports nor the NJCM shadow reports as well as the concluding observations of the Committee offer a definitive answer. Nevertheless, on average, women still are not paid equal salaries for equal work. The majority of the top positions in corporate and academic life are still occupied by men rather than women. One of the reasons for this situation may be insufficient or far too expensive childcare facilities. There is a lack of paid maternity leave for members of representative bodies. This may be seen as a curious aberration in what otherwise seems to be an overall situation of genuine attempts to provide equal rights for men and women.

NJCM has criticized the so-called "voluntary tuition fees" in primary and secondary schools: if this tuition fee was not paid, schools could refuse to permit pupils to take part in extra-curricular activities financed mainly by these voluntary fees.[32]

NJCM called attention to the lack of employment opportunities for older and disabled persons. It requested in particular clarification as to the responsibility of the Government for the disproportionate unemployment of disabled persons and the status of possible measures with a view to improving employment of the disabled.[33] It criticized the Dutch Government for not mentioning in its report protective measures against discrimination of disabled persons, a phenomenon that was increasing, partly as a result of the privatization of social security services.

NJCM has also mentioned the position of elderly women in relation to health care. It criticized the Netherlands Government for not dealing with this issue in its report, in particular referring to longer waiting lists for special care in hospitals; difficulties in obtaining home care when required as a result of problems related to the financing of care; increasing financial contributions to health care and higher health care insurance premiums; the shortage of general practitioners, especially in the larger cities; and longer waiting lists for institution-alized care for the elderly.[34]

The main problems in the field of ESC rights deal with illegal migrants, ethnic minorities and asylum seekers. De facto school segregation ("black schools") is on the increase in the major cities. This is partly a consequence of the fact that the members of ethnic minorities who belong to the lower socio-economic strata, are forced, if only for financial reasons, to live in the same vicinities. The quality of these schools is on the whole perceived as lower than that of "white" schools. Nevertheless, the percentage of university students with an ethnic minority origin is rising, though not the percentage that continues for a doctoral degree. As far as educational opportunities are concerned, as NJCM has noted, the situation is worst for the girls, who suffer both for lacking a Dutch background and for being females.

The most pressing, though hardly documented, problem is, however, that of the illegal residents. These vary from persons who are brought to the Netherlands by traffickers, mainly for economic reasons, to asylum-seekers whose claim for asylum has been rejected (*"uitgeprocedeerd"*), but who for various – including humanitarian – reasons are not deported. They find it difficult to obtain employment, housing, health services or social benefits. Estimates vary from 100,000 to 200,000 or more, but the precise size of this problem is virtually unknown. Here lies the main deficiency of the Netherlands in the area of economic, social and cultural rights, which according to the ESC Covenant, supposedly apply to "everyone".

In its report the Government referred to a government-sponsored assessment of the general Association of Employment Agencies' code of conduct aimed at preventing racial discrimination in employment agencies.[35] But NJCM pointed out that the Government neglected to report that this assessment resulted in the conclusion that the code was insufficiently effective: "Moreover, it remained unclear to what extent the Government accepted responsibility for racial discrimination on the labour market."[36] Furthermore, NJCM noted that there was nothing in the Government report about the limitations of access to the labour market for non-citizens among ethnic minorities. It also criticized the absence of specific information on the policy of the Government to tackle the problem of dropping out of school and criminal activities by young people from ethnic minorities.[37] Also not mentioned in the Government report was the so-called Matching Bill

("Koppelingswet"); this bill excludes illegal immigrants from, amongst others, socialized medical care. Although the Government did mention that "in principle" everybody had access to trained personnel for the treatment of common diseases and injuries,[38] NJCM pointed to the financial barrier that in practice obstructed this access for illegal immigrants. Illegally residing immigrants themselves had to pay themselves for these medical expenses. It feared therefore that the health of illegal immigrants in the Netherlands would suffer from these new regulations.[39] NJCM suggested that the Netherlands was thus in violation of Article 12 of the ICESCR [International Covenant on Economic, Social and Cultural Rights] and Article 12 of the Convention on the Elimination of All Forms of Discrimination against Women.

NJCM was further concerned that participation in primary, secondary and higher education of girls and women from ethnic minorities lagged behind the educational participation of girls and women with a Dutch background.: "[G]irls from ethnic minorities face a double educational back-log: as members of a minority who have no Dutch background, and as being girls."[40]

Some of the points raised by NJCM were clearly of a very sensitive nature. They detracted from the picture presented by the Government that the economic, social and cultural rights in the Netherlands were quite positive. The Netherlands clearly is not yet a "Walhalla of human rights".[41]

Universal Periodic Review

Of a nature similar to the shadow reports, are the reports by NGOs to the Human Rights Council's Universal Periodic Review. In 2006, the UN General Assembly mandated the Human Rights Council to "undertake a universal periodic review, based on objective and reliable information, of the fulfilment by each State of its human rights obligations and commitments in a manner which ensures universality of coverage and equal treatment with respect to all States; the review shall be a cooperative mechanism, based on an interactive dialogue, with the full involvement of the country concerned and with consideration given to its capacity-building needs; such a mechanism shall complement and not duplicate the work of treaty bodies."[42] During the negotiations about the establishment of the Human Rights Council Amnesty International had campaigned for a review mechanism with human rights expertise at its centre, thorough analysis of each situation, a dedicated follow-up mechanism and a greater role for civil society.[43]

At its sixth session, on 21 September 2007, the Human Rights Council adopted a calendar in relation to the consideration of the 192 member states of the United Nations to be considered during the first four-year cycle of the UPR mechanism, and decided on the precise order of consideration of reviewed states in 2008.

In accordance with resolution 5/1, the documents on which the review would be based are:

- Information prepared by the state concerned, which can take the form of a national report, and any other information considered relevant by the State concerned. States are encouraged to prepare the information through a broad consultation process at the national level with all relevant stakeholders;
- Additionally a compilation prepared by the Office of the UN High Commissioner for Human Rights of the information contained in the reports of treaty bodies, special procedures, including observations and comments by the State concerned, and other relevant official United Nations documents;
- Additional, credible and reliable information provided *by other relevant stakeholders* to the universal periodic review which should also be taken into consideration by the Council in the review, which will be summarized by the Office of the UN High Commissioner of Human Rights. Stakeholders include, inter alia, *NGOs*, National Human Rights Institutions, human rights defenders, academic institutions and research institutes, regional organizations, as well as civil society representatives.[44]

The report by 13 Dutch NGOs is an example of such "additional, credible and reliable information".[45] In addition, three other NGOs submitted separate reports on the Netherlands.[46] The following subjects were dealt with:

- The legal status of UN-human rights instruments;
- The role of the Netherlands in setting standards in international human rights law;
- Structural delays in reporting;

- Reports on all parts of the Kingdom of the Netherlands (including the Netherlands Antilles and Aruba;
- Assessment of policies and laws;
- Coordination of gender policy, gender mainstreaming and implementation of the CEDAW-convention;
- Counter-terrorism;
- Aliens;
- Health;
- Education.

A number of the recommendations of the NGOs were adopted by the Human Rights Council, some of which were also accepted by the Netherlands Government.

The NGOs have the right to speak during the plenary session of the Human Rights Council when the report of its working group is adopted. The NGOs have only two minutes of speaking time with a maximum of ten NGOs per country. That is very short indeed. Moreover, the NGOs speaking about the Netherlands were often interrupted on points of order, which even further limited their time to speak.[47] Two NGOs[48] organized a "side-event" during which the NGOs discussed matters with delegates of the Dutch government; it was generally seen as successful.[49] NGOs from other countries operated under more difficult circumstances. For instance. during the debate over the report on Pakistan, members of the Pakistani delegation were seen to take photographs of Pakistani NGO representatives, which must have put them under considerable strain.[50]

Some of the points that had been raised by Dutch NGOs were mentioned by other governmental delegations. The Universal Periodic Review has just started (2008) and it remains to be seen to what extent it will be successful. It would seem, however, that it offers NGOs an opportunity to raise their concerns in an international context that compels the government, if not necessarily to accede to their concerns, at least to pay attention to some. As was pointed out by Amnesty International: "Transparency is among the founding principles of the UPR."[51] Moreover, issues that were raised in one round of discussions may be brought up in the next round, three years later. It would certainly seem to be an improvement over the situation during the Commission on Human Rights, the predecessor of the Human Rights Council, where NGOs could only raise issues that could be safely disregarded by governments. In the case of the Netherlands (as well as other countries), NGOs might consider to combine their efforts rather than submit four separate reports.

Globalization

A survey of human rights NGOs that was conducted in 1996 lists few issues that now would be considered as belonging to globalization.[52] The researchers report that less than one-quarter of the NGOs surveyed indicated that they had changed their mission statements within the last five years.[53] Most of the NGOs reported no contact with international financial institutions, particularly with the International Monetary Fund.[54] The interest of human rights organizations in the role and function of the international financial institutions seems to be a relatively recent phenomenon.

NGOs that concentrate their activities on economic, social and cultural rights, have a natural interest in issues of globalization. One such is the FoodFirst International and Action Network (FIAN). The effects of economic globalization, according to this NGO, threaten the rights relevant to its interests. In many campaigns on the right to food, FIAN fights what it deems negative outcomes of economic globalization.[55] It has recently expanded its activities related to the fast changes that disintegrate traditional agricultural structures in Third World countries.[56]

Some NGOs that traditionally concentrate their activities on violations of civil and political rights also pay attention to issues of globalization. The International Commission of Jurists, for instance, has recognized a decline in the role of the state and the concomitant emergence and rise of powerful global economic actors that affect the rule of law. It decided, in 1998, to develop strategies for monitoring the activities of global actors, in particular international financial institutions and trade and investment organizations. It decided to lobby in order to ensure that international trade and investments agreements conform to international human rights standards.[57]

The US-based Human Rights Watch also emphasizes issues of globalization. The opening paragraph of its World Report 2001 reads as follows:

> The scope of today's *global* human rights problems far exceeds the capacity of *global* institutions to address them. The problem is most acute in the *global* economy, where a disturbing institutional void frequently leaves human rights standards unenforced.

(...) Yet the capacity to meet these demands has not kept up with the challenges. A reinforced *global* architecture is needed. (...) [A] world integrated on commercial lines does not necessarily lead to human rights improvements. (...) Experience shows that global economic integration is no substitute for a firm parallel commitment to defending human rights.[58]

Six years later, globalization was still on its agenda. In an entry, entitled "Globalization Comes Home: Protecting Migrant Domestic Workers' Rights," Nisha Varian wrote: "The situation of migrant domestic workers is a particularly stark illustration of the need for transnational governance in an era of globalization."[59]

Amnesty International and globalization

Amnesty has long resisted attempts to broaden its mandate. If it were to become a general human rights organization, it would risk dispersing its efforts and therewith its power to influence.[60] There was also the understandable fear, as earlier noted, that its International Secretariat would not be able to cope with such an expanded mandate and maintain its reputation of preciseness and reliability. However, times are changing – also in the case of Amnesty International. Morton Winston, former chair of the Board of Directors of Amnesty International USA, writing around the turn of the century, listed as one of the major challenges for the organization its "selectivity of human rights", particularly as concerns economic, social, and cultural rights.[61] He criticized the organization for "systematically ignor[ing] economic rights" giving the impression that they regard violations of these rights as less grave than violations of the civil and political rights that have been the focus of AI's work."[62]

In its 2002 annual report, Amnesty International highlighted the issue of globalization as follows:

As globalisation spreads, bringing greater wealth to some and destitution and despair to others, human rights activists must promote not just legal justice, but also social justice. An ethical approach to globalisation can mean nothing less than a rights based approach to development. We must struggle not only against torture, arbitrary detention and unfair trials, but also against hunger, illiteracy and discrimination if human rights are to be meaningful in developing countries.[63]

For many years, the Statute of Amnesty International had begun with a section on "Object and Mandate". That section was expanded over the years, leading to the following mandate of the organization:

> – to promote awareness of and adherence to the Universal Declaration of Human Rights and other internationally recognized human rights instruments, the values enshrined in them , and the indivisibility and interdependence of all human rights and freedoms;
> – to oppose grave violations of the rights of every person freely to hold and to express his or her convictions, and to be free from discrimination and of the right of every person to physical and mental integrity and, in particular, to oppose by all appropriate means irrespective of political considerations:
>
> a) the imprisonment, detention or other physical restrictions imposed on any person by reason of his or her political, religious or other conscientiously held beliefs or by reason of his or her ethnic origin, sex, colour, language, national or social origin, economic status, birth or other status, provided that he or she has not used or advocated violence (hereinafter referred to as "prisoners of conscience"; AMNESTY INTERNATIONAL shall work towards the release of and shall provide assistance to prisoners of conscience);
> b) the detention of any political prisoner without fair trial within a reasonable time or any trial procedures relating to such prisoners that do not conform to internationally recognized norms;
> c) the death penalty, and the torture or other cruel, inhuman or degrading treatment or punishment or prisoners or other detained or restricted persons, whether or not the persons affected have used or advocated violence;
> d) the extrajudicial execution of persons whether or not imprisoned, detained or restricted, and "disappearances", whether or not the persons affected have used or advocated violence.[64]

This traditional mandate came under increasing criticism both from inside and outside the organization, claiming that it was far too limited and did not do justice to the appeal, expressed among others by the second World Conference on Human Rights, held in Vienna in 1993, to work for the promotion and protection of *all* human rights.[65] Eventually, this led to the adoption of a radically amended Statute which now begins with a section on 'Vision and Mission' as follows:

1. Amnesty International's vision is of a world in which every person enjoys *all of the human rights enshrined in the Universal Declaration of Human Rights and other international human rights standards.*

   In pursuit of this vision, Amnesty International's mission is to undertake research and action focussed on preventing and ending grave abuses of these rights.[66]

This change of the Statute has opened the possibility for the organization to work on all human rights, including economic, social and cultural rights.

At the time of writing (summer 2008) Amnesty is conducting campaigns in the following areas:

Control Arms
The unregulated global arms trade inflicts misery worldwide. Every year thousands of people are killed, injured, raped and forced to flee their homes as a result.

Counter Terror with Justice
The so-called "war on terror" has led to an erosion of a whole host of human rights. States are resorting to practices which have long been prohibited by international law, and have sought to justify them in the name of national security.

Stop Violence Against Women
Violence against women is often ignored and rarely punished. Women and girls suffer disproportionately from violence – both in peace and in war, at the hands of the state, the community and the family. A life free from violence is a basic human right.[67]

So far, the change of the mandate has not yet led to a dramatic expansion of activities on behalf of economic, social and cultural rights. It would seem that economic factors are taken into account, if and as far as they have an impact on civil and political rights, as under the old mandate of the organization. In fact, the organization dealt already with corporations before the change of the Statute. Yet, read literally, work to promote all human rights could mean campaigns on behalf of the right to food, the right to housing, the right to health etc. Thus far, this interpretation seems not to be the one adopted by the International Secretariat. However, there can be little doubt that in principle the change of the Statute, as adopted in 2001, could mean considerably more work in the field of economic and social rights – including issues of globalization.

Conclusions

Globalization in the sense of increased border crossing flows of trade and finance and all sorts of international communication, is here to stay. In step with the progressive development of technology (and a corresponding decrease of financial costs) it is likely to expand. Part of this globalization involves multinational corporations (MNCs) whose decisions to invest or operate affect the lives of millions of people all over the world.[68] Many of these MNCs show themselves, more than in the past, prepared to take notice of the consequences of their activities for international human rights. The dialogues between MNCs and human rights organizations are a positive development, as long as the latter bear in mind that their basic objectives will remain vastly different from those of the MNCs. Human rights organizations are the only bodies that can permit themselves to be single-minded in the pursuit of the maximation of respect for human rights. Neither states, nor MNCs, nor international financial institutions (IFIs) can do so. Whatever they may say, they have always other, in their eyes more important, interests to pursue. Nevertheless, IFIs and the World Trade Organization (WTO) are and should be affected by international human rights standards. As UN bodies they are subject to the rules of the UN Charter (which lists the promotion and encouragement of respect for human rights as one of the purposes of the organization).

This chapter has listed a great number of human rights that are or may be affected by globalization. They include economic, social and cultural rights, such as the right to food, to work, to education, and to medical care. But also a great number of the traditional civil and political rights may be affected by globalization, such as freedom of expression, freedom of assembly, and the right to association. The process of globalization can stimulate well-known phenomena such as traffic in women, children and migrants as well as modern forms of slavery are major violations of human rights. These violations especially affect people living in the poorest regions of the world, in Africa, parts of Asia and Latin America.

A critical civil society[69] as represented by international NGOs is indispensable for raising concerns about global developments affecting human rights. Many of these NGOs do not necessarily belong to the "grassroots" of society. But they can serve as spokesmen for the interests of the underprivileged and downtrodden. Indeed the "fathers of socialism", Karl Marx and Friedrich Engels, far from being workers in industry, were members of the German bourgeoisie. Yet, they spoke for the rights and the welfare of the underprivileged working class. Many of the social-democratic and communist political leaders who succeeded them, were not industrial workers, either. Yet, their role in raising public awareness of the dismal situation in industry at the time is indisputable. Similarly, activists of international human rights NGOs, even if belonging to the "elite" in their societies, call attention to the situation at the "grassroots". The fact that many of the most important human rights NGOs have a "Western image" if not a "Western origin", seems so far unavoidable. Amnesty International, for instance, has put a great deal of effort, including financial means, into "development", i.e. recruiting members in the non-Western world – so far without great success. If NGOs were able to shed this Western image, it might perhaps contribute to their effectiveness in Third World countries. This may, however, be a matter of time. For the time being, while continuing their efforts on development, NGOs are well advised to concentrate more on the contents of their message than on their image.

NGOs themselves have no "power" in the sense that they lack the financial and political, let alone the military, means to persuade governments, MNCs and IFIs of the correctness of their position. Their only tool of persuasion is in the end the so-called "mobilization of shame". That may be easier in the case of states that have ratified the international human rights conventions, than in the case of MNCs that have no standing in international law. Therefore, a likely venue to the latter is through the channels of the state.

National legislation that is based on international human rights treaties can help to compel MNCs to honour those very human rights standards. Governmental delegations to international meetings may help to persuade IFIs to do likewise. NGOs, for their part, can call attention to, and provide information on alleged violations of human rights through the activities (or the lack of activities) of MNCs or IFIs. In this way, NGOs can make use of, and operate within the sphere of globalization.

In the case of the largest human rights organization, Amnesty International, the change of its mandate has in principle further opened ways to be active in the field of globalization. These ways are now being studied by the organization. Expanding its activities in the sphere of economic and social rights will mean a greater load on the shoulders of its professional staff in the International Secretariat in London. Obviously, the organization would not want to fall into the trap that such expansion would be to the detriment of its reputation for accuracy and reliability of its reports. What is true for Amnesty International is also true for many of the other NGOs that have so far concentrated their activities in the field of civil and political rights. At the moment, many of them tend to pay lip service to issues of globalization, without engaging in a great deal of activities in that field.

The emphasis in this chapter has been on globalization's negative consequences for human rights and what to do about it. There are, however, also positive consequences. For example, the increase in communication technology and possibilities for international transportation has undoubtedly also contributed to the possibilities of NGOs to work on behalf of human rights.

7
Non-Governmental Entities

Introduction

According to classical doctrine, governments are accountable under international law for violations of human rights and must see to it that international standards are applied. These standards have been codified in international treaties, and states as parties to such treaties must meet their related obligations.[1] This doctrine is the approach that a HRNGO may take in confronting a government, once it becomes aware of human rights violations in its territory. However, some governments are barely able to exert their authority in their own capital city, let alone the remainder of the territory they are supposed to govern. Examples are the governments of Colombia, the Democratic Republic of the Congo, Nepal, Sri Lanka, and Sudan. In the case of Somalia, a government in the formal sense hardly exists. In these nations, circumstances may differ, but they usually include one or more of the following characteristics:

- A civil war: two or more groups fighting each other, claiming central or partial political control.
- A threat of break-up: that is, the chance of the country dissolving, while the allocation of governmental authority remains at least temporarily unresolved (as has happened in the Soviet Union and the former Yugoslavia).
- A certain degree of control by the armed opposition: it may control part of the territory and the population, either on a permanent or temporary basis.

Such situations pose a number of questions. Should non-governmental entities such as insurrectionary movements be expected to honour the same commitments in the field of human rights as the formal government of their country? Should they be asked to give their prisoners fair and prompt trials? Apart from the technical difficulty of identifying a central authority in many of these cases, how realistic is it to treat such groups as if they were governments? And to what extent would the making of such demands imply some sort of recognition? Governments regard such armed opposition groups as rebels or terrorists, if not outright criminals. These governments usually adopt a somewhat ambivalent attitude with regard to the question of upholding human rights standards. Although they want the armed opposition to be judged by the same human rights criteria as they are, they also do not want to publicly offer the opposition this kind of recognition.

Most international human rights organizations, finding it difficult to decide how to approach such entities, have struggled with the dilemma of confronting non-governmental entities whose abuses are as bad or even worse than the violations committed by governments. Amnesty International, for example, has taken for a long time the position that it would condemn the torture or killing of prisoners by opposition groups, but not directly confront such groups. According to some critics, directly addressing such groups would signify that the organization was moving into the area of crime fighting, because when an individual or opposition group commits a killing, perpetrates torture, or takes a hostage, the act should be regarded as a crime rather than as an abuse of human rights. International human rights instruments bind only states parties, that is, governments. On the other hand, however, some governments have accused Amnesty of being less forceful in pursuing its aims with regard to non-governmental entities than with governments. As a consequence, the organization began to deal with abuses by non-governmental entities but refused to deal with them on the same level as with governments.

For a number of years, Amnesty distinguished a separate category of non-governmental entities, what it chose to call "quasi-governmental entities", having a number of characteristics that made them look very much like governments. These characteristics are:

• Having effective authority over territory and peoples such that individuals may be subject to abuses, whereas the formal government is excluded as a source of protection.

- Being political organizations in the sense of acting in pursuit of a political program.

In practice, however, Amnesty has found it difficult to maintain the distinction between non-governmental entities in general and quasi-governmental entities. The authority exerted by the quasi-governmental entity is often rather transient in nature. It may control parts of the population for a while, then lose that control or take over the government according to the fortunes of war. Some entities may gain control of part of a territory at night, only to have to relinquish it during daytime. In some cases, deciding the following can also be rather arbitrary: whether an entity pursues a political program, thus distinguishing it from groups that are purely criminal such as the Mafia or dealers in narcotic drugs. In actuality, political groups may engage in criminal activities to support their cause, whereas criminals may opt for some kind of semi-political control. Amnesty does address abuses by political non-governmental entities, whether or not the entity has the attributes of a government, in effect abolishing the distinction between non-governmental and quasi-governmental entities.

A continuum of political non-governmental organizations may exist, ranging from those that are very similar to governments to those organizations having little in common with governments. The organization decided that as a priority Amnesty would concentrate its resources on those entities having greater control over people, territory, and the use of force and develop criteria by which political non-governmental entities might be distinguished from groups falling outside the scope of Amnesty's work.

The question of how to approach non-governmental entities received special emphasis in relation to hostages taken by non-governmental entities. Originally, Amnesty did not condemn the taking of hostages but only torturing or killing them. As sometimes hostages are taken for political reasons, that posed the question of whether Amnesty should call for their release. Moreover, whether it was logical to condemn hostage taking, but not killings by those same non-governmental entities posed another question. Amnesty decided both to bring the taking of hostages by non-governmental entities into the scope of its activities as well as other deliberate and arbitrary killings such as the killings of people under the non-governmental entity's immediate control or carried out solely by reason of the victim's ethnic origin, sex, colour of skin, language, religion, or political or other beliefs.

The following sections illustrate how the two major international human rights NGOs, Amnesty International and Human Rights Watch, have reacted to human rights abuses by non-governmental entities in the following five countries: Somalia, Colombia, the Democratic Republic of the Congo, Spain and Afghanistan. By way of comparison reference is also made to the most recent US State Department's report on these countries.

Somalia

According to Amnesty International, during most recent years, violations of international humanitarian law and human rights law have been widespread throughout central and southern Somalia. The Transitional Federal Government of Somalia (TFG) is hardly able to protect itself, let alone the civilian population in the country. Civilians are being routinely targeted; rape, killings and looting have become widespread. Civilians have been violently attacked in the conflict areas of southern and central Somalia, on the roads as they tried to escape and in the camps and settlements to which they fled.[2] Amnesty International's assessment was confirmed by the country report of the United States State Department:

> The country's poor human rights situation deteriorated further during the year, exacerbated by the absence of effective governance institutions and the rule of law, the widespread availability of small arms and light weapons, and ongoing conflicts. As a consequence citizens were unable to change their government. Human rights abuses included unlawful and politically motivated killings; kidnapping, torture, rape, and beatings; official impunity; harsh and life-threatening prison conditions; and arbitrary arrest and detention. In part due to the absence of functioning institutions, the perpetrators of human rights abuses were rarely punished. Denial of fair trial and limited privacy rights were problems, and there were restrictions on freedoms of speech, press, assembly, association, religion, and movement. Discrimination and violence against women, including rapes; female genital mutilation (FGM); child abuse;

recruitment of child soldiers; trafficking in persons; abuse and discrimination against clan and religious minorities; restrictions on workers' rights; forced labour, including by children; and child labour were also problems.[3]

Amnesty's report concentrates on the role of the federal government and the Ethiopian military forces in the country, but it also mentions that informal armed groups were responsible for human rights abuses. Manifold are the references to "all parties to the conflict" committing human rights abuses and violations of international humanitarian law. The report contains recommendations to the Transitional Federal Government, the Government of Ethiopia, armed groups in Somalia and the "international community".

Armed groups in Somalia, according to Amnesty, are many and varied:

> They include remnants of the Islamic Courts Union (ICU), supporters of the Alliance for the Re-Liberation of Somalia (ARS), and various factions of the Shabab ("youth") militia – formerly young ICU fighters. As long as members of these armed groups are taking direct part in the conflict, they do not enjoy civilian status. Sub-clan and other local political leaders have also committed crimes against civilians, as have bandits and clan militias. Some are involved as combatants in the armed conflict of TFG and Ethiopian forces against armed opposition groups, while some are not. Many are committing acts of robbery, extortion, rape and violence against civilians throughout southern and central Somalia. The FRG has provided virtually no protection from such acts.[4]

The humanitarian and human rights situation in Somalia has grown worse. *Clan militias, remnants of the former ICU, Shabab militia and armed bandits* as well as TFG and Ethiopian security forces, have all perpetrated abuses against civilians.[5] Sections of the report deal with violations by TFG forces and by Ethiopian forces. A separate section deals with "human rights abuses by armed groups". These also include clan, sub-clan and local political leaders and militias who act as bandits, carrying out raids and robberies and perpetrating abuses against civilians, including rape and other forms of sexual violence. Terms that are used locally include "the resistance", "those who are defending the land", "the opposition", and "terrorists". The Amnesty reports uses the term "armed groups" to refer to "groups that have declared their violent opposition to TFG and Ethiopian forces, as well as non-governmental militias serving as proxies for the TFG forces." All of these groups were reported to have targeted and killed civilians.[6] Every day, humanitarian workers face checkpoints, roadblocks, extortion, car jacking and a lack of acceptance of the impartial nature of their assistance. These obstructions hamper humanitarian access, travel and humanitarian supplies.[7]

Though the TFG as the recognized government of Somalia bears principal responsibility for ensuring the human rights of the people of Somalia, there are numerous references to "all parties to the conflict" as having committed war crimes and crimes against humanity. These include "the leaders of non-state armed groups": "With regard to war crimes and crimes against humanity, the question of whether the perpetrators belonged to an army or a state, an armed group or any other entity is of little relevance; anyone responsible for such crimes may and should be brought to justice."[8]

Although in the past Amnesty avoided identification as a "crime fighting organization", there are references to "unidentified robbers". Obviously, in the Somali situation it is very difficult, if not impossible to distinguish robberies for political ends from purely criminal activities.

As to the application of relevant international law, the report points to the Geneva conventions:

> [A]ll parties to the armed conflict, *including armed groups that are not part of the forces of a state,* must respect certain fundamental laws of international humanitarian law applicable to non-international armed conflict, including those applicable to the conduct of hostilities under customary international law. (...) All parties to armed conflict, *including armed groups that are not part of the state armed forces,* have a responsibility to distinguish between civilians and civilian objects, which may not be attacked, and military objectives, which, subject to certain conditions, may be attacked.[9]

The report ends with specific recommendations to the TFG, the Ethiopian government, the armed groups, the UN Security Council and what is called "the international community". There are also recommendations "to armed groups opposing TFG and Ethiopian forces in Somalia". These deserve to be quoted in full, as one may wonder whether the authors of the report really thought that these would ever reach the addressees, let alone that they would follow up on them:

- halt immediately all violations of international humanitarian war;
- issue instructions clearly prohibiting all unlawful attacks, including those targeting civilians, those which do not attempt to distinguish between military targets and civilians or civilian objects, and those which, although aimed at a legitimate military target, have a disproportionate impact on civilians or civilian objects;
- cease all use of death threats, rape, looting and intimidation of civilians, and abide fully with the provisions of Common Article 3 of the Geneva Conventions;
- take all other necessary measures to protect the civilian population from the dangers arising from military operations, including not locating military objectives among civilian concentrations.[10]

The other major international human rights organization, Human Rights Watch, has reached similar conclusions. In its report it refers to violations by "insurgent forces". That term is used to describe a range of anti-TFG and anti-Ethiopian forces. These include the extremist al-Shabaab militia, supporters of the Alliance for the Re-Liberation of Somalia, and clan-based fighters loosely known among many Somalis as *muquawaama* (resistance).[11] Human Rights Watch describes them as having repeatedly and indiscriminately attacked civilians, killed and mutilated captured combatants, killed government officials, and threatened civilians, including journalists and aid workers.[12]

Human Rights Watch reported that Somalia had been wracked by violence and lawlessness, numerous serious crimes by members of the state armed forces *and non-state armed groups*. It asked the Security Council to set up a commission of inquiry, which could draw public attention to the responsibility *of all parties to the conflict*

to uphold human rights standards in Somalia. Individuals responsible for the crimes should be held to account.[13]

Both human rights NGOs have reached the conclusion that in the
Somali situation, there is no point in only approaching whatever
body claims to be the official government. That "government" is
clearly not able – if willing – to carry out their international obligations. That is why the organizations were forced to include "all
parties to the conflict" is its deliberations, casting aside its former
reluctance to deal with what could be seen as "criminal organizations". Whether or not such recommendations carry any effect
whatsoever is of course an entirely different matter that encourages
little optimism.

Colombia

According to Amnesty International, all the parties to the 40-year
internal conflict in Colombia continued to bear responsibility for
widespread abuses of international human rights and humanitarian
law, mostly committed against civilians. The human rights and
humanitarian situation deteriorated during 2007 in some regions.
Amnesty International was particularly concerned about increases
in extrajudicial executions committed by the security forces and in
the increased number of civilians forcibly displaced by the armed
conflict.[14] Amnesty International's assessment was confirmed by the
country report of the United States State Department:

> The 43-year internal armed conflict continued between the govern-
> ment and terrorist organizations, particularly the Revolutionary
> Armed Forces of Colombia (FARC) and the National Liberation
> Army (ELN). While civilian authorities generally maintained effect-
> ive control of the security forces, there were instances in which
> elements of the security forces acted in violation of state policy.

> The FARC and ELN committed the following human rights abuses:
> political killings; killings of off-duty members of the public security
> forces and local officials; kidnappings and forced disappearances;
> massive forced displacements; subornation and intimidation of
> judges, prosecutors, and witnesses; infringement on citizens' pri-
> vacy rights; restrictions on freedom of movement; widespread

recruitment of child soldiers; attacks against human rights activists; and harassment, intimidation, and killings of teachers and trade unionists.[15]

The Amnesty report dealt with the legal framework for the demobilization of paramilitary groups, reparation for victims of human rights abuses, the Rome Statute of the International Criminal Court, children and armed conflict, human rights violations by paramilitary groups, extrajudicial executions, enforced disappearances, forced displacement, attacks on human rights defenders and trade unionists and human rights abuses and violations of international humanitarian law by guerrilla groups. The latter provides an excellent illustration of how Amnesty has dealt with this at the time relatively strong armed opposition group:

> Guerrilla groups continue to commit human rights abuses and to violate international humanitarian law, including deliberate killings of civilians, abductions and hostage-taking. The FARC is believed to hold 700 hostages, often in appalling conditions. Amnesty International is also concerned about the dispute between the FARC and the National Liberation Army (ELN) in Arauca Department, which has resulted in the killing of hundreds of civilians over the last ten years, and about the continued use of anti-personnel mines by guerrilla groups, which has resulted in numerous casualties, including civilians. The FARC were also alleged responsible for many of the around 29 killings of candidates in the run-up to the October 2007 local elections. Amnesty International continues to receive numerous testimonies about forced recruitment of children by both guerrilla and paramilitary groups. Amnesty International is also concerned about the indiscriminate bomb attacks that have taken place in several urban areas, some of which the authorities attributed to the FARC.[16]

The last sentence of the quoted text is remarkable, as Amnesty International would seem to accept an allegation by the Colombian government, without making an assessment of its own.

Human Rights Watch also reported widespread abuses by irregular armed groups, including both left-wing guerrillas and paramilitaries who remained active. Targeted killings, forced disappearances, use of anti-personnel landmines, recruitment of child combatants, and threats against trade unionists, human rights defenders and journalists remained serious problems. Due to the abuses, Colombia had the second largest population of internally displaced persons in the world.[17]

About guerrilla abuses Human Rights Watch asserted:

> Both the FARC and ELN guerrillas continue to engage in abuses against civilians. The FARC's widespread use of antipersonnel land mines has resulted in a dramatic escalation in new reported casualties from these indiscriminate weapons in recent years. The FARC also continues to engage in kidnappings. In June 2007, the FARC announced that 11 congressman from the state of Valle del Cauca that it had been holding for more than five years had been shot to death while under their control.[18]

Again, as in the case of Somalia, both international NGOs gave attention to the actions of non-governmental entities in Colombia. The FARC controls a large part of the countryside, where it can be termed as a quasi-governmental agency. Such quasi-governments are of course not parties to international human rights treaties. Yet, for their victims it does not make any difference whether they are being tortured or shot to death by government forces or by guerrillas.

Democratic Republic of the Congo

According to Amnesty International, in the Democratic Republic of the Congo human rights of civilians were constantly violated. Extrajudicial executions and other unlawful killings, arbitrary arrests, unlawful detentions, acts of torture or ill-treatment, and life-threatening prison conditions made up a daily routine. Decades of neglect, poor governance and mismanagement of resources, compounded in the east by war, left essential services and infrastructure, including the justice, health and education sectors, in near-collapse. Widespread violations of human rights took place, including enforced disappearances, arbitrary arrests, ethnic violence, excessive use of force by the security forces, and restrictions of freedom of expression and assembly.[19]

Amnesty's assessment was confirmed by the United States State Department:

> In all areas of the country the government's human rights record remained poor, and security forces acted with impunity during the year, committing numerous serious abuses, including unlawful killings, disappearances, torture, and rape, and engaged in arbitrary arrests and detention. Harsh and life-threatening conditions in prison and detention facilities, prolonged pretrial detention, lack of an independent and effective judiciary, and arbitrary interference with privacy, family, and home also remained serious problems. Security forces recruited and retained child soldiers and compelled forced labor by adults and children. Members of the security forces also continued to abuse and threaten journalists, contributing to a decline in freedom of the press. Government corruption remained pervasive. Security forces at times harassed local human rights advocates and UN human rights investigators. Discrimination against women and ethnic minorities, trafficking in persons, child labor, and lack of protection of workers' rights continued to be pervasive throughout the country." Armed groups continued to commit numerous, serious abuses – some of which may have constituted war crimes – including unlawful killings, disappearances, and torture. They also recruited and retained child soldiers, compelled forced labor, committed widespread crimes of sexual violence and other possible war crimes.[20]

Also armed groups were opposed to the peace process and to integration in the armed forces of the Congo (FARDC), responsible for numerous grave human rights abuses in the provinces of North- and South-Kivu, Katanga and Orientale (Ituri). These abuses, some of which appeared to be ethnically motivated, included rapes, unlawful killings and torture. In January 2007, forces of Laurent Nkunda's armed group, opposed to the government and composed mainly of Kinyarwanda-speaking fighters, launched attacks against government forces and civilian centres in North-Kivu province. They allegedly committed numerous unlawful killings and raped scores of women from non-Kinyarwanda-speaking communities.[21]

Human Rights Watch confirmed Amnesty's findings, referring to "all sides in the conflict" as inflicting atrocities against civilians, especially women. It mentioned in particular the Forces for the Liberation of Rwanda (FDLR), composed largely of Rwanda combatants. The FDLR is supposedly committed to overthrowing the current government of Rwanda, but "in recent years its members have attacked Congolese civilians more than they have engaged the Rwandan army."[22]

Spain

According to Amnesty International, reports of human rights violations and subsequent impunity involving Spanish law enforcement officers continued to be widespread in 2007. Asylum seekers and migrants were denied access to Spanish territory and were processed in extra-territorial centres in conditions that did not comply with international standards. Unaccompanied minors were expelled without adequate guarantees for their safety. Victims of domestic violence continued to face obstacles in obtaining protection, justice and reparation, with migrant women facing additional difficulties in accessing essential resources. The armed Basque group Euskadi Te Askatasuna (ETA) declared its "permanent ceasefire" over in June and resumed bomb attacks.[23]

Amnesty's report was basically confirmed by the State Department's report:

> The government generally respected the human rights of its citizens, and the law and judiciary provided effective means of addressing individual instances of abuse. There were some reports that security forces abused suspects and that migrant children in detention centers were mistreated. There were reports of delays in arraignment of arrested persons before a judge and delays in providing legal assistance to arrested persons. There were reports that authorities at times expelled illegal immigrants without adequate screening for potential asylees. On June 5, the terrorist group Basque Fatherland and Liberty (ETA) declared an end to its March 2006 "permanent ceasefire," and continued its terrorist campaign of bombings during the year, in addition to killing two Spanish Civil Guards in southern France. Societal problems included the following: Jewish groups reported isolated acts of vandalism and anti- Semitism, Muslim groups reported some societal discrimination, and there were incidents of

societal violence against other minorities; domestic violence and trafficking in persons were also reported.[24]

Under the heading "armed groups" Amnesty reported that ETA had resumed its attacks in Spain. In June 2007, ETA officially ended the ceasefire that was effectively broken in December 2006 by a bomb attack on Madrid's airport which killed two people. In August, a car bomb exploded outside the Civil Guard station in Durango in the Basque country, causing damage but no casualties. In October, the bodyguard of Basque councillor was injured in a further bomb attack. In December, two unarmed Spanish Civil Guard officers were shot and killed by suspected ETA members in Capbreton, France.[25]

The 2008 World Report of Human Rights Watch did not contain an entry on Spain, nor had HRW any detailed reports on ETA activities.

Afghanistan

According to Amnesty International, in 2007 increasing conflict and insecurity affected large parts of Afghanistan and, aggravated by drought and floods, it led to large-scale displacement of people throughout the year. At least 6,500 people were estimated to have been killed in the context of the conflict. With impunity all parties, including Afghan and international security forces *and insurgent groups,* committed violations of international humanitarian and human rights law. All sides carried out indiscriminate attacks, which included aerial bombardments by the International Security Assistance Force (ISAF) and US-led Operation Enduring Freedom (OEF) forces, as well as suicide attacks by armed groups. According to the Afghanistan NGO Security Office, there were around 2,000 non-combatant civilian deaths, with international forces causing over a quarter of casualties *and insurgent groups* just under half. Rights associated with education, health and freedom of expression were violated, particularly for women. Human rights defenders and journalists, many of them women, were threatened, physically intimidated, detained or killed. Reforms of key government institutions, including the police and intelligence service, made limited progress. Government officials and local power-holders were not held accountable for reported abuses and there was little or no access to justice in many areas.[26]

Amnesty's report was basically confirmed by the State Department:

The country's human rights record remained poor due to a deadly insurgency, weak governmental and traditional institutions, corruption, drug trafficking, and the country's legacy of two-and-a-half decades of conflict. Human rights problems continued, including extrajudicial killings; torture; poor prison conditions; official impunity; prolonged pretrial detention; increased restrictions on freedom of press; restrictions on freedoms of religion, movement, and association; violence and societal discrimination against women, religious converts, and minorities; trafficking in persons; abuse of worker rights; and child labor. While civilian authorities generally maintained effective control of the security forces, there were instances in which members of the security forces acted independently of government authority.

While the government deepened its authority in provincial centers, the Taliban or factions operating outside government authority controlled some areas. During the year more than 6,500 persons died as a result of the insurgency, including by suicide attacks, roadside bombs, and gun assassinations, in contrast to 2006, when more than 1,400 individuals died. The overwhelming majority of the casualties were insurgent fighters killed in combat. The Taliban and antigovernment elements continued to threaten, rob, attack, and kill villagers, government officials, foreigners, and non-governmental organization (NGO) workers. The Taliban increasingly attacked civilian and international targets using the tools of terrorism, including targeted suicide bombings, automatically and remotely detonated bombs and landmines, and the use of civilians as shields. Also during the year, the number of NGO representatives who were threatened and kidnapped increased significantly. The instability caused by the continuing insurgency and the difficult operating environment caused by the Taliban's strategy of targeting government offices and workers contributed to weaknesses in government institutions.[27]

Under the heading "Abuses by armed groups" Amnesty reported on abductions and killings, suicide attacks and killings following quasi-judicial processes. Armed groups, including the Taliban, Hiz-e Islami and al-Qa'ida, deliberately targeted civilians. This included killing people perceived to be working or co-operating with the Afghan government or international military forces. Armed groups carried out 140 suicide attacks against military and civilian targets, killing around 300 civilians. The Taliban and other groups unlawfully killed people following quasi-judicial processes.[28]

In April 2007, Amnesty International issued a report, entitled *Afghanistan: All who are not Friends are Enemies: Taleban[29] Abuses against Civilians*.[30] The report stated that Taliban attacks on civilians were widespread and systematic and were used to instil fear and exert control over the local population. Taliban insurgents had deliberately killed scores of civilians in the past two years, apparently because they were branded as "spies". Targets included women's rights activists, clerics, government and health workers and teachers. At least 183 schools were burned in arson attacks across the country between 2005 and 2006. The report contained a number of recommendations, referring to the Taliban and other armed groups:

Amnesty International calls on armed groups in Afghanistan to immediately cease:

- attacks targeting civilians and civilian objects, attacks that do not attempt to distinguish between military objectives and civilians or civilian objects; all disproportionate attacks;
- in particular attacks on teachers, students, education officials and school buildings, all attacks against members of local and international humanitarian organizations and agencies, and ensure unhindered and safe access for humanitarian agencies to all areas;
- locating military objectives among civilian concentrations and take all other necessary measures to protect the civilian population from the dangers arising from military operations;
- killing civilians, as a result of quasi-judicial procedures; and holding such procedures;
- all abductions and hostage-taking;
- all torture and other ill-treatment;
- all harassment and threats of death or abduction against civilians.

Amnesty International calls on armed groups in Afghanistan to:

- publicly condemn all attacks against civilians and indiscriminate and disproportionate attacks, abduction, hostage-taking, unlawful killings, torture and other ill-treatment and use instructions to members strictly prohibiting such acts in all circumstances;
- give immediate and clear instructions from the highest levels of leadership that all of their combatants are bound by all provisions of applicable international humanitarian law;
- remove any members suspected of abuses from positions and situations where they might continue to perpetrate abuses.[31]

Human Rights Watch reported that Afghans faced in 2007 escalating violations of their human rights at the hands of a variety of abusers: the Taliban and other anti-government insurgent groups, including Gulbuddin Hekmatyar's Hezb-e Islami and tribal militias, criminal groups and local warlords. The Taliban began using anti-personnel mines in Helmand province again, complicating efforts to eradicate mines from one of the most mine-infested countries in the world. The Taliban increasingly relied on public executions to terrorize and rule populations living in areas under their influence. They carried out at least 28 beheadings, several of them filmed and broadcast on the internet. The Taliban targeted humanitarian aid workers, journalists, doctors, religious leaders, and civilian government employees, condemning them as spies or collaborators.[32]

In August 2007, Human Rights Watch issued a report, entitled: *Afghanistan: Taliban Should Immediately Free Hostages*. It considered the recent abduction and hostage-taking of at least five Afghan, two German, and 23 South Korean civilians, and the reported killing of several of them, as war crimes.[33] Human Rights Watch furthermore documented what it called increasingly abusive behaviour by the Taliban in a series of reports; *The Human Cost: The Consequences of Insurgent Attacks in Afghanistan*[34] (April 2007), describing how Taliban and associated forces sharply escalated suicide bombings and other attacks in 2006 and early 2007, killing hundreds of civilians. Its report *Lessons in Terror: Attacks on Education in Afghanistan*[35] (July 2006) described the Taliban's increasing attacks on schools and teachers.

Conclusions

The five cases described here differ in detail from each other. Afghanistan is subject to international intervention in support of the central government that can barely exert its authority in many parts of the country. The case of Somalia is somewhat similar in that there is hardly a central government as well as because of foreign intervention by Ethiopia. Likewise, large parts of the Democratic Republic of the Congo are not controlled by the central government. The government of Colombia controls larger parts of the country, though it has not been able to defeat the guerrilla forces that dispute its authority. In Spain, there is only the local conflict in the Basque region, but the central government has not been able to put an end to the challenges made by ETA.

In all of these cases non-governmental entities (NGEs) challenge the central government's authority and abuse human rights. Some NGEs could be called "quasi governments" or "governments in aspiration". The Taliban in Afghanistan earlier formed the central government, from which they were ousted in 2001 Yet, they might conceivably return to their former position of power.

These NGEs have not accepted international human rights conventions and cannot be formally held accountable. Yet, wherever they are in a position of power, they may be obligated not to violate basic human rights. That is at least the position of the two major international NGOs, Amnesty International and Human Rights Watch. As said before, for the victims of human rights abuses, it does not make much difference whether they are being tortured, raped, summarily killed or made to "disappear" by forces serving the central government or an NGE.

The two major human rights organizations find it difficult to approach the leaders of the "armed opposition". The opposing forces often lack a central site of authority and it is often difficult to determine who exactly can act on their behalf. Nevertheless, both in the case of Somalia and Afghanistan Amnesty International has formulated recommendations to these forces to the effect that they should stop their violent actions against the civilian population. While neither organization has taken a position with regard to the raging military conflicts in these countries, they have emphasized the need to protect the civilian population. So far, little is known of any reaction by the armed opposition, except for the Taliban who stress the need to do away with "spies" and "collaborators".

The two NGOs appear to have ended their former hesitations about dealing with such non-governmental entities. At least in these cases, they do deal with hostage taking and abductions by the groups mentioned. In other countries, such as Mexico and other Latin-American countries, most abductions would still be considered of a criminal rather than a political nature. Yet, it may not always easy to make this distinction.

In the remaining decades of the twenty-first century the activities of non-governmental entities will well receive greater attention from human rights organizations. The dilution of state power seems to be on the increase. With the weakening of state power and even the demise of governments comes an upsurge of new, "non-government" groups who seem to have little in common except an abundant supply of weapons and a striving for power. Together with that come killings of civilians, torture, extrajudicial executions, and other abuses of international human rights standards. The existence and contents of those standards are usually little known to the perpetrators. This only further complicates the already daunting tasks of human rights organizations.

8
Conclusions

Introduction

In an earlier publication that appeared some eight years ago, I raised six controversial themes about human rights then under debate.[1] These themes were:

- the universality of human rights;
- the promotion of economic, social and cultural rights;
- the place of collective human rights;
- how to deal with past violations of human rights and humanitarian law;
- the role of large multinational enterprises;
- the place of refugees and displaced persons.

None of these issues has been satisfactorily resolved, but some of them are less strongly debated than others, certainly if seen from the perspective of human rights NGOs.

The universality of human rights and the related problem of cultural relativism are less of today's focus. Many human rights NGOs assume the universality of human rights as a point of departure. This assumption provides them with the right to challenge governments' performance in the field of human rights. It also provides the background to their main weapon, the "mobilization of shame". Governments that accept the notion of the universality of human rights would be compelled to react to the challenges made by NGOs and sometimes be willing to do something about it. Claims based on notions of "cultural relativism" or "Asian values" that are sup-posedly different from universal human rights are now heard less often than in the 1990s.

Almost all governments (the United States being a notable excep-tion) pay at least lip service to the promotion of economic, social and cultural rights on an equal level with civil and political rights. That issue was more or less settled at the second World Conference on Human Rights in Vienna in 1993, where agreement was reached on the importance of the respect for *all* human rights. Although the major human rights NGOs still tend to put more emphasis on civil and political rights, they do pay attention to economic, social and cultural rights as well. Amnesty International made a major move in this direction, when it decided in 2001 to go "full spectrum", a notion that had for many years received much resistance from many segments of the organization.

The notion of collective rights has also become less controversial than it used to be. Though the concept of "peoples" as holders of the right to self-determination remains undefined, the indigenous now receive more attention. Major countries such as Canada and Australia, under constant pressure from international and domestic NGOs, have decided to pass legislation granting major rights to their indigenous populations. That does not mean that the issue has been settled once and for all, but it has lost some of its principled character.

Major progress has been achieved on methods, some of them novel, to deal with past violations of human rights and humanitar-ian law. Truth and reconciliation commissions have sprung up in many parts of the world. A major NGO, the International Centre for Transitional Justice, provides information and spreads knowledge on the subject. The international tribunals on Yugoslavia and Rwanda have become politically accepted. The International Criminal Court, which was established thanks to great pressure from important NGOs at the founding conference in Rome in 1998,[2] has started operations and is also gaining political acceptance, although again, the United States remains an important and challenging opponent.

Many major multinational enterprises pay increasing attention to human rights. This has been partly achieved through the efforts of international human rights NGOs that have focused their attention on these actors. A wide variety of dialogues have sprung up and remind enterprises of their responsibility in this field. Codes of conduct have been formulated to establish standards of behaviour. Although a great deal of work remains to be done, the issue has become less controversial than it used to be.

Finally, the issue of refugees and displaced persons remains a major problem. Recent conflicts as in West Darfur and in Georgia have led to a constant stream of refugees. Even if the United Nations High Commissioner for Refugees (UNHCR) does his best, the agency lacks the funds and facilities to deal adequately with the matter. The close link between the number of refugees and the violation of fundamental human rights is insufficiently realized. Supporting efforts by NGOs remain underfinanced and inadequate.

The question of what exactly constitutes an NGO in good standing remains. Consultative status with the ECOSOC may offer an indication, but among the NGOs that have received that status, some might be termed "GONGOs". It remains hard to distinguish such GONGOs from fully independent organizations. The existence of GONGOs nevertheless illustrates the importance NGOs have gained in the eyes of governments. On the other hand, not all truly independent NGOs may aim for achieving consultative status. In the end, the only true test whether an NGO has an independent character is by its colleagues, the other NGOs.

At the end of Chapter 1 a number of questions were raised. In the subsequent chapters an effort was made to find answers to these questions. These answers are recapitulated in this chapter by way of conclusions.

Legitimacy

Human rights NGOs base their actions mainly on their knowledge and expertise in the field of human rights. They gather reliable information that is eagerly sought by governments and on what they must base their accountability. The question of accountability is often raised by those who do not take kindly to the activities of NGOs, such as governments that come in for criticism because of their human rights record.

If an organization has a membership, the members to whom it is formally accountable will usually elect its leadership directly or indirectly. This may help to establish the transparency of the organization. Not all "members" are, however, *active* members. Being a member of a human rights organization often means not much more than registering as a financial donor. Many of the human rights NGOs are not necessarily, as they claim to be, closer to the "grass roots" than the governments. From the point of view of accountability, far more important than the membership is, as Van Bijsterveld has put it, the representation of values and interests, rather than of persons.[3]

Impact

Human rights NGOs have been crucial in the development of human rights since the end of the Second World War. They advanced the major ideas about standard setting that led to the manifold international treaties on human rights. They also continuously exert pressure on governments to remind them of their commitments. Left to their own devices, most governments would be reluctant to enter into the field of human rights. It would seem fair to state that without the NGOs, human rights would have drifted to the bottom of international agendas.

The standard answer to the often-asked question about the precise impact of the activities of a human rights organization is: "We don't really know."[4] The number of its activities and of its publications, both of which have grown enormously over the years, is no indication of its impact. Expansion of these activities proves neither that the number of human rights violations covered by the organization has grown, nor that its effectiveness has increased or decreased. It only shows that the *information*, which is made available, has grown. All other inferences are a matter of speculation.

Welch distinguishes between "claimed" and "real" effectiveness. He asks: "Ultimately, should we be more persuaded by the successes that NGOs have claimed, or did they contribute only marginally to changes that would have occurred "naturally"?[5] NGOs actually do not often claim major successes. Most of them are quite modest in making such claims. Whether the changes referred to by Welch would have occurred anyway, is of course difficult to say. It is therefore safer and probably closer to the truth to limit oneself to the "marginal successes".

Despite the abundance of non-governmental human rights organizations little is actually known about their effectiveness or impact, except for the fact that they tend to rely on what is commonly known as the "mobilization of shame". Yet, it is hard to put a finger on what exactly constitutes such mobilization. It refers to governments being "shamed" into observing human rights standards. Governments are not eager to admit that they are being influenced by human rights NGOs (or any other NGOs for that matter). Kamminga has rightly observed that governments are reluctant to cede power and influence to NGOs that could pose a threat to their own power and influence.[6]

Governments and NGOs need each other: governments, because they can use the information supplied by NGOs; NGOs, because their objective – the promotion and protection of human rights in the world – can only be attained through the activities of governments. They are as it were two sides of the same coin.

A major source of influence of human rights NGOs is the supply of reliable information, for example to governments. That does not of course necessarily mean that governments will also do whatever the NGO asks them to do. But once they have digested the information supplied by the NGO, it may also colour their views on the matter. But another aspect of NGO activities comes close to the exercise of influence. By continuously harping on a particular issue, NGOs may be able to change the officials' view of the matter: *gutta cavat lapidem.*[7] Thus it has been suggested that the continuous pressure by NGOs has helped to change official views of the death penalty from seeing it in particular as a matter of a severe means of punishment to mainly a matter of human rights.[8] This does not mean that the death penalty will be immediately abolished by the state in question, but that it may lead to results in the long run. For example, Chinese officials, when questioned on the issue of the death penalty, have suggested that eventually it will be abolished in China, but "that the country is not yet ready for it".[9]

NGO representatives and government officials both welcome personal contacts. They find it on the whole useful to exchange views, though they will of course often not agree. Probably the threshold for access to government officials has been lowered for NGO representatives. Yet, it would seem to be of vital importance that the latter always remain aware of why these contacts are taking place. Obviously, the government representatives will express views that serve the interests of the government, while the NGO representatives can afford to be single minded on the issue of human rights. In the words of one NGO representative: "The limit is when I am expected to say things I do not really agree with."[10]

Particularly striking to an outsider is the warmth and positive feelings with which many representatives of the two parties often speak of each other – in particular persons involved in the activities of global international organizations such as the United Nations in New York and Geneva. Many of them like each other and speak in terms of working for the same goals – albeit from a different perspective.

Sometimes, a close personal relationship builds up, in particular if individuals in the course of their career have "switched sides". Such individuals are familiar with the other side of the coin and can help to smooth matters over. A danger is that the NGO representatives may become so familiar with the problems faced by the government representatives, by fully "understanding" the latter's position, that their actions may lose some of the required acumen.

Quiet versus public diplomacy

To choose between quiet diplomacy and making statements in public is not always easy. Quiet diplomacy will be preferred, if it will make it easier to persuade a government to mend its ways, without losing face. A matter of prestige is then at issue on both sides. The NGO may want to show to its adherents that it is really effective in its struggle for human rights, while the government may prefer not to be seen as giving in to NGO pressure. If an NGO chooses quiet diplomacy on a particular issue, it will always have the threat of "going public" in reserve.

Quiet diplomacy requires trust. Can one trust the public official to do what he or she has promised to do? Can the NGO representative be trusted not to speak out on confidential arrangements? Such mutual trust can only be built up in the course of time. A change of personnel may mean that both parties have to start all over again. And finally, not all individuals are by their personality equally suited to such proceedings. Indeed, one may wonder whether many NGO representatives have the experience and expertise to play what is essentially a diplomats' game.

If they use the practice of "quiet diplomacy" to achieve their goals, NGO representatives must have a good personal relationship with their interlocutors. Government representatives may be willing to help, for example, in facilitating the release of a victim of human rights violations, if their country is not openly attacked and can thus avoid losing face in an international forum. "Naming and shaming" does not help quiet diplomacy. However, the former may still be necessary, if quiet diplomacy does not deliver the results requested.

The use of quiet diplomacy may be easier for NGOs that do not have a membership. Members of NGOs are eager to see results and may not be impressed by references by their representatives to "actions behind the scenes". The same is true of NGOs working together in *ad hoc* coalitions. The members may not be impressed by invisible activities of their own organizations in New York or Geneva, or with other, similar organizations.

The rank and file of the NGOs wants to see results. That is one of the reasons why the NGOs must produce "good news stories" to maintain the morale of the membership. If no such stories are produced, the rank and file may lose its enthusiasm for the cause and may even leave the organization.

Public action needs cooperation on the part of the news media. The latter will be more interested in reporting on an NGO's activities if there is actually "news" involved. Therefore NGOs sometimes take recourse to publicity stunts that may not be to everybody's taste but have the advantage of attracting attention.

Public officials

Why do public officials pay attention at all to whatever actions of human rights NGOs? It would be by far easier to ignore such actions and that is of course what many governments would prefer to do. However, the threat of the "mobilization of shame" remains. All governments want to be seen as civilized and as respecting human rights. No government in the world will easily admit that its officials practice torture or make their victims "disappear".

The main condition for success or failure of human rights NGOs is the reliability of its reporting. It may take years to build up a reputation of reliability, but a few failures can demolish that reputation in a much shorter period of time. Once it is gone, it will be very difficult to regain it.

Some exchange of personnel between the staffs of governments, intergovernmental organizations and NGOs is normal. Although such individuals may not "betray" the secrets of their former employers, they can of course use the experience and expertise that they have built up in their new jobs.

The United Nations

The treaty-based monitoring committees and the Charter-based special procedures could hardly have functioned, if not fed by the information that is supplied by NGOs. Initially, NGOs feared that governments might use the newly created Human Rights Council to undo some of the privileges they had received under its predecessor, the Commission on Human Rights. So far, this fear has not materialized. On the contrary, the newly created Universal Periodic Review of states has provided NGOs with new opportunities to influence the decision-making process. However, NGOs must always watch for possible negative developments. Although they may at times need each other, in the end there is no love lost between NGOs and governments (especially of course the ones that are being criticized for their human rights performance).

The NGOs benefit from close mutual cooperation. The voice of many will be heard more clearly than the voice of one organization and the information many gather will be greater than what solitary efforts can find. Yet, the NGOs find it as hard to achieve such cooperation as governments. Each organization has its own axes to grind and would reject a compromise that might damage some of its cherished objectives. Governments for their part are not unwilling to encourage such cooperation, as it may limit the number of NGO representatives taking the floor in meetings of United Nations bodies. In the end, it should not be governments, but the NGOs themselves that should regulate their activities in terms of efficiency and effectiveness.

Governments have regrettably so far not accepted the Cardozo Committee's recommendations. The Commission saw the great possibilities offered by NGOs to contribute to a greater role of civil society in the United Nations system. The new UN Secretary-General Ban Ky Moon could, if he wanted to, revive the panel's recommendations, but so far he seems not very likely to do so.

Standard-setting

Many treaties in the field of human rights that expand the Universal Declaration of Human Rights and the two international covenants would not have come about without the initiatives taken by and the material provided by human rights NGOs. They drafted texts for governments and international organizations and commented on drafts produced by governments. Here the expertise of NGOs serves handily, as the NGO representatives often know much more about the subject than governmental delegates. Typically, NGO representatives stay in their jobs for many years, while the government representatives are periodically rotated. Here also the cooperation between general human rights organizations and organizations that are specialized in a particular topic may produce important results. While the former know more about procedures in intergovernmental organizations, the latter possess the necessary specialized knowledge of the subject.

Protection of human rights

Human rights organizations strive energetically to offer protection to the victims of human rights violations. They may work on behalf of "prisoners of conscience", other political prisoners, victims of torture practices and similar abuses. It is hard to say whether, and to what extent, their activities have helped to improve the situation. Clearly in the absence of their efforts things would not be better.

Human rights organizations provide important material to truth and reconciliation commissions and to the newly established tribunals as well as the International Criminal Court. It is far too early to reach a conclusion as to whether these new phenomena should be considered a success. NGOs certainly have made considerable efforts to turn them into a success.

"Shadow reports" are another important instrument used by NGOs. They accompany the official reports submitted by governments and thus provide international monitoring committees with the necessary additional information. This also benefits the Universal Periodic Review initiated by the United Nations Human Rights Council that has just started. Again, it is far too early to judge the degree of its effectiveness.

Non-governmental entities

Human rights NGOs find it easier now than in the past to deal with the activities of non-governmental entities, such as "armed opposition groups". The NGOs are now less concerned that reacting to such activities would mean a kind of informal recognition, which would not be appreciated by the formal government in power. In some "failing states" a complete absence of such formal government means that the NGOs have little alternative to proceeding. For the victims of human rights violations it does not make much difference whether armed groups working for the government or for the armed opposition commit the violations. The number of such non-governmental entities may even increase as time goes by, which will make it even more important for the human rights NGOs to deal with them.

The future of human rights NGOs

Will the future hold in store a role for human rights NGOs? As the old saying goes: "Prediction is difficult, especially about the future." There is no reason to expect that human rights NGOs will wither away, but will they continue to occupy the relatively important positions they now hold as actors in international relations? That will depend on the quality of their work and the extent to which they will be able to mobilize public opinion as they have done in recent years. The aim of most human rights NGOs is to make themselves superfluous by turning the world into a true "international community" that respects human rights. But to expect this to happen in the near future would be a sign of greater optimism than this author can accept.

Appendix 1 ECOSOC Resolution E/1996/31: Consultative Relationship Between the United Nations and Non-Governmental Organizations

The Economic and Social Council,

Recalling Article 71 of the Charter of the United Nations,

Recalling also its resolution 1993/80 of 30 July 1993, in which it requested a general review of arrangements for consultation with non-governmental organizations, with a view to updating, if necessary, Council resolution 1296 (XLIV) of 23 May 1968, as well as introducing coherence in the rules governing the participation of non-governmental organizations in international conferences convened by the United Nations, and also an examination of ways and means of improving practical arrangements for the work of the Committee on Non-Governmental Organizations and the Non-Governmental Organizations Section of the Secretariat,

Recalling further its decision 1995/304 of 26 July 1995,

Confirming the need to take into account the full diversity of the non-governmental organizations at the national, regional and international levels,

Acknowledging the breadth of non-governmental organizations' expertise and the capacity of non-governmental organizations to support the work of the United Nations,

Taking into account the changes in the non-governmental sector, including the emergence of a large number of national and regional organizations,

Calling upon the governing bodies of the relevant organizations, bodies and specialized agencies of the United Nations system to examine the principles and practices relating to their consultations with non-governmental organizations and to take action, as appropriate, to promote coherence in the light of the provisions of the present resolution,

Approves the following update of the arrangements set out in its resolution 1296 (XLIV) of 23 May 1968:

ARRANGEMENTS FOR CONSULTATION WITH NON-GOVERNMENTAL ORGANIZATIONS

I. Principles to be applied in the establishment of consultative relations

II. Principles governing the nature of the consultative arrangements

III. Establishment of consultative relationships

IV. Consultation with the Council

V. Consultation with commissions and other subsidiary organs of the Council resources

VI. Consultations with ad hoc committees of the Council

VII. Participation of non-governmental organizations in International Conferences convened by the United Nations and their preparatory process

VIII. Suspension and withdrawal of consultative status

IX. Council committee on non-governmental Organizations

X. Consultation with the secretariat

XI. Secretariat support

Part I   PRINCIPLES TO BE APPLIED IN THE ESTABLISHMENT OF CONSULTATIVE RELATIONS

The following principles shall be applied in establishing consultative relations with non-governmental organizations:

1. The organization shall be concerned with matters falling within the competence of the Economic and Social Council and its subsidiary bodies.

2. The aims and purposes of the organization shall be in conformity with the spirit, purposes and principles of the Charter of the United Nations.

3. The organization shall undertake to support the work of the United Nations and to promote knowledge of its principles and activities, in accordance with its own aims and purposes and the nature and scope of its competence and activities.

4. Except where expressly stated otherwise, the term "organization" shall refer to non-governmental organizations at the national, subregional, regional or international levels.

5. Consultative relationships may be established with international, regional, subregional and national organizations, in conformity with the Charter of the United Nations and the principles and criteria established under the present resolution. The Committee, in considering applications for consultative status, should ensure, to the extent possible, participation of non-governmental organizations from all regions, and particularly from developing countries, in order to help achieve a just, balanced, effective and genuine involvement of non-governmental organizations from all regions and areas of the world. The Committee shall also pay particular attention to non-governmental organizations that have special expertise or experience upon which the Council may wish to draw.

6. Greater participation of non-governmental organizations from developing countries in international conferences convened by the United Nations should be encouraged.

7. Greater involvement of non-governmental organizations from countries with economies in transition should be encouraged.

8. Regional, subregional and national organizations, including those affiliated to an international organization already in status, may be admitted provided that they can demonstrate that their programme of work is of direct relevance to the aims and purposes of the United Nations and, in the case of national organizations, after consultation with the Member State concerned. The views expressed by the Member State, if any, shall be communicated to the non-governmental organization concerned, which shall have the opportunity to respond to those views through the Committee on Non-Governmental Organizations.

9. The organization shall be of recognized standing within the particular field of its competence or of a representative character. Where there exist a number of organizations with similar objectives, interests and basic views in a given field, they may, for the purposes of consultation with the Council, form a joint committee or other body authorized to carry on such consultation for the group as a whole.

10. The organization shall have an established headquarters, with an executive officer. It shall have a democratically adopted constitution, a copy of which shall be deposited with the Secretary-General of the United Nations, and which shall provide for the determination of policy by a conference, congress or other representative body, and for an executive organ responsible to the policy-making body.

11. The organization shall have authority to speak for its members through its authorized representatives. Evidence of this authority shall be presented, if requested.

12. The organization shall have a representative structure and possess appropriate mechanisms of accountability to its members, who shall exercise effective control over its policies and actions through the exercise of voting rights or other appropriate democratic and transparent decision-making processes. Any such organization that is not established by a governmental entity or intergovernmental agreement shall be considered a non-governmental organization for the purpose of these arrangements, including organizations that accept members designated by governmental authorities, provided that such membership does not interfere with the free expression of views of the organization.

13. The basic resources of the organization shall be derived in the main part from contributions of the national affiliates or other components or from individual members. Where voluntary contributions have been received, their amounts and donors shall be faithfully revealed to the Council Committee on Non-Governmental Organizations. Where, however, the above criterion is not fulfilled and an organization is financed from other sources, it must explain to the satisfaction of the Committee its reasons for not meeting the requirements laid down in this paragraph. Any financial contribution or other support, direct or indirect, from a Government to the organization shall be openly declared to the Committee through the Secretary-General and fully recorded in the financial and other records of the organization and shall be devoted to purposes in accordance with the aims of the United Nations.

14. In considering the establishment of consultative relations with a non-governmental organization, the Council will take into account whether the field of activity of the organization is wholly or mainly within the field of a specialized agency, and whether or not it could be admitted when it has, or may have, a consultative arrangement with a specialized agency.

15. The granting, suspension and withdrawal of consultative status, as well as the interpretation of norms and decisions relating to this matter, are the prerogative of Member States exercised through the Economic and Social Council and its Committee on Non-Governmental Organizations. A non-governmental organization applying for general or special consultative status or a listing on the Roster shall have the opportunity to respond to any objections being raised in the Committee before the Committee takes its decision.

16. The provisions of the present resolution shall apply to the United Nations regional commissions and their subsidiary bodies mutatis mutandis.

17. In recognizing the evolving relationship between the United Nations and non-governmental organizations, the Economic and Social Council, in

consultation with the Committee on Non-Governmental Organizations, will consider reviewing the consultative arrangements as and when necessary to facilitate, in the most effective manner possible, the contributions of non-governmental organizations to the work of the United Nations.

Part II PRINCIPLES GOVERNING THE NATURE OF THE CONSULTATIVE ARRANGEMENTS

18. A clear distinction is drawn in the Charter of the United Nations between participation without vote in the deliberations of the Council and the arrangements for consultation. Under Articles 69 and 70, participation is provided for only in the case of States not members of the Council, and of specialized agencies. Article 71, applying to non-governmental organizations, provides for suitable arrangements for consultation. This distinction, deliberately made in the Charter, is fundamental and the arrangements for consultation should not be such as to accord to non-governmental organizations the same rights of participation as are accorded to States not members of the Council and to the specialized agencies brought into relationship with the United Nations.

19. The arrangements should not be such as to overburden the Council or transform it from a body for coordination of policy and action, as contemplated in the Charter, into a general forum for discussion.

20. Decisions on arrangements for consultation should be guided by the principle that consultative arrangements are to be made, on the one hand, for the purpose of enabling the Council or one of its bodies to secure expert information or advice from organizations having special competence in the subjects for which consultative arrangements are made, and, on the other hand, to enable international, regional, subregional and national organizations that represent important elements of public opinion to express their views. Therefore, the arrangements for consultation made with each organization should relate to the subjects for which that organization has a special competence or in which it has a special interest. The organizations given consultative status should be limited to those whose activities in fields set out in paragraph 1 above qualify them to make a significant contribution to the work of the Council and should, in sum, as far as possible reflect in a balanced way the major viewpoints or interests in these fields in all areas and regions of the world.

Part III ESTABLISHMENT OF CONSULTATIVE RELATIONSHIPS

21. In establishing consultative relationships with each organization, regard shall be had to the nature and scope of its activities and to the assistance it may be expected to give to the Council or its subsidiary bodies in carrying out the functions set out in Chapters IX and X of the Charter of the United Nations.

22. Organizations that are concerned with most of the activities of the Council and its subsidiary bodies and can demonstrate to the satisfaction of the Council that they have substantive and sustained contributions to make to the achievement of the objectives of the United Nations in fields set out in paragraph 1 above, and are closely involved with the economic and social life of the peoples of the areas they represent and whose membership, which should be considerable, is broadly representative of major segments of society in a large number of countries in different regions of the world shall be known as organizations in general consultative status.

23. Organizations that have a special competence in, and are concerned specifically with, only a few of the fields of activity covered by the Council and its subsidiary bodies, and that are known within the fields for which they have or seek consultative status shall be known as organizations in special consultative status.

24. Other organizations that do not have general or special consultative status but that the Council, or the Secretary-General of the United Nations in consultation with the Council or its Committee on Non-Governmental Organizations, considers can make occasional and useful contributions to the work of the Council or its subsidiary bodies or other United Nations bodies within their competence shall be included in a list (to be known as the Roster). This list may also include organizations in consultative status or a similar relationship with a specialized agency or a United Nations body. These organizations shall be available for consultation at the request of the Council or its subsidiary bodies. The fact that an organization is on the Roster shall not in itself be regarded as a qualification for general or special consultative status should an organization seek such status.

25. Organizations to be accorded special consultative status because of their interest in the field of human rights should pursue the goals of promotion and protection of human rights in accordance with the spirit of the Charter of the United Nations, the Universal Declaration of Human Rights and the Vienna Declaration and Programme of Action.

26. Major organizations one of whose primary purposes is to promote the aims, objectives and purposes of the United Nations and a furtherance of the understanding of its work may be accorded consultative status.

Part IV   CONSULTATION WITH THE COUNCIL

Provisional agenda

27. The provisional agenda of the Council shall be communicated to organizations in general consultative status and special consultative status and to those on the Roster.

28. Organizations in general consultative status may propose to the Council Committee on Non-Governmental Organizations that the Committee request the Secretary-General to place items of special interest to the organizations in the provisional agenda of the Council.

Attendance at meetings

29. Organizations in general consultative status and special consultative status may designate authorized representatives to sit as observers at public meetings of the Council and its subsidiary bodies. Those on the Roster may have representatives present at such meetings concerned with matters within their field of competence. These attendance arrangements may be supplemented to include other modalities of participation.

Written statements

30. Written statements relevant to the work of the Council may be submitted by organizations in general consultative status and special consultative status on subjects in which these organizations have a special competence. Such statements shall be circulated by the Secretary-General of the United Nations to the members of the Council, except those statements that have become obsolete, for example, those dealing with matters already disposed of and those that had already been circulated in some other form.

31. The following conditions shall be observed regarding the submission and circulation of such statements:

(a) The written statement shall be submitted in one of the official languages;

(b) It shall be submitted in sufficient time for appropriate consultation to take place between the Secretary-General and the organization before circulation;

(c) The organization shall give due consideration to any comments that the Secretary-General may make in the course of such consultation before transmitting the statement in final form;

(d) A written statement submitted by an organization in general consultative status will be circulated in full if it does not exceed 2,000 words. Where a statement is in excess of 2,000 words, the organizations shall submit a summary which will be circulated or shall supply sufficient copies of the full text in the working languages for distribution. A statement will also be circulated in full, however, upon a specific request of the Council or its Committee on Non-Governmental Organizations;

(e) A written statement submitted by an organization in special consultative status or on the Roster will be circulated in full if it does not exceed 500 words.

Where a statement is in excess of 500 words, the organization shall submit a summary which will be circulated; such statements will be circulated in full, however, upon a specific request of the Council or its Committee on Non-Governmental Organizations;

(f) The Secretary-General, in consultation with the President of the Council, or the Council or its Committee on Non-Governmental Organizations, may invite organizations on the Roster to submit written statements. The provisions of subparagraphs (a), (b), (c) and (e) above shall apply to such statements;

(g) A written statement or summary, as the case may be, will be circulated by the Secretary-General in the working languages, and, upon the request of a member of the Council, in any of the official languages.

Oral presentations during meetings

32. (a) The Council Committee on Non-Governmental Organizations shall make recommendations to the Council as to which organizations in general consultative status should make an oral presentation to the Council and on which items they should be heard. Such organizations shall be entitled to make one statement to the Council, subject to the approval of the Council. In the absence of a subsidiary body of the Council with jurisdiction in a major field of interest to the Council and to organizations in special consultative status, the Committee may recommend that organizations in special consultative status be heard by the Council on the subject in its field of interest;

(b) Whenever the Council discusses the substance of an item proposed by a non-governmental organization in general consultative status and included in the agenda of the Council, such an organization shall be entitled to present orally to the Council, as appropriate, an introductory statement of an expository nature. Such an organization may be invited by the President of the Council, with the consent of the relevant body, to make, in the course of the discussion of the item before the Council, an additional statement for purposes of clarification.

Part V CONSULTATION WITH COMMISSIONS AND OTHER SUBSIDIARY ORGANS OF THE COUNCIL

Provisional agenda

33. The provisional agenda of sessions of commissions and other subsidiary organs of the Council shall be communicated to organizations in general consultative status and special consultative status and those on the Roster.

34. Organizations in general consultative status may propose items for the provisional agenda of commissions, subject to the following conditions:

(a) An organization that intends to propose such an item shall inform the Secretary-General of the United Nations at least 63 days before the commencement of the session and before formally proposing an item shall give due consideration to any comments the Secretary-General may make;

(b) The proposal shall be formally submitted with the relevant basic documentation not later than 49 days before the commencement of the session. The item shall be included in the agenda of the commission if it is adopted by a two-thirds majority of those present and voting.

Attendance at meetings

35. Organizations in general consultative status and special consultative status may designate authorized representatives to sit as observers at public meetings of the commissions and other subsidiary organs of the Council. Organizations on the Roster may have representatives present at such meetings that are concerned with matters within their field of competence. These attendance arrangements may be supplemented to include other modalities of participation.

Written statements

36. Written statements relevant to the work of the commissions or other subsidiary organs may be submitted by organizations in general consultative status and special consultative status on subjects for which these organizations have a special competence. Such statements shall be circulated by the Secretary-General to members of the commission or other subsidiary organs, except those statements that have become obsolete, for example, those dealing with matters already disposed of and those that have already been circulated in some other form to members of the commission or other subsidiary organs.

37. The following conditions shall be observed regarding the submission and circulation of such written statements:

(a) The written statement shall be submitted in one of the official languages;

(b) It shall be submitted in sufficient time for appropriate consultation to take place between the Secretary-General and the organization before circulation;

(c) The organization shall give due consideration to any comments that the Secretary-General may make in the course of such consultation before transmitting the statement in final form;

(d) A written statement submitted by an organization in general consultative status will be circulated in full if it does not exceed 2,000 words. Where a statement is in excess of 2,000 words, the organization shall submit a summary, which will be circulated, or shall supply sufficient copies of the full text in the working languages for distribution. A statement will also be circulated in full, however, upon the specific request of the commission or other subsidiary organs;

(e) A written statement submitted by an organization in special consultative status will be circulated in full if it does not exceed 1,500 words. Where a statement is in excess of 1,500 words, the organization shall submit a summary, which will be circulated, or shall supply sufficient copies of the full text in the working languages for distribution. A statement will also be circulated in full, however, upon the specific request of the commission or other subsidiary organs;

(f) The Secretary-General, in consultation with the chairman of the relevant commission or other subsidiary organ, or the commission or other subsidiary organ itself, may invite organizations on the Roster to submit written statements. The provisions in subparagraphs (a), (b), (c) and (e) above shall apply to such statements;

(g) A written statement or summary, as the case may be, will be circulated by the Secretary-General in the working languages and, upon the request of a member of the commission or other subsidiary organ, in any of the official languages.

Oral presentations during meetings

38. (a) The commission or other subsidiary organs may consult with organizations in general consultative status and special consultative status either directly or through a committee or committees established for the purpose. In all cases, such consultations may be arranged upon the request of the organization;

(b) On the recommendation of the Secretary-General and at the request of the commission or other subsidiary organs, organizations on the Roster may also be heard by the commission or other subsidiary organs.

Special studies

39. Subject to the relevant rules of procedure on financial implications, a commission or other subsidiary organ may recommend that an organization that has special competence in a particular field should undertake specific studies or investigations or prepare specific papers for the commission. The limitations of paragraphs 37 (d) and (e) above shall not apply in this case.

Part VI   CONSULTATIONS WITH AD HOC COMMITTEES OF THE COUNCIL

40. The arrangements for consultation between ad hoc committees of the Council authorized to meet between sessions of the Council and organizations in general consultative status and special consultative status and on the Roster shall follow those approved for commissions of the Council, unless the Council or the committee decides otherwise.

Part VII   PARTICIPATION OF NON-GOVERNMENTAL ORGANIZATIONS IN INTERNATIONAL CONFERENCES CONVENED BY THE UNITED NATIONS AND THEIR PREPARATORY PROCESS

41. Where non-governmental organizations have been invited to participate in an international conference convened by the United Nations, their accreditation is the prerogative of Member States, exercised through the respective preparatory committee. Such accreditation should be preceded by an appropriate process to determine their eligibility.

42. Non-governmental organizations in general consultative status, special consultative status and on the Roster, that express their wish to attend the relevant international conferences convened by the United Nations and the meetings of the preparatory bodies of the said conferences shall as a rule be accredited for participation. Other non-governmental organizations wishing to be accredited may apply to the secretariat of the conference for this purpose in accordance with the following requirements.

43. The secretariat of the conference shall be responsible for the receipt and preliminary evaluation of requests from non-governmental organizations for accreditation to the conference and its preparatory process. In the discharge of its functions, the secretariat of the conference shall work in close cooperation and coordination with the Non-Governmental Organizations Section of the Secretariat, and shall be guided by the relevant provisions of Council resolution 1296 (XLIV) as updated.

44. All such applications must be accompanied by information on the competence of the organization and the relevance of its activities to the work of the conference and its preparatory committee, with an indication of the particular areas of the conference agenda and preparations to which such competence and relevance pertain, and should include, *inter alia*, the following information:

(a) The purpose of the organization;

(b) Information as to the programmes and activities of the organization in areas relevant to the conference and its preparatory process and the country or countries in which they are carried out. Non-governmental organizations seeking accreditation shall be asked to confirm their interest in the goals and objectives of the conference;

(c) Confirmation of the activities of the organization at the national, regional or international level;

(d) Copies of the annual or other reports of the organization with financial statements, and a list of financial sources and contributions, including governmental contributions;

(e) A list of members of the governing body of the organization and their countries of nationality;

(f) A description of the membership of the organization, indicating the total number of members, the names of organizations that are members and their geographical distribution;

(g) A copy of the constitution and/or by-laws of the organization.

45. In the evaluation of the relevance of applications of non-governmental organizations for accreditation to the conference and its preparatory process, it is agreed that a determination shall be made based on their background and involvement in the subject areas of the conference.

46. The secretariat shall publish and disseminate to Member States on a periodic basis the updated list of applications received. Member States may submit comments on any of the applications on the list 14 days from receipt of the above-mentioned list by Member States. The comments of Member States shall be communicated to the non-governmental organization concerned, which shall have the opportunity to respond.

47. In cases where the secretariat believes, on the basis of the information provided in accordance with the present resolution, that the organization has established its competence and the relevance of its activities to the work of the preparatory committee, it shall recommend to the preparatory committee that the organization be accredited. In cases where the secretariat does not recommend the granting of accreditation, it shall make available to the preparatory committee its reasons for not doing so. The secretariat should ensure that its recommendations are available to members of the preparatory committee at least one week prior to the start of each session. The secretariat must notify such applicants of the reasons for non-recommendation and provide an opportunity to respond to objections and furnish additional information as may be required.

48. The preparatory committee shall decide on all recommendations for accreditation within 24 hours after the recommendations of the secretariat

have been taken up by the preparatory committee in plenary meeting. In the event of a decision not being taken within this period, interim accreditation shall be accorded until such time as a decision is taken.

49. A non-governmental organization that has been granted accreditation to attend a session of the preparatory committee, including related preparatory meetings of regional commissions, may attend all its future sessions, as well as the conference itself.

50. In recognition of the intergovernmental nature of the conference and its preparatory process, active participation of non-governmental organizations therein, while welcome, does not entail a negotiating role.

51. The non-governmental organizations accredited to the international conference may be given, in accordance with established United Nations practice and at the discretion of the chairperson and the consent of the body concerned, an opportunity to briefly address the preparatory committee and the conference in plenary meetings and their subsidiary bodies.

52. Non-governmental organizations accredited to the conference may make written presentations during the preparatory process in the official languages of the United Nations as they deem appropriate. Those written presentations shall not be issued as official documents except in accordance with United Nations rules of procedure.

53. Non-governmental organizations without consultative status that participate in international conferences and wish to obtain consultative status later on should apply through the normal procedures established under Council resolution 1296 (XLIV) as updated. Recognizing the importance of the participation of non-governmental organizations that attend a conference in the follow-up process, the Committee on Non-Governmental Organizations, in considering their application, shall draw upon the documents already submitted by that organization for accreditation to the conference and any additional information submitted by the non-governmental organization supporting its interest, relevance and capacity to contribute to the implementation phase. The Committee shall review such applications as expeditiously as possible so as to allow participation of the respective organization in the implementation phase of the conference. In the interim, the Economic and Social Council shall decide on the participation of non-governmental organizations accredited to an international conference in the work of the relevant functional commission on the follow-up to and implementation of that conference.

54. The suspension and withdrawal of the accreditation of non-governmental organizations to United Nations international conferences at all stages shall be guided by the relevant provisions of the present resolution.

Part VIII   SUSPENSION AND WITHDRAWAL OF CONSULTATIVE STATUS

55. Organizations granted consultative status by the Council and those on the Roster shall conform at all times to the principles governing the establishment and nature of their consultative relations with the Council. In periodically reviewing the activities of non-governmental organizations on the basis of the reports submitted under paragraph 61 (c) below and other relevant information, the Council Committee on Non-Governmental Organizations shall determine the extent to which the organizations have complied with the principles governing consultative status and have contributed to the work of the Council, and may recommend to the Council suspension of or exclusion from consultative status of organizations that have not met the requirements for consultative status as set forth in the present resolution.

56. In cases where the Committee on Non-Governmental Organizations has decided to recommend that the general or special consultative status of a non-governmental organization or its listing on the Roster be suspended or withdrawn, the non-governmental organization concerned shall be given written reasons for that decision and shall have an opportunity to present its response for appropriate consideration by the Committee as expeditiously as possible.

57. The consultative status of non-governmental organizations with the Economic and Social Council and the listing of those on the Roster shall be suspended up to three years or withdrawn in the following cases:

(a) If an organization, either directly or through its affiliates or representatives acting on its behalf, clearly abuses its status by engaging in a pattern of acts contrary to the purposes and principles of the Charter of the United Nations including unsubstantiated or politically motivated acts against Member States of the United Nations incompatible with those purposes and principles;

(b) If there exists substantiated evidence of influence from proceeds resulting from internationally recognized criminal activities such as the illicit drugs trade, money-laundering or the illegal arms trade;

(c) If, within the preceding three years, an organization did not make any positive or effective contribution to the work of the United Nations and, in particular, of the Council or its commissions or other subsidiary organs.

58. The consultative status of organizations in general consultative status and special consultative status and the listing of those on the Roster shall

be suspended or withdrawn by the decision of the Economic and Social Council on the recommendation of its Committee on Non-Governmental Organizations.

59. An organization whose consultative status or whose listing on the Roster is withdrawn may be entitled to reapply for consultative status or for inclusion on the Roster not sooner than three years after the effective date of such withdrawal.

Part IX   COUNCIL COMMITTEE ON NON-GOVERNMENTAL ORGANIZATIONS

60. The members of the Committee on Non-Governmental Organizations shall be elected by the Council on the basis of equitable geographical representation, in accordance with the relevant Council resolutions and decision[1] and rules of procedure of the Council.[2] The Committee shall elect its Chairman and other officers as necessary.

61. The functions of the Committee shall include the following:

(a) The Committee shall be responsible for regular monitoring of the evolving relationship between non-governmental organizations and the United Nations. With a view to fulfilling this responsibility, the Committee shall hold, before each of its sessions, and at other times as necessary, consultations with organizations in consultative status to discuss questions of interest to the Committee or to the organizations relating to the relationship between the non-governmental organizations and the United Nations. A report on such consultations shall be transmitted to the Council for appropriate action;

(b) The Committee shall hold its regular session before the substantive session of the Council each year and preferably before the sessions of functional commissions of the Council to consider applications for general consultative status and special consultative status and for listing on the Roster made by non-governmental organizations and requests for changes in status, and to make recommendations thereon to the Council. Upon approval by the Council, the Committee may hold other meetings as required to fulfil its mandated responsibilities. Organizations shall give due consideration to any comments on technical matters that the Secretary-General of the United Nations may make in receiving such applications for the Committee. The Committee shall consider at each such session applications received by the Secretary-General not later than 1 June of the preceding year, on which sufficient data have been distributed to the members of the Committee not later than six weeks before the applications are to be considered. Transitional arrangements, if possible, may be made during the current year only. Reapplication by an organization for status, or a request for a change in status, shall be considered by the Committee at the earliest at its first session in the second year following the session at which the substance of the previous application or request was considered, unless at the time of such consideration it was decided otherwise;

(c) Organizations in general consultative status and special consultative status shall submit to the Council Committee on Non-Governmental Organizations through the Secretary-General every fourth year a brief report of their activities, specifically as regards the support they have given to the work of the United Nations. Based on findings of the Committee's examination of the report and other relevant information, the Committee may recommend to the Council any reclassification in status of the organization concerned as it deems appropriate. However, under exceptional circumstances, the Committee may ask for such a report from an individual organization in general consultative status or special consultative status or on the Roster, between the regular reporting dates;

(d) The Committee may consult, in connection with sessions of the Council or at such other times as it may decide, with organizations in general consultative status and special consultative status on matters within their competence, other than items in the agenda of the Council, on which the Council or the Committee or the organization requests consultation. The Committee shall report to the Council on such consultations;

(e) The Committee may consult, in connection with any particular session of the Council, with organizations in general consultative status and special consultative status on matters within the competence of the organizations concerning specific items already in the provisional agenda of the Council on which the Council or the Committee or the organization requests consultation, and shall make recommendations as to which organizations, subject to the provisions of paragraph 32 (a) above, should be heard by the Council or the appropriate committee and regarding which subjects should be heard. The Committee shall report to the Council on such consultations;

(f) The Committee shall consider matters concerning non-governmental organizations that may be referred to it by the Council or by commissions;

(g) The Committee shall consult with the Secretary-General, as appropriate, on matters affecting the consultative arrangements under Article 71 of the Charter, and arising therefrom;

(h) An organization that applies for consultative status should attest that it has been in existence for at least two years as at the date of receipt of the application by the Secretariat. Evidence of such existence shall be furnished to the Secretariat.

62. The Committee, in considering a request from a non-governmental organization in general consultative status that an item be placed in the agenda of the Council, shall take into account, among other things:

(a) The adequacy of the documentation submitted by the organization;

(b) The extent to which it is considered that the item lends itself to early and constructive action by the Council;

(c) The possibility that the item might be more appropriately dealt with elsewhere than in the Council.

63. Any decision by the Council Committee on Non-Governmental Organizations not to grant a request submitted by a non-governmental organization in general consultative status that an item be placed in the provisional agenda of the Council shall be considered final unless the Council decides otherwise.

Part X   CONSULTATION WITH THE SECRETARIAT

64. The Secretariat should be so organized as to enable it to carry out the duties assigned to it concerning the consultative arrangements and the accreditation of non-governmental organizations to United Nations international conferences as set forth in the present resolution.

65. All organizations in consultative relationship shall be able to consult with officers of the appropriate sections of the Secretariat on matters in which there is a mutual interest or a mutual concern. Such consultation shall be upon the request of the non-governmental organization or upon the request of the Secretary-General of the United Nations.

66. The Secretary-General may request organizations in general consultative status and special consultative status and those on the Roster to carry out specific studies or prepare specific papers, subject to the relevant financial regulations.

67. The Secretary-General shall be authorized, within the means at his disposal, to offer to non-governmental organizations in consultative relationship facilities that include:

(a) Prompt and efficient distribution of such documents of the Council and its subsidiary bodies as shall in the judgement of the Secretary-General be appropriate;

(b) Access to the press documentation services provided by the United Nations;

(c) Arrangement of informal discussions on matters of special interest to groups or organizations;

(d) Use of the libraries of the United Nations;

(e) Provision of accommodation for conferences or smaller meetings of consultative organizations on the work of the Economic and Social Council;

(f) Appropriate seating arrangements and facilities for obtaining documents during public meetings of the General Assembly dealing with matters in the economic, social and related fields.

Part XI   SECRETARIAT SUPPORT

68. Adequate Secretariat support shall be required for fulfilment of the mandate defined for the Committee on Non-Governmental Organizations with respect to carrying out the wider range of activities in which the enhanced involvement of non-governmental organizations is envisaged. The Secretary-General is requested to provide the necessary resources for this purpose and to take steps for improving the coordination within the Secretariat of units dealing with non-governmental organizations.

69. The Secretary-General is requested to make every effort to enhance and streamline as appropriate Secretariat support arrangements, and to improve practical arrangements on such matters as greater use of modern information and communication technology, establishment of an integrated database of non-governmental organizations, wide and timely dissemination of information on meetings, distribution of documentation, provision of access and transparent, simple and streamlined procedures for the attendance of non-governmental organizations in United Nations meetings, and to facilitate their broad-based participation.

70. The Secretary-General is requested to make the present resolution widely known, through proper channels, to facilitate the involvement of non-governmental organizations from all regions and areas of the world.

Appendix 2   International Non-Governmental Organizations: Accountability Charter

Endorsed by:
ActionAid International
Amnesty International
CIVICUS World Alliance for Citizen Participation
Consumers International
Greenpeace International
Oxfam International
International Save the Children Alliance
Survival International
International Federation Terre des Hommes
Transparency International
World YWCA

Who we are

We, international non-government organisations (INGOs) signatory to this Charter, are independent non-profit organisations that work globally to advance human rights, sustainable development, environmental protection, humanitarian response and other public goods.

Our organisations are proud and privileged to work across a wide range of countries and cultures, with a diverse range of peoples and in varied eco- and social and political systems.

Our right to act is based on universally-recognised freedoms of speech, assembly and association, on our contribution to democratic processes, and on the values we seek to promote.

Our legitimacy is also derived from the quality of our work, and the recognition and support of the people with and for whom we work and our members, our donors, the wider public, and governmental and other organisations around the world.

We seek to uphold our legitimacy by responding to inter-generational considerations, public and scientific concerns, and through accountability for our work and achievements.

By signing this Charter we seek to promote further the values of transparency and accountability that we stand for, and commit our INGO to respecting its provisions.

How we work

INGOs can complement but not replace the over-arching role and primary responsibility of governments to promote equitable human development and wellbeing, to uphold human rights and to protect ecosystems.

We also seek to promote the role and responsibilities of the private sector to advance human rights and sustainable development, and protect the environment.

We can often address problems and issues that governments and others are unable or unwilling to address on their own. Through constructive challenge, we seek to promote good governance and foster progress towards our goals.

We seek to advance our mission through research, advocacy and programmes. It is common for our work to be at the international, national, regional and local levels, either directly or with partners.

We work with other organisations where this is the best way to advance our individual missions.

The Charter's purpose

This Charter outlines our common commitment to excellence, transparency and accountability. To demonstrate and build on these commitments, we seek to:

* identify and define shared principles, policies and practices;
* enhance transparency and accountability, both internally and externally;
* encourage communication with stakeholders; and
* improve our performance and effectiveness as organisations.

We recognise that transparency and accountability are essential to good governance, whether by governments, businesses or non-profit organisations.

Wherever we operate, we seek to ensure that the high standards which we demand of others are also respected in our own organisations.

The Charter complements and supplements existing laws. It is a voluntary charter, and draws on a range of existing codes, norms, standards and guidelines.

We agree to apply the Charter progressively to all our policies, activities and operations. The Charter does not replace existing codes or practices to which signatories may also be party, except as specified by them. Its adoption does not prevent signatories from supporting or using other tools to promote transparency and accountability.

We will refine the Charter through experience, taking into account future developments, particularly those that improve accountability and transparency.

Our stakeholders

Our first responsibility is to achieve our stated mission effectively and transparently, consistent with our values. In this, we are accountable to our stakeholders.

Our stakeholders include:

- Peoples, including future generations, whose rights we seek to protect and advance;
- Ecosystems, which cannot speak for or defend themselves;
- Our members and supporters;
- Our staff and volunteers;
- Organisations and individuals that contribute finance, goods or services;
- Partner organisations, both governmental and non-governmental, with whom we work;
- Regulatory bodies whose agreement is required for our establishment and operations;
- Those whose policies, programmes or behaviour we wish to influence;
- The media; and
- The general public.

In balancing the different views of our stakeholders, we will be guided by our mission and the principles of this Charter.

Principles

Respect for Universal Principles
INGOs are founded on the rights to freedom of speech, assembly and association in the Universal Declaration of Human Rights. We seek to advance

international and national laws that promote human rights, ecosystem protection, sustainable development and other public goods.

Where such laws do not exist, are not fully implemented, or abused, we will highlight these issues for public debate and advocate appropriate remedial action.

In so doing, we will respect the equal rights and dignity of all human beings.

Independence

We aim to be both politically and financially independent. Our governance, programmes and policies will be non-partisan, independent of specific governments, political parties and the business sector.

Responsible advocacy

We will ensure that our advocacy is consistent with our mission, grounded in our work and advances defined public interests.

We will have clear processes for adopting public policy positions, (including for partners where appropriate,) explicit ethical policies that guide our choices of advocacy strategy, and ways of identifying and managing potential conflicts of interest among various stakeholders.

Effective Programmes

We seek to work in genuine partnership with local communities, NGOs and other organisations aiming at sustainable development responding to local needs.

Non-Discrimination

We value, respect and seek to encourage diversity, and seek to be impartial and nondiscriminatory in all our activities. To this end, each organisation will have policies that promote diversity, gender equity and balance, impartiality and non-discrimination in all our activities, both internal and external.

Transparency

We are committed to openness, transparency and honesty about our structures, mission, policies and activities.

We will communicate actively to stakeholders about ourselves, and make information publicly available.

Reporting

We seek to comply with relevant governance, financial accounting and reporting requirements in the countries where we are based and operate.

We report at least once a year on our activities and achievements. Reports will describe each organisation's:

- Mission and values;
- Objectives and outcomes achieved in programme and advocacy;
- Environmental impact;
- Governance structure and processes, and main office bearers;
- Main sources of funding from corporations, foundations, governments, and individuals;
- Financial performance;
- Compliance with this Charter; and
- Contact details.

Audit

The annual financial report will conform to relevant laws and practices and be audited by a qualified independent public accountant whose statement will accompany the report.

Accuracy of information

We will adhere to generally-accepted standards of technical accuracy and honesty in presenting and interpreting data and research, using and referencing independent research.

Good Governance

We should be held responsible for our actions and achievements. We will do this by: having a clear mission, organisational structure and decision-making processes; by acting in accordance with stated values and agreed procedures; by ensuring that our programmes achieve outcomes that are consistent with our mission; and by reporting on these outcomes in an open and accurate manner.

The governance structure of each organisation will conform to relevant laws and be transparent. We seek to follow principles of best practice in governance. Each organisation will have at least:

- A governing body which supervises and evaluates the chief executive, and oversee programme and budgetary matters. It will define overall strategy, consistent with the organisational mission, ensure that resources are used efficiently and appropriately, that performance is measured, that financial integrity is assured and that public trust is maintained;
- Written procedures covering the appointment, responsibilities and terms of members of the governing body, and preventing and managing conflicts of interest;
- A regular general meeting with authority to appoint and replace members of the governing body.
- We will listen to stakeholders' suggestions on how we can improve our work and will encourage inputs by people whose interests may be directly

affected. We will also make it easy for the public to comment on our programmes and policies.

Ethical Fundraising

Donors

We respect the rights of donors: to be informed about causes for which we
are fundraising; to be informed about how their donation is being used; to
have their names deleted from mailing lists; to be informed of the status and
authority of fundraisers; and to anonymity except in cases where the size of
their donation is such that it might be relevant to our independence.

Use of Donations

In raising funds, we will accurately describe our activities and needs. Our
policies and practices will ensure that donations further our organisation's
mission. Where donations are made for a specific purpose, the donor's
request is honoured. If we invite the general public to donate to a specific
cause, each organisation will have a plan for handling any shortfall or
excess, and will make this known as part of its appeal.

Gifts in kind

Some donations may be given as goods or services. To retain our effectiveness and independence, we will: record and publish details of all major institutional gifts and gifts-in-kind; clearly describe the valuation and auditing
methods used; and ensure that these gifts contribute towards our mission.

Agents

We seek to ensure that donations sought indirectly, such as through third
parties, are solicited and received in full conformity with our own practices.
This will normally be the subject of written agreement between the parties.

Professional Management

We manage our organisations in a professional and effective manner. Our
policies and procedures seek to promote excellence in all respects.

Financial controls

Internal financial control procedures will ensure that all funds are effectively
used and minimise the risk of funds being misused. We will follow principles
of best practice in financial management.

Evaluation

We seek continuously to improve our effectiveness. We will have defined
evaluation procedures for our boards, staff, programmes and projects on the
basis of mutual accountability.

Public Criticism

We will be responsible in our public criticisms of individuals and organisations, ensuring such criticism amounts to fair public comment.

Partners
We recognise our that organisational integrity extends to ensuring that our partners also meet the highest standards of probity and accountability, and will take all possible steps to ensure that there are no links with organisations, or persons involved in illegal or unethical practices.

Human Resources
We recognise that our performance and success reflect the quality of our staff and volunteers and management practices, and are committed to investing in human resource development.

Remuneration and benefits should strike a balance between public expectations of voluntary-based, not-for-profit organisations and the need to attract and retain the staff we need to fulfil our mission. Our human resources policies seek to conform fully with relevant international and national labour regulations and apply the best voluntary sector practices in terms of employee and volunteer rights and health and safety at work. Human resources policies will include procedures for evaluating the performance of all staff on a regular basis.

Bribery and Corruption
Human resources policies will specifically prohibit acts of bribery or corruption by staff or other persons working for, or on behalf of, the organisation.

Respect for Sexual Integrity
We condemn sexual exploitation, abuse and discrimination in all its forms. Our policies will respect sexual integrity in all our programmes and activities, and prohibit gender harassment, sexual exploitation and discrimination.

Whistle-blowers
Staff will be enabled and encouraged to draw management's attention to activities that may not comply with the law or our mission and commitments, including the provisions in this Code.

****

Notes

Chapter 1   Introduction

1 A recently published collection contains 84 documents on human rights and the United Nations, human rights at a regional level and other relevant international treaties and resolutions (P. van Dijk, C. Flinterman and P.E.L. Janssen (eds) *International Law, Human Rights*, The Hague: SDU Uitgevers, 5th revised edition, 2006.

2 See: Rachel Brett, "Non-Governmental Actors in the Field of Human Rights," in: Raija Hanski and Markku Suski (eds), *An Introduction to the International Protection of Human Rights: A Textbook*, Turku/Åbo: Institute for Human Rights, Åbo Akademi University, 2nd rev. ed., 1999, 399–413. See also: Menno T. Kamminga, "The Evolving Status of NGOs under International Law: A Threat to the Inter-State System?" in: Philip Alston (ed.), *Non-State Actors and Human Rights*, Oxford: Oxford University Press, 2005, 93–111 at 95: "[I]nternational law does not offer an authoritative definition of a non-governmental organization."

3 Rainer Lagoni. "Article 71," in: Bruno Simma (ed.), *The Charter of the United Nations*, Oxford: Oxford University Press, 1994, 902–915 at 905, note 29.

4 Resolution 1996/31, 49th plenary meeting, 25 July 1996. For its text see Appendix 1.

5 *Ibid.*, par. 12.

6 Henry J. Steiner & Philip Alston, *International Human Rights in Context: Law, Politics, Morals*, Oxford: Oxford University Press, 2nd ed., 2000, 980.

7 UN Charter article 71: "The Economic and Social Council may make suitable arrangements for consultation with non-governmental organizations which are concerned with matters within its competence. Such arrangements may be made with international organizations and, where appropriate, with national organizations after consultation with the Member of the United Nations concerned."

8 http://www.un.org/esa/coordination/ngo/table2007.html.;   accessed 21 September 2008.

9 Ruth B. Russell, *A History of the United Nations Charter: The Role of the United States 1940–1945*, Washington D.C.: The Brookings Institution, 1958, 800.

10 GONGOs: Government-organized non-governmental organizations, which achieved notoriety during the Cold War because they owed their very existence and entire financial support to communist governments in the Soviet bloc or authoritarian ones in the Third World. QUANGOs: Quasi-non-governmental organizations: many Nordic and Canadian NGOs and a handful of US ones, as well as the ICRC receive the bulk of

their resources from public funds. DONGOs: Donor-organized non-governmental organizations are also distinguished by their source of funds, from donor governments or intergovernmental organizations to promote or to carry out tasks established by their financial backers (Leon Gordenker and Thomas Weiss, "Pluralizing Global Governance: Analytical Approaches and Dimensions," in Thomas Weiss and Leon Gordenker, *NGOs, the UN and Global Governance*, Boulder/London: Lynne Rienner, 1996, 20–21). This list is by no means exhaustive, as indicated by the following additions by a Japanese scholar: AGOs: Anti-Government Organizations, TRANGOs: Transnational NGOs, GRINGOs: Government Regulated and Initiated NGOs, BINGOs: Business and Industry NGOs, DODONGOs: Donor Dominated NGOs, ODANGOs: ODA Financed NGOs, and FLAMINGOs: Flashy Minded NGOs representing the rich. (Tatsuro Kunugi, "The United Nations and Civil Society – NGOs Working towards the 21st Century," unpublished paper). Christian Tomuschat, *Human Rights: Between Idealism and Realism*, Oxford: Oxford University Press, 2003, 231 prefers the name GRINGOS.

11 *We the Peoples: Civil Society, the United Nations and Global Governance, Report of the Panel of Eminent Persons on United Nations-Civil Society Relations,* "Cardozo Report" UNGA, United Nations General Assembly, A/58/817, 11 June 2004, par. 127.

12 For example, as recently as September 2008, Oxfam International published a report on climate change and human rights, entitled *Climate Wrongs and Human Rights*. Typically, Mary Robinson, the former UN High Commissioner for Human Rights, is honorary president of Oxfam International.

13 Laurie S. Wiseberg, "Protecting Human Rights Activists and NGOs: What More Can Be Done?" *Human Rights Quarterly*, vol. 13 (1991), 525–544 at 529. See also: *Panel of Eminent Persons on United Nations-Civil Society Relations (the "Cardozo Report")* (A/58/817), 13 that defined non-governmental organizations as follows: "All organizations of relevance to the United Nations that are not central Governments and were not created by intergovernmental decision, including associations of businesses, parliamentarians and local authorities."

14 Gordenker and Weiss, *supra*, note 10, 24. Cf. also Bob Reinalda, "Private in Form, Public in Purpose: NGOs in International Relations Theory," in: Bas Arts, Math Noortman and Bob Reinalda, *Non-State Actors in International Relations*, Aldershot: Ashgate, 2001, 12: "The main characteristics of proper NGOs is that they result from private initiatives and on principle act independently of governments."

15 Cf. Daniel A. Bell and Jean-Marc Coicaud (eds), *Ethics in Action: The Ethical Challenges of International Human Rights Nongovernmental Organizations*, Cambridge: Cambridge University Press, 2007, 1, note 2: "An INGO [International Non-Governmental Organization] is defined here as an organization with substantial autonomy to decide on and carry out human rights and/or humanitarian projects in various regions around the world."

16 As quoted by Diane Otto, "Nongovernmental Organizations in the United Nations System: The Emerging Role of International Civil Society," *Human Rights Quarterly*, vol. 18 (1996), 107–141 at 111, note 22.

17 See also: the European Convention on the Recognition of the Legal Personality of International Non-Governmental Organisations (of 1986), which uses the following definition: "[A]ssociations, foundations and other private institutions which satisfy the following conditions: a) have a non profit-making aim of international utility; b) have been established by an instrument governed by the internal law of a Party; c) carry on their activities in at least two States and d) have their statutory office in the territory of a Party and the central management and control in the territory of that Party or another Party." Cf. also Bob Reinalda, "Private in Form, Public in Purpose: NGOs in International Relations Theory," in: Arts, Noortman and Reinalda, *supra*, note 14, 12: "The main characteristics of proper NGOs is that they result from private initiatives and on principle act independently of governments. (...) In this chapter I use the term 'NGO' for international private organisations and social movements which are public in purpose, and the term 'private actor' for all international non-governmental actors, both public and private in purpose."

18 Brett, *supra*, note 2, 399–400.

19 Amnesty International which aspires to have national sections all over the world, thus being truly "international", has been trying for many years to persuade international news agencies to delete the affix "'the London-based human rights organization". So far, however, with little success.

20 Makau Mutua, "Standard Setting in Human Rights: Critique and Prognosis," *Human Rights Quarterly*, vol. 29 (2007), 547–630 at 580.

21 *Ibid.*, 591.

22 Peter Willetts , "Introduction" in: Peter Willetts (ed.) *"Conscience of the World": The Influence of Non-Governmental Organisations in the UN System.* Washington D.C.: The Brookings Institution, 1996, 1–14 at 11. Cf. Ann C. Hudock, *NGOs and Civil Society: Democracy by Proxy?* (Cambridge: Polity Press, 1999), 20–21: "One of the most fundamental weaknesses of the NGO literature is the suggestion that NGOs possess a value base that drives them to act on 'altruistic' motives. This absolutely contradicts one of the key tenets of organizational analysis; namely that, to survive, an organization *must place its own interests before those of others,* especially those which are potential competitors." [italics supplied]. See also: Anna-Karin Lindblom, *Non-governmental Organizations in International Law,* Cambridge etc.: Cambridge University Press, 2005, 525: "What has been stated above may give the impression that it has been assumed here that NGOs are 'good'. This is not the case. It is recognized that NGOs are self-appointed, single-issue oriented and often not accountable to the people on whose behalf they claim to speak."

23 See: John Sankey, "Conclusions," in: Willetts, *supra*, note 22, 270–276 at 270.

24 *Ibid.*, 274.
25 Helmut Anheier, Marlies Glasius and Mary Kaldor, *Global Civil Society 2001*, New York: Oxford University Press, 2001, 4.
26 Margaret E. Keck and Kathryn Sikkink, *Activists Beyond Borders: Advocacy Networks in International Politics*, Ithaca N.Y.: Cornell University Press, 1998, 41–72.
27 Theo van Boven, "The Role of Non-Governmental Organisations in International Human Rights Standard-Setting: A Prerequisite of Democracy," in: Fons Coomans, Cees Flinterman, Fred Grünfeld, Ingrid Westendorp and Jan Willems (eds), *Human Rights from Exclusion to Inclusion; Principles and Practice: An Anthology from the Work of Theo van Boven*, The Hague/London/Boston: Kluwer Law International 2000, 347–361 at 349.
28 Rachel Brett, *supra*, note 2, 399, calls this "education in its broadest sense": "developing a human rights culture by making people aware of their rights, of their responsibility not to violate the rights of others, and of the possibilities of redress, including supporting individuals to bringing cases, whether within the national system or under regional or international procedures."
29 Jackie Smith and Ron Pagnucco with George A. Lopez, "Globalizing Human Rights: The Work of Transnational Human Rights NGOs in the 1990s," *Human Rights Quarterly*, vol. 20 (1998), 379–412 at 383.
30 46% in Western Europe and 17% in North America, see: Smith *et al.*, *supra*, note 29, 387. Anheier c.s., *supra*, note 25, 7 make the point that more in general, "global civil society is heavily concentrated in northwestern Europe, especially in Scandinavia, the Benelux-countries, Austria, Switzerland, and the United Kingdom."
31 The more than 2.4 million members worldwide (information provided by the International Secretariat) include: US section: 360,000 members; Dutch section 300,000; UK section: 250,000 financial supporters of which 175,000 members and French section 250,000 donors of which 23,000 "militants" (information provided by the secretariat of the Dutch section). Some sections regard all members who support the organization financially as members, while other sections require an explicit declaration of will in order for a person to become a member.
32 Smith and Pagnucco, *supra*, note 29, 390.
33 $1,937,581.- as compared to $ 389,748.-, *ibid.*, 410.
34 Lindblom, *supra*, note 22, 526.

Chapter 2   Legitimacy

1 Dianne Otto, "Non-Governmental Organizations in the United Nations System: The Emerging Role of International Civil Society," *Human Rights Quarterly*, vol. 18 (1996), 107–141 at 112, note 25.
2 According to its own website (accessed 22 September 2008) Amnesty International has "more than 2.2 million members and subscribers in more than 150 countries and regions".

3 A. Fowler, "The Role of NGOs in Changing State-Society Relations: Perspectives from Eastern and Southern Africa," *Development Policy Review*, vol. 9 (1991), 67 as quoted by Peter Uvin "Scaling Up the Grassroots and Scaling Down the Summit: The Relations Between Third World NGOs and the UN," in: Thomas Weiss and Leon Gordenker (eds), *NGOs, the UN and Global Governance*, Boulder/London: Lynne Rienner, 1996, 159–176 at 169. Fowler concludes: "Maintaining accountability to its grassroots constituency while simultaneously building competencies and credibility with decision-makers is perhaps the overriding challenge facing NGOs that would influence policy." (Uvin, 169–170).

4 Resolution 1996/31, 49th plenary meeting, 25 July 1996; for text see Appendix 1. Peter Willetts has observed: "The term consultative status was deliberately chosen to indicate a secondary role – being available to give advice but not being part of the decision making process." (Peter Willetts, "From 'Consultative Arrangements' to 'Partnership': The Changing Status of NGOs in Diplomacy at the UN," *Global Governance*, vol. 6 (2000), 191–213 at 191.

5 ECOSOC Resolution 1996/31, par. 12; see Appendix 1.

6 Menno Kamminga, "What Makes an NGO 'Legitimate' in the Eyes of States?" in: Anton Vedder (ed.), *NGO Involvement in International Governance and Policy: Sources of Legitimacy*, Leiden/Boston: Martinus Nijhoff, 2007, 175–195 at 186.

7 Cf. Vivien Collingwood and Louis Logister, "Perceptions of the Legitimacy of Traditional NGOs," in: Vedder, *supra*, note 6, 21–57 at 30.

8 Leon Gordenker and Thomas G. Weiss, "NGO Participation in the International Policy Process," in: Weiss and Gordenker, *supra*, note 3, 209–221 at 219.

9 *Ibid.*

10 Statute of Amnesty International, as amended by the 27th International Council, meeting in Morelos, Mexico, 11–17 August, 2007, Article 5.

11 *Ibid.*, Article 17.

12 Peter Baehr and Menno Kamminga, "Een Gedragscode voor Mensenrechten NGOs?" ["A Code of Behaviour for Human Rights NGOs?"] in: C. Flinterman and W. van Genugten (eds), *Niet-statelijke Actoren en de Rechten van de Mens: Gevestigde Waarden, Nieuwe Wegen*, 67–80 at 68; translated from the original Dutch.

13 Otto, *supra*, note 1, 138.

14 *Ibid.*

15 Jem Bendell, *Debating NGO Accountability*. New York and Geneva: United Nations, 2006, 13.

16 Cf. Anton Vedder, "Questioning the Legitimacy of Non-Governmental Organizations," in Vedder, *supra*, note 6, 4: "Some international NGOs (...) also refer to themselves as being grass roots organizations. What is usually meant with this is that the local perspective is taken into account and that actions are initiated locally and not somewhere far away." See also: Peter Willetts, "What Is a Non-Governmental Organization?" http://www.staff.city.ac.uk/p.willetts/CS-NTWKS/NGO-AKT.HTM,

accessed 10 February 2007, 4: "NGOs are so diverse and so controversial that it is not possible to support, or be opposed to, all NGOs. They may claim to be the voice of the people to have greater legitimacy than governments, but this can only be a plausible claim under authoritarian governments. However, their role as participants in democratic debate does not depend upon any claim to representative legitimacy."

17   See: Hugo Slim, "By What Authority? The Legitimacy and Accountability of Non-Governmental Organisations," The International Council on Human Rights Policy, International Meeting on Global Trends and Human Rights, Before and After September 11th, Geneva, January 10–12, 2002.

18   Sophie C. van Bijsterveld, "Tussen Burger en Internationale Organisatie: NGO's als Vehikel voor Veranderende Internationale Constitutionele Verhoudingen,"["Between the Citizen and International Organizations: NGOs as Vehicles for Changing International Constitutional Relations"] in: C. Flinterman and W. van Genugten (eds), *Niet-statelijke Actoren en de Rechten van de Mens; Gevestigde Waarden, Nieuwe Wegen,* Den Haag: Boom Juridische Uitgevers, 2003, 81–92 at 90; translated from the original Dutch. Cf. Also the [Dutch] Advisory Council on International Affairs [AIV], *The Role of NGOs and the Private Sector in International Relations,* The Hague: Ministry of Foreign Affairs, 2006, 29: "[T]he AIV feels that the fundamental question of legitimacy is best approached on the basis that NGOs represent certain values or interests rather than certain (groups of) individuals."

19   Slim, *supra*, note 17, 3.

20   Jan Aart Scholte, "Civil Society and Democratically Accountable Global Governance," *Government and Opposition* (2004), 211–233 at 230.

21   For text see Appendix 2.

22   www.ingoaccountabilitycharter.org/about-the-charter.php; accessed on 19 March 2008.

23   *Ibid.*, 3.

24   *Ibid.*

25   Whitney Brown, "Human Rights Watch: An Overview," in: Claude E. Welch Jr. (ed.), *NGOs and Human Rights: Promise and Performance,* Philadelphia: University of Pennsylvania Press, 2001, 72–84 at 74; italics supplied. For a similar view about Amnesty International see: Helena Cook, "Amnesty International at the United Nations," in: Peter Willetts, (ed.), *"The Conscience of the World": The Influence of Non-Governmental Organisations in the UN System,* Washington D.C.: The Brookings Institution, 1996, 181–213 at 183: "As an outsider in their governmental club [i.e. the UN], Amnesty's most potent weapon is *awareness raising* – bring human rights concerns into the public arena and using the momentum created by public opinion as a catalyst for international action." (italics supplied).

26   Michael Longford has noted: "The members of the NGO group generally had greater professional expertise in the field of children's rights than many of the governmental delegations." (Michael Longford, "NGOs and the Rights of the Child," in Willetts, *supra*, note 25, 214–240 at 224. See

also: Hilde Reiding, *The Netherlands and the Development of International Human Rights Instruments*, Antwerp: Intersentia, 2007, 258: "The proposals that it [the NGO Ad Hoc Group] made were meant to be non-political and professional, and paid attention to civil and political as well as economic, social and cultural rights. As a consequence, the proposals of the NGO Ad Hoc Group could be utilized as a tool to diminish political tensions."

27 Jem Bendell, *supra*, note 15, 39, referring to Alison Van Rooy, *The Global Legitimacy Game: Civil Society, Globalization and Protest,* London: Palgrave Macmillan, 2004.

28 Amnesty International, *Iraq/Occupied Kuwait: Human Rights Violations since 2 August*, AI Index: MDE 14/16/90, December 1990, 56.

29 Amnesty International News release, "Kuwait: Amnesty International Calls on Emir to Intervene over Continuing Torture and Killings," AI Index: MDE 17/03/91, 19 April 1991; *International Herald Tribune* (Paris), 8 January 1992. See also: Ann Marie Clark, *Diplomacy of Conscience: Amnesty International and Changing Human Rights Norms*, Princeton: Princeton University Press, 2001, 132.

30 Shanthi Dairiam, "From Global to Local: the Involvement of NGOs," in: Hanna Beate Schöpp-Schilling and Cees Flinterman (eds) *The Circle of Empowerment: Twenty-five Years of the UN Committee on the Elimination of Discrimination against* Women, New York: The Feminist Press at the City University of New York, 2007, 313–325 at 319.

31 Antonio Donini, "The Bureaucracy and the Free Spirits: Stagnation and Innovation in the Relationship in Weiss and Gordenker, *supra*, note 3, 83–101 at 86.

32 Cf. Anna-Karin Lindblom, *Non-governmental Organisations in International Law*, Cambridge etc.: Cambridge University Press, 2005, 477: "Many NGOs decided never to 'loan' their staff to governments like this, as it might compromise the independence of their organisation."

33 It actually led to some difficulties with a Minister of Immigration who used to wear publicly his Amnesty badge at a time when his decisions seemed contrary to human rights principles supported by Amnesty. In March 2000, the national President of Amnesty International said publicly that the Minister had been asked not to wear the badge, but that he had not agreed to this request. (I thank Elizabeth Evatt for this information.)

34 Alston has remarked on the permanent tension between governments and NGOs: "Despite the fact that NGOs are indispensable to the effective functioning of the [UN Human Rights] Commission, their position will never be accepted more than grudgingly by the states that make up the Commission. If it were otherwise, it would be safe to say that NGOs were not behaving as they should: in an informed, independent, critical, and uncompromising manner." (Philip Alston, "The Commission on Human Rights," in: Alston (ed.), *The United Nations and Human Rights*, Oxford: Clarendon Press, 1992, 126–210 at 203–204.) However, Gordenker and Weiss suggest that the decline of oppressive regimes and the rise of

democracy mainly since the end of the Cold War "… has tempered the former automatic hostility by governments toward the activities of local and international NGOs. Previously, NGO-government relationships were often ones of benign neglect at best, or of suspicion and outright hostility at worst." (Leon Gordenker and Thomas G. Weiss, "Pluralizing Global Governance: Analytical Approaches and Dimensions," in: Weiss and Gordenker, *supra*, note 3, 30.)

35 Personal interview, 4 August 2008; translated from the original Dutch.

36 J. Herman Burgers, "Dutch Nongovernmental Organizations and Foreign Policy in the Field of Human Rights," in: P.J. van Krieken and Ch.O. Pannenborg (eds), *Liber Akkerman: In- and Outlaws in War*, Apeldoorn/Antwerpen: MAKLU Publishers, 1992, 157–168 at 168.

37 Reiding, *supra*, note 26, 421.

38 Faced with these adverse comments, I – reluctantly – decided to give up the position of chairman of the Advisory Committee.

39 Victoria Berry and Allan McChesney, "Human Rights and Foreign Policy-Making," in: Robert O. Matthews and Cranford Pratt (eds), *Human Rights in Canadian Foreign Policy*, Kingston and Montreal: McGill-Queen's University Press, 1988, 59–76 at 60; John W. Foster, "The UN Commission on Human Rights," in: *ibid.*, 79–100 at 94–97.

40 Cf. Peter Willetts, *supra*, note 16, 11–12: "In each case the NGOs tend to feel dissatisfied, because they have worked hard and long to achieve less than they would have wished. In each case, the governments involved and outside observers tend to feel the NGOs have achieved more than would seem possible for relatively small organisations working with limited resources on complex problems."

41 I thank Andrew Thompson for this information.

42 The other topics were: development cooperation, the European Union, trade and international economic cooperation, the common foreign and security policy of the European Union, the foreign service and the United Nations.

43 *Challenges and Opportunities Abroad: White Paper on Foreign Policy*, Dublin: Department of Foreign Affairs, 1996, 2–3. The author of the present volume, who attended the meeting on human rights at the University of Galway, can confirm that the meeting provided an excellent opportunity for dialogue.

44 Kerstin Martens, "An Appraisal of Amnesty International's Work at the United Nations: Established Areas of Activities and Shifting Priorities since the 1990s," *Human Rights Quarterly*, vol. 26 (November 2004), 1050–1070 at 1064.

45 Gordenker and Weiss, *supra*, note 34, 36.

46 An African participant in a human rights seminar in The Hague, which was opened by then Foreign Minister Kooijmans, observed in private that it was a remarkable country that had a human rights activist for foreign minister!

47 The pun is lost in translation: "Knowledge is power, but acquaintances give even more power."

48   Gordenker and Weiss, *supra*, note 34, 28.
49   Cyril Ritchie, "Coordinate? Cooperate? Harmonise? NGO Policy and Operational Coalitions," in Weiss and Gordenker, *supra*, note 3, 177–188 at 181.
50   Jody Williams and Stephen Goose, "The International Campaign to Ban Landmines," in: Maxwell A. Cameron, Brain W. Tomlin and Robert J. Lawson (eds), *To Walk without Fear: The Global Movement to Ban Landmines*, Toronto: Oxford University Press, 1998, 20–47.
51   William R. Pace, "The Relationship between the International Criminal Court and Non-governmental Organizations," in: Herman A.M. von Hebel, Johan G. Lammers and Jolien Schukking (eds), *Reflections on the International Criminal Court: Essays in Honour of Adriaan Bos*, The Hague: T.M.C. Asser Press, 1999, 189–211.
52   Kamminga, *supra*, note 6, 192.
53   http://www.act4europe.org/code/en/about.asp? Accessed 14 September 2008.
54   *Ibid.*
55   The current members of the network are: Amnesty International EU Office (AI): Coalition for the International Criminal Court (CICC); December 18; Club of Madrid; Euro-Mediterranean Human Rights Network (EMHRN); European Association for Human Rights (AEDH), associated member of FIDH; European Council on Refugees and Exiles (ECRE); European Peacebuilding Liaison Office (EPLO); FIACAT – International Federation of the Action by Christians for the Abolition of Torture; Front Line Defenders; Human Rights Watch (HRW); Humanist Committee on Human Rights (HOM); International Center for Transitional Justice (ICTJ); International Dalit Solidarity Network (IDSN); International Federation for Human Rights (FIDH); International Federation for Human Rights – European Association (FIDH-EU); International Federation Terres des Hommes (IFTDH); International Helsinki Federation; International Lesbian and Gay Association – Europe (ILGA-Europe); International Rehabilitation Council for Torture Victims (IRCT); International Rescue Committee Belgium (IRC-Belgium); Minority Rights Group International; Open Society Institute-Brussels (OSI-Brussels); Partners for Democratic Change International (PDCI); Penal Reform International (PRI); PLAN International; Peace Brigades International – European Office; POLLEN; Quaker Council for European Affairs (QCEA); Reporters sans frontieres; Save the Children EU Office; Search for Common Ground (SFCG); Trade Unions Institute For The Co-Operation To Development (ISCOS-CISL); La Strada International; World Organisations Against Torture (OMCT); World Vision; World Vision UK.
56   *We the Peoples: Civil Society, the United Nations and Global Governance: Report of the Panel of Eminent Persons on United Nations-Civil Society Relations*, UNGA A/58/817, 11 June 2004, 59; italics supplied. See also the earlier Principles for Consultation with Non-Governmental Organizations, adopted by the ECOSOC: "Where there exist a number of organizations with similar objectives, interests and basic views in a given field,

they may, for the purposes of consultation with the Council, form a joint committee or other body authorized to carry on such consultations for the group as a whole." (ECOSOC Resolution 1996/31, 49th plenary meeting, 25 July 1996, par. 9. For text see Appendix 1.)

57 Felice D. Gaer, "Reality Check: Human Rights NGOs Confront Governments at the UN," in: Weiss and Gordenker, *supra*, note 3, 51–66 at 64.

58 Stephen Hopgood, *Keepers of the Flame: Understanding Amnesty International*, Ithaca and London: Cornell University Press, 2006, 139: "[T]his cooperation on country strategies, research missions and public statements is termed by some 'co-opetition'."

59 Ann C. Hudock, *NGOs and Civil Society: Democracy by Proxy?* Cambridge: Polity Press, 1999, 21.

60 NGOs from the Global South represent 33% of the 3052 NGOs that enjoy consultative status with ECOSOC and can participate fully in the sessions of the Human Rights Council. See: Lucia Nader, "The Role of NGOs in the UN Human Rights Council," *SUR-International Journal on Human Rights*, vol. 4 (2007), 7–27 at 10. Longford, writing about the rights of the child, has observed: "The non-participation of NGOs from poorer countries seems to be a serious defect in the present system, but many 'southern' NGOs will not be able to send delegates to UN meetings without financial help. It may also be the case that most of the NGOs which are really representative of the developing countries are too poor to operate in more than one country, and therefore feel themselves excluded by the broad requirement that NGOs should be international or regional in order to qualify for consultative status." (Michael Longford, "NGOs and the Rights of the Child," in: Willetts, *supra*, note 16, 214–240 at 232).

61 Cf. Peter Uvin, "Scaling up the Grassroots and Scaling down the Summit: The Relations between Third World NGOs and the UN," in: Weiss and Gordenker, *supra*, note 3, 159–176 at 166. Falk has called such meetings "counter-conferences" [Richard Falk, "The Global Promise of Social Movements: Explorations at the Edge of Time," *Alternatives*, vol. 12 (1987), 187, as quoted by Otto, *supra*, note 1, 120.] See also Cook, *supra*, note 25, 188.

62 Ritchie, *supra*, note 49, 183; see also Manfred Nowak (ed.), *World Conference on Human Rights: The Contribution of NGOs, Reports and Documents*, Wien: Manzsche Verlags- und Universitätsbuchhandlung, 1994, 7. Cf. also Christian Tomuschat, *Human Rights: Between Idealism and Realism*, Oxford: Oxford University Press, 2003, 236, who, referring to the World Conference against Racism, Racial Discrimination, Xenophobia and Related Intolerance, held in Durban in 2001, observes: "It is well-known that NGOs had indeed a great impact on that conference , setting the tone for sharp attacks against the human rights policies of the State of Israel." The author of this volume attended some of the NGO meetings, which he recalls as having been strongly manipulated in an anti-Zionist and anti-Israel direction. Remarkable was also the acclaim Cuban leader Fidel Castro received when he addressed a large gathering of NGOs in Durban's cricket stadium. Most of the NGOs present would not have received permission to operate in Cuba itself.

63 Cf. Gaer, *supra*, note 57, 59.
64 Among these were: *Albertina Sisulu*, President of the Women's League of the African National Congress; *Ibrahima Fall*, Director of the UN Centre of Human Rights; *Adama Dieng*, Secretary-General of the International Commission of Jurists; and Nobel Prize Winner *Adolfo Perez Esquivel*. However, among the attending NGOs the atmosphere was not always serene, as appeared when a number of Latin American representatives succeeded in shouting down former President *Jimmy Carter*, when he tried to deliver his address. In the somewhat euphemistic rendering in the NGO Newsletter relating to the World Conference, Carter was "... prevented by a number of NGO representatives to effectively communicate his message to the NGO community." (Nowak, *supra*, note 62, 224).
65 Gaer, *supra*, note 57, 58.
66 *Ibid.*, 59.
67 *Ibid.*, 60.
68 A/CONF.157/23, par. 5, italics supplied.
69 Gaer, *supra*, note 57, 61.
70 Cf. Peter R. Baehr, "Human Rights Organizations and the UN: A Tale of Two Worlds," in: Dimitris Bourantonis and Jarrod Wiener (eds), *The United Nations in the New World Order: The World Organization at Fifty*, Houndmills, Basingstoke: Macmillan, 1995, 170–189. See also: Theo van Boven, "The United Nations High Commissioner for Human Rights: The History of a Contested Project," in: Thomas Skouteris and Annemarieke Vermeer-Künzli (eds), *The Protection of the Individual in International Law: Essays in Honour of John Dugard*, Cambridge: Cambridge University Press, 2007, 767–784.
71 Gaer, *supra*, note 57, 60.
72 Andrew Clapham, "Creating the High Commissioner for Human Rights: The Outside Story," *European Journal of International Law*, vol. 5, (1994), 556–568 at 563.
73 Nowak, *supra*, note 62, 8.
74 Personal communication from Laurie Wiseberg.
75 Gaer, *supra*, note 57, 64.
76 ECOSOC resolution 1996/31, par. 9; see Appendix 1.
77 Keck and Sikkink have rightly called attention to the importance of international human rights advocacy networks. The diverse entities that make up the international human rights issue-network include parts of IGOs at both the international and regional levels, international NGOs on human rights. domestic NGOs on human rights and private foundations. (Margaret E. Keck and Kathryn Sikkink, *Activists Beyond Borders: Advocacy Networks in International Politics*, Ithaca and London: Cornell University Press, 1998.)

Chapter 3 Independence

1 For examples of anti-Amnesty publications, see Samuel Zivs, *Anatomy of a Lie* (1982); Oleg Vakulovsky, *The False Bottom of Amnesty International*

(1987); Oleg Vakulovsky, '*Amnesty*' *with and without its Greasepaint* (1988). This author was the subject of a strong verbal attack by the chairman of the Supreme Soviet of the Nationalities, when he raised the subject of Amnesty International during a visit to the Kremlin in 1979.

2 For other similar descriptions of Amnesty International, see: *Amnesty Citaten* ("Amnesty Quotations"): "an extension of communist prop-aganda" (the prime minister of Queensland, Australia, 1981); "(...) com-pletely financed by imperialistic security services"(*Izvestia*, USSR, 1980), "(..."frustrated old women and young people"(attorney-general of Kenya 1977); "All satanic superpowers and all bootlickers of satanic powers, such as Amnesty International and other organizations are aiming for the death by suffocation of our Islamic republic "(ayatollah Ruhollah Khomeini, 1981); all translated from the original Dutch. Former legal advisor Helena Cook observes: "(...) it is not uncommon for Amnesty to be vilified at the UN by a government it has criticized, only to be approached by that same government seeking information it can use against another government." (Helena Cook, "Amnesty International at the United Nations," in: Peter Willetts (ed.), *Conscience of the World*, Washington D.C.: The Brookings Institution, 1996, 181–213 at 181.)

3 "China's human rights conditions are making progress, and the Human Rights Watch should view the progress with an unbiased and just atti-tude," said Chinese Foreign Ministry Spokesman Liu Jianchao. He said the organization has always stuck to a biased view about China and its report has always been harbouring political purposes and not reflecting the true conditions. "China Slams Human Rights Report Released by U.S.-based Group," *One World One Dream*, 11 January 2007; www.human rights-china.org/en/CSHRS/Developments/t200; accessed 17 August 2008.

4 See: *Reuter Textline: Bangkok Post*, April 1, 1993.

5 Lucia Nader, "The Role of NGOs in the UN Human Rights Council," *SUR International Journal on Human Right*, vol. 4 (2007), 7–27 at 10.

6 These examples are given by Menno Kamminga in "What Makes an NGO 'Legitimate' in the Eyes of States?" in: Anton Vedder (ed.), *NGO Involvement in International Governance and Policy: Sources of Legitimacy*, Leiden/Boston: Martinus Nijhoff, 2007, 175–195 at 187–188.

7 Jurij Daniel Aston, "The United Nations Committee on Non-governmental Organizations: Guarding the Entrance to a Politically Divided House," *European Journal of International Law*, vol. 12 (2001), 943–962.

8 Peter Willetts, "From 'Consultative Arrangements' to 'Partnership': The Changing Status of NGOs in Diplomacy at the UN," "*Global Gov-ernance*, vol. 6 (2000), 191–213. But the Dutch Government in its official reaction to the Advisory Council's report on NGOs (*infra*, note 12) notes that the NGO Committee of the ECOSOC, where the first selection of NGOs with a consultative status takes place, "has been strongly politicized".

9 Kamminga, *supra*, note 6, 177.

10 "Rights Group Says Kremlin Hinders Work," *International Herald Tribune* (Paris), 21 February 2008.

11 Peter Willetts (ed.), "Introduction," in Peter Willetts (ed.), *"Conscience of the World": The Influence of Non-Governmental Organizations in the UN System*, Washington D.C.: The Brookings Institution, 1996, 1–14 at 6.

12 Vivien Collingwood and Louis Logister, "Perceptions of the Legitimacy of International NGOs," in: Vedder, *supra*, note 6, 21–57 at 30–31. The Dutch Advisory Council on International Affairs has noted: "At the moment, very many NGOs are directly or indirectly financed by governments or other organisations in the West. This makes them inherently less trustworthy to many leaders in developing countries and undermines their legitimacy." (Advisory Council on International Affairs, *The Role of NGOs and the Private Sector in International Relations*, advisory report nr. 51, official English version, The Hague: Ministry of Foreign Affairs, 2006, 30).

13 Howard B. Tolley Jr., *The International Commission of Jurists: Global Advocates for Human Rights*, Philadelphia: University of Pennsylvania Press, 1994, 42.

14 Canadian International Development Agency, Canada Department of Foreign Affairs and International Trade, Permanent Mission of Denmark at the UN, European Commission Brussels, European Commission Bogota, Finland Ministry for Foreign Affairs, Finland Embassy Pretoria, Institut fuer Auslandsbeziehungen, Irish Aid, Japan International Cooperation Agency, Permanent Mission of Liechtenstein to the UN, Luxembourg Ministry of Foreign Affairs, Permanent Mission of Luxembourg to the UN, Netherlands Ministry of Foreign Affairs, Netherlands Embassy Kabul, Norwegian Ministry of Foreign Affairs, Spain Ministry of Foreign Affairs and Cooperation, Swedish International Development Agency, Swedish Ministry for Foreign Affairs, Swiss Agency for Development and Cooperation, Swiss Federal Department for Foreign Affairs, UK Department for International Development, UK Foreign and Commonwealth Office. See: International Center for Transitional Justice, *Challenges Legacies of Impunity*, New York, 2006/2007, 36.

15 Stephen Hopgood, *Keepers of the Flame: Understanding Amnesty International*, Ithaca and London: Cornell University Press, 2006, 70.

16 Cf. Jan Aart Scholte, "Civil Society and Democratically Accountable Global Governance," *Government and Opposition* (2004), 211–233 at 229: "Indeed, in contacts where citizens tend to regard all governance as corrupt, many people may look skeptically on the notions of civil society organizations as well, doubting that civil society could be a space where persons of integrity could pursue public interests."

17 *Ibid.*, 224.

18 Cited by Hopgood, *supra*, note 15, 101–102.

19 *Ibid.*, 11.

20 *Ibid.*, 107.

21 Hilde Reiding, *The Netherlands and the Development of International Human Rights Instruments*, Antwerp: Intersentia, 2007, 272–273.

22 Helena Cook, "Amnesty International at the United Nations," in: Willets, *supra*, note 11, 209; italics supplied. Cf. Anna-Karin Lindblom,

Non-governmental Organisations in International Law, Cambridge etc.: Cambridge University Press, 2005, 476: "A matter that was mentioned by state representatives was that the tendency of NGOs to go for the 'maximum position' or formulate 'wish lists' sometimes caused irritation among governmental delegations, especially when they were subjected to heavy criticism for making compromises. In their view, compromises were necessary, and NGOs did not always understand this." Cf. also Anton Vedder, "Questioning the Legitimacy of Non-governmental Organizations," in Vedder, *supra*, note 6, 1–20 at 10: "Most internationally operating NGOs have their institutional bases and members and sponsors in the North, whereas the people affected by their actions live in other parts of the world."

23 See: Jan Aart Scholte, "Civil Society and Democratically Accountable Global Governance," *Government and Opposition*, 39 (2004), 211–233 at 223. See also the Cardozo report: "In particular, civil society speakers come largely from the global North and their organizations are headquartered there; speakers are largely male; most civil society organizations (both Northern and Southern) have unclear accountability to the grass roots; and the voices of vulnerable groups are underrepresented." (*We the Peoples: Civil Society, the United Nations and Global Governance: Report of the Panel of Eminent Persons on United Nations-Civil Society Relations*, UNGA, A/58/817, 11 June 2004, 65).

24 *Ibid.*, 216.

25 United States, United Kingdom, the Netherlands, France, Germany, Switzerland, Sweden, Canada (English speaking), Italy, Australia and Norway. See: Hopgood, *supra*, note 15, 197.

26 This author, when on a visit to the Amnesty section of Sierra Leone in the early 1990s, felt somewhat embarrassed when his companion from the International Secretariat handed out wads of "leones" (the local currency) to members of the local board. He felt even more embarrassed when he found out that one night's stay in the hotel at the airport – modest by Western standards – was equal to the annual salary of the treasurer of the local Amnesty group.

27 Daniel A. Bell, "Reflections on Dialogues between Practitioners and Theorists of Human Rights," in: Daniel A. Bell and Jean-Marc Coicaud (eds), *Ethics in Action: The Ethical Challenges of International Human Rights Nongovernmental Organizations*, Cambridge etc.: Cambridge University Press/United Nations University Press, 2007, 1–22 at 5.

28 See: Scholte, *supra*, note 23, 228.

29 See for instance: Joanne R. Bauer and Daniel Bell (eds) *The East Asian Challenge for Human Rights,* Cambridge: Cambridge University Press, 1999.

30 United Nations General Assembly, A/CONF.157/23, 12 July 1993, *Vienna Declaration and Programme of Action*, par. 5.

31 *Our Voice: Bangkok NGO Declaration on Human Rights*, Bangkok: Asian Cultural Forum on Development, 1993, 199; bold in original text, italics supplied.

32 Hanna Beate Schöpp-Schilling, "The Nature and Mandate of the Committee," in: Hanna Beate Schöpp-Schilling and Cees Flinterman (eds), *The Circle of Empowerment: Twenty-five Years of the UN Committee on the Elimination of Discrimination against Women,* New York: The Feminist Press at the City University of New York, 2007, 248–261 at 257.

33 Cynthia Price Cohen, "The Role of Nongovernmental Organizations in the Drafting of the Convention on the Rights of the Child," *Human Rights Quarterly,* 12 (1990), 137–147 at 137.

34 Ineke Boerefijn, Alex van Geuns and Rolanda Oostland, "De Rol van Niet-Gouvernementele Organisaties in de Toezichtsprocedures op Basis van VN Mensenrechten Verdragen,"["The Role of Non-Governmental Organizations in the Supervisory Procedures of the UN Human Rights Treaties"] in: C. Flinterman and W. van Genugten (eds), *Niet-statelijke Actoren en de Rechten van de Mens: Gevestigde Waarden, Nieuwe Wegen,* Den Haag: Boom Juridische Uitgevers, 2003, 121–133 at 126.

35 See: Ineke Boerefijn, 'Towards a Strong System of Supervision: The Human Rights Committee's Role in Reforming the Reporting Procedure under Article 40 of the Covenant on Civil and Political Rights,' *Human Rights Quarterly,* vol. 17 (1995), 766–793 at 784.

36 *Ibid.,* 785

37 Felice D. Gaer, "Reality Check: Human Rights NGOs Confront Governments at the UN," in: Thomas Weiss and Leon Gordenker (eds), *NGOs, the UN and Global Governance,* Boulder/London: Lynne Rienner, 1996, 51–66 at 56.

38 Anna-Karin Lindblom, *Non-governmental Organizations in International Law,* Cambridge etc.: Cambridge University Press, 2005. 482.

39 John Sankey, "Conclusions," in: Willetts, *supra,* note 11, 270–276 at 272.

40 *Ibid.,* 273–274.

41 Manfred Nowak and Ingeborg Schwarz, The Contribution of Non-Governmental Organizations," in: Manfred Nowak, (ed.), *World Conference on Human Rights, Vienna, June 1993: The Contribution of NGOs Reports and Documents,* Wien: Manzsche Verlags- und Universitätsbuchhandlung, 1993, 1–11 at 11.

42 Cyril Ritchie, "Coordinate? Cooperate? Harmonise? NGO Policy and Operational Coalitions," in Weiss and Gordenker, *supra,* note 37, 186.

43 See: James Henke, *Human Rights Now! The Official Book of the Concerts for Human Rights Foundation World Tour,* London: Bloomsbury, 1988, p. 16. At the occasion of the London concert, pop star Bruce Springsteen commented: "I think people come out to see the rock show, to dance and have fun. But if you reach a small percent, if you reach just one person, you've done something." (*New York Times,* 3 September 1988).

44 Reebok Athletic Shoe Corporation.

45 Cf. Martha Alter Chen, "Engendering World Conferences: The International Women's Movement and the UN," in: Weiss and Gordenker, *supra,* note 37, 143.

46 Johan Kaufmann, *Conference Diplomacy: An Introductory Analysis,* Dordrecht: Martinus Nijhoff Publishers, 2nd rev. ed., 1988, 52.

47 For this and similar techniques for solving foreign policy dilemmas, see: Philip P. Everts *et al.*, *Dilemmas in de Buitenlandse Politiek van Nederland* ["Dilemmas in Dutch Foreign Policy"], Leiden: DSWO Pers. 1996.
48 Cook, *supra*, note 22, 191.
49 Cynthia Price Cohen, "The Role of Non-Governmental Organizations in the Drafting of the Convention on the Rights of the Child," *Human Rights Quarterly*, 12 (1990), 137–147.
50 Menno Kamminga, "The Evolving Status of NGOs under International Law: A Threat to the Inter-State System?" in: Philip Alston, (ed.), *Non-State Actors and Human Rights*, Oxford: Oxford University Press, 2005, 93–111 at 101.
51 UN Charter, art. 2, par. 7: "Nothing contained in the present Charter shall authorize the United Nations to intervene in matters which are essentially within the domestic jurisdiction of any state..."
52 On the eve of the 2008 Olympic Games, President George Bush, speaking from Bangkok, criticized the governments of China and Myanmar for their human rights record. A spokesman for the Chinese Foreign Ministry responded by saying that no one should interfere in other countries' internal affairs. ["Bush Faults China over Human Rights and Detentions," *International Herald Tribune* (Paris), 7 August, 2008 and "Bush Puts Heat on Myanmar and China from Thailand," *International Herald Tribune* (Paris), 8 August 2008.]
53 On the notion of "international community" see further Chapter 4.
54 Jem Bendell, *Debating NGO Accountability*, New York and Geneva: United Nations, 2006, 55, referring to Stephen J. Larrabee, "Restrictive Proposals in Kazakhstan," *The International Journal of Not-for-Profit Law*, vol. 7 (2005).
55 *Ibid.*, 56.
56 Lindblom, *supra*, note 22.
57 *Ibid.*, 473.
58 Edmund Burke, *Speech on Conciliation with America.* 22 March 1775 (J.M. and M.J. Cohen, *Dictionary of Quotations*, London: Penguin Books, 1960, 80).
59 *Supra*, note 22, 478.
60 Peter Baehr, Monique Castermans-Holleman and Fred Grünfeld, *Human Rights in the Foreign Policy of the Netherlands*, Antwerp/Oxford/New York: Intersentia, 2002. The following is based on the conclusions of that study, 228–230.
61 *Ibid.*, 195–216.
62 *Ibid.*, 43–72.
63 *Ibid.*, 23–42.
64 *Ibid.*, 99–121. In the final document of the third follow-up meeting of the OSCE in Vienna (1989), the participating states created a far-reaching new supervisory mechanism of human rights consisting of four phases: exchange of information, discussion of the situation in bilateral meetings, bringing a human rights situation to the attention of other OSCE states, and finally providing information at the next follow-up meeting.

65 *Ibid.*, 123–147. "Refuseniks" were Russian Jews wanting to leave the Soviet Union for Israel or the United States and were refused exit visas.
66 *Ibid.*, 173–194.
67 *Ibid.*, 195–216.
68 The United States asked for a (highly unusual) formal vote and then voted against her.
69 See: Peter R. Baehr, "Human Rights in Foreign Policy and International Relations: Shifting Emphasis after 9/11? The Cases of the United States and the Netherlands," (in print).

Chapter 4   The United Nations

1 For more information on the Universal Periodic Review and the way it is used by NGOs see *infra* Chapter 6.
2 *Dutch NGOs Contribution to the First Universal Periodic Review of the Netherlands by the UN Human Rights Council*, November 2007. That report had been submitted on behalf of the following NGOs: Dutch section of the International Commission of Jurists (NJCM), Art. 1, Netwerk VN-Vrouwenverdrag, Dutch CEDAW Network, Johannes Wier Stichting, Aim for Human Rights, E-Quality, Movisie, International Information Centre and Archives for the Women's Movement, Justice and Peace Netherlands, Defence for Children International Nederland, Stichting Buitenlandse Partner, Vereniging voor Vrouw en Recht Clara Wichmann, Stichting Landelijk Ongedocumenteerden Steunpunt, Stichting LOS.
3 UN General Assembly, Human Rights Council, Res. A/RES/60/251, 3 April 2006, par. 11; italics supplied.
4 Lucia Nader, "The Role of NGOs in the UN Human Rights Council," *SUR International Journal on Human Rights*, vol. 7 (2007), 7–27 at 9.
5 T. Hill, "Three Generations of UN-Civil Society Relations: A Quick Sketch," Geneva: UN-NGLS, 2004, 1 quoted by Jem Bendell, *Debating NGO Accountability*, New York and Geneva: United Nations, 2006, 51.
6 Bendell, *supra*, note 5, 51.
7 P. Willetts, "From 'Consultative Arrangements' to 'Partnership': The Changing Status of NGOs in Diplomacy at the UN," *Global Governance*, vol. 6 (2000), 191–213 at 191.
8 UN Charter art. 1, par. 3.
9 Articles 13(1b), 55(c), 56, 62(2), 68 and 76(c).
10 The International Covenant on Civil and Political Rights and the International Covenant on Economic, Social and Cultural Rights.
11 As of 26 September 2008, the treaties had the following number of ratifications:
International Covenant on Economic, Social and Cultural Rights: 159;
International Covenant on Civil and Political Rights: 162;
Optional Protocol to the International Covenant on Civil and Political Rights: 111;
Second Optional Protocol to the International Covenant on Civil and Political Rights: 68.

12 Jan Herman Burgers, "The Road to San Francisco: The Revival of the Human Rights Idea in the Twentieth Century," *Human Rights Quarterly*, vol. 14 (1992), 447–478. For even earlier developments see: Glen Mitona, "Civil Society and Human Rights: The Commission to Study the Organization of Peace and the Origins of the UN Human Rights Regime," *Human Rights Quarterly*, vol. 30 (2008), 607–630.

13 See also: Paul Gordon Lauren, *Power and Prejudice: The Politics and Diplomacy of Racial Discrimination*, Boulder and London: Westview Press, 1988 who emphasizes another source for the human rights idea: the irritation on the part of non-Western countries over Western colonialism and racial discrimination.

14 See: Helena Cook, "Amnesty International at the United Nations," in: Peter Willetts (ed.), *The Conscience of the World: The Influence of Non-Governmental Organisations in the UN System*, Washington D.C.: The Brookings Institution, 1996, 181–213, at 184: "It is difficult to quantify precisely what impact Amnesty has within the United Nations. It is impossible to attribute specific results solely to a particular NGO initiative. NGOs can and do set a political process in motion and shape the outcome, but one cannot isolate the impact of NGOs from that of other players or factors."

15 "The Economic and Social Council may make suitable arrangements for consultation with non-governmental organizations which are concerned with matters within its competence. Such arrangements may be made with international organizations and, where appropriate, with national organizations after consultation with the Member of the United Nations concerned." (United Nations Charter, article 71).

16 Anna-Karin Lindblom, *Non-Governmental Organisations in International Law*, Cambridge etc.: Cambridge University Press, 2005, 457: "The total number of participants amounted to around 7,000. Of these, 3,691 persons were NGO representatives from 841 organisations; 593 NGOs were not in consultative status with ECOSOC."

17 Their access to the conference was, however, limited, as Helena Cook, former legal advisor of Amnesty International reports: "Despite intensive lobbying and vociferous protests NGOs were effectively excluded even from silently observing the drafting of the final document of the 1993 World Conference on Human Rights, both in the Preparatory Committee and at the Conference itself. Governments' unease about the exclusion was reflected in the fact that 'formal' sessions of the drafting group were declared open to NGOs, but then neatly circumvented by having all the real work go on in closed informal meetings." (Cook, *supra*, note 14, 192).

18 Henry J. Steiner, *Diverse Partners: Non-Governmental Organizations in the Human Rights Movement, the Report of a Retreat of Human Rights Activists*, Cambridge, Mass.: Harvard Law School Human Rights Program and Human Rights Internet, 1990, 5–15 at 7.

19 *Ibid.*

20 Vienna Declaration and Programme of Action, par. 38; italics supplied.

21 J. Herman Burgers, "Dutch Nongovernmental Organizations and Foreign Policy in the Field of Human Rights," in: P.J. van Krieken and Ch. O. Pannenborg (eds), *Liber Akkerman: In- and Outlaws in War*, Apeldoorn/Antwerp: MAKLU, 1992, 157–168 at 157.

22 *Ibid.*, 157–158.

23 Peter R. Baehr, "The General Assembly: Negotiating the Convention on Torture," in: David P. Forsythe (ed.), *The United Nations in the World Political Economy: Essays in Honour of Leon Gordenker*, London: Macmillan, 1989, 36–53 at 47.

24 William Korey, *NGOs and the Universal Declaration of Human Rights: "A Curious Grapevine"*, Dobbs Ferry, N.Y.: St. Martin's Press, 1998, 5.

25 Ineke Boerefijn, Alex van Gans en Rolanda Oostland, "De Rol van Niet-Gouvernementele Organisaties in de Toezichtprocedures op Basis van VN-Mensenrechten Verdragen," ["The Role of Non-Governmental Organizations in the Supervision Procedures on the Basis of UN-Human Rights Treaties"], in: C. Flinterman and W. Van Genugten (eds), *Niet-statelijke Actoren en de Rechten van de Mens: Gevestigde Waarden, Nieuwe Wegen*, Den Haag: Boom Juridische Uitgevers, 2003, 121–133 at 127.

26 Cook, *supra*, note 14, 192.

27 Interview with Theo van Boven in: Margaret E. Keck and Kathryn Sikkink, *Activists Beyond Borders: Advocating Networks in International Politics*, Ithaca and London: Cornell University Press, 1998, 96.

28 *Report of the Working Group on Enforced or Involuntary Disappearances*, A/HRC/4/41, 25 January 2007, 12.

29 *Ibid.*, 2.

30 Michael Longford, "NGOs and the Rights of the Child," in: Willetts (ed.), *supra*, note 14, 231.

31 Hilde Reiding, *The Netherlands and the Development of International Human Rights Instruments*, Antwerp: Intersentia, 2007, 257.

32 Shanti Dairiam, "From Global to Local: the Involvement of NGOs," in: Hanna Beate Schöpp-Schilling and Cees Flinterman (eds), *The Circle of Empowerment: Twenty-five Years of the UN Committee on the Elimination of Discrimination Against Women*, New York: The Feminist Press at the City University of New York, 2007, 313–325 at 315.

33 *Strengthening of the United Nations: An Agenda for Further Change*, UNGA A/57/387, 9 September 2002, 23–25.

34 UNGA A/58/817, 11 June 2004, 1.

35 Transmitted letter, dated 7 June 2004 from the Chair of the Panel of Eminent Persons on United Nations-Civil Society Relations addressed to the Secretary-General; *ibid.*, 3.

36 Michael Longford has made the point that "(...) different organizations in the UN system use different understandings of the term when accrediting organizations for participation in its processes." (Longford, *supra*, note 30, 48.

37 *Report of the Panel of Eminent Persons on United Nations-Civil Society Relations*, A/58/817, 11 June 2004. The Arria formula, named after Venezuelan ambassador Diego Arria, is an informal arrangement that

allows Security Council members to meet with non-member states, and recently also with representatives of NGOs, in informal sessions, to be briefed about international peace and security issues. See also: Kerstin Martens, "An Appraisal of Amnesty International's Work at the United Nations: Established Areas of Activities and Shifting Priorities since the 1990s," *Human Rights Quarterly*, 26 (2004), 1050–1070 at 1059, notes 40–44.

38 *Report of the Secretary-General in response to the report of the Panel of Eminent Persons on United Nations-Civil Society Relations*, A/59/354, 13 September 2004, 1.
39 See: Lindblom, *supra*, note 16, 519.
40 *Supra*, note 34, 53.
41 Menno Kamminga, "What Makes an NGO 'Legitimate' in the Eyes of States?" in: Anton Vedder (ed.), *NGO Involvement in International Governance and Policy: Sources of Legitimacy*, Leiden/Boston: Martinus Nijhoff Publishers, 2007, 188.
42 "Loud Voice for Rights Exits with Optimism," *International Herald Tribune* (Paris), 2 July 2008.
43 Theo C. van Boven, 'The Role of the United Nations Secretariat,' in: Philip Alston (ed.), *The United Nations and Human Rights: A Critical Appraisal*, Oxford: Clarendon Press, 1992, 549–579 at 561.
44 *Ibid.*
45 With regard to this subject the Vienna Declaration uses similar words: 'The Centre for Human Rights should play an important role in coordinating system-wide attention for human rights. The focal role of the Centre can best be realized if it is enabled to cooperate fully with other United Nations bodies and organs. The coordinating role of the Centre for Human Rights also implies that the office of the Centre for Human Rights in New York is strengthened.' (*Vienna Declaration and Programme of Action*, IIA, par. 14).
46 Cambodia, Uganda, Chile, Iran, El Salvador and Guatemala. Cf. Howard Tolley Jr., *The UN Commission on Human Rights*, Boulder and London: Westview Press, 1987, 107.
47 Iain Guest, *Behind the Disappearances: Argentina's Dirty War Against Human Rights and the United Nations*, Philadelphia: University of Pennsylvania Press, 1990.
48 See: R.S. Clark, *A United Nations High Commissioner for Human Rights*, The Hague: Martinus Nijhoff, 1972.
49 John P. Humphrey, *Human Rights and the United Nations: A Great Adventure*, Dobbs Ferry N.Y.: Transnational Publishers, 1983, 296 ff.
50 W.J.M. van Genugten, "Hoge Commissaris voor de Rechten van de Mens: de Langzame Dood van een Goede Gedachte." ["The High Commissioner for Human Rights: Slow Death of a Good Idea"], *Internationale Spectator*, vol. 41 (1987), 463–467.
51 Amnesty International, *World Conference on Human Rights, Facing Up to the Failures: Proposals for Improving the Protection of Human Rights by the United Nations*, AI Index: IOR 41/16/92, December 1992.

52 It was envisaged from the beginning that the new function could be fulfilled by either a man or a woman.

53 Although formally launched only in December 1992, it had been discussed before on an informal basis.

54 *Vienna Declaration and Programme of Action* II A. 'Increased coordination on human rights within the United Nations system,' par. 18.

55 See for instance: "Time Running Out in Afghanistan," *International Herald Tribune* (Paris), 22 August 2008: "The *international community* needs to provide more – and more carefully monitored – resources to build up Afghanistan's security forces and administrative capacity and accelerate rural development." "France Shaken by Gloating Taliban," *International Herald Tribune* (Paris), 5 September 2008: "[France's Defense Minister Hervé Morin said:] 'They [the Taliban] have understood that public opinion is probably the Achilles' heel of the *international community* that is present in Afghanistan.'" "Republic of Blowback,", *International Herald Tribune* (Paris), 5 September 2008: "Thus began the schooling of the *international community* on the law of unintended consequences in Somalia ..." [(italics supplied]. See also: Bruno Simma and Andreas L. Paulus, "The 'International Community': Facing the Challenge of Globalization," *European Journal of International Law*, 9 (1998), 266–277.

56 George Schwarzenberger, *Power Politics: A Study of World Society* (London: Stevens & Sons Ltd., 3rd ed. 1964), 12.

57 *Srebrenica Report of the Secretary-General pursuant to General Assembly resolution 53/35 (1998)*, A/54/549, New York: United Nations, 1999, pars. 6, 45, 49, 71, 127, 129, 130, 195, 321, 371, 372, 408, 415, 446, 452, 465, 474, 487, 497, 501, 502, 503, and 504; see also: Peter R. Baehr, "Accountability of the United Nations: The Case of Srebrenica," in print.

58 UNSG Report, par. 132; italics supplied.

59 "Human Rights Watch, Bosnia-Herzegovina: The Fall of Srebrenica and the Failure of UN Peace-keeping, 7 (13) (October 1995), 2 See also: Human Rights Watch World Report 2001 Bosnia and Herzegovina, 1: "The international community 's close involvement continued to be necessary to move the peace process along (...) However, many in the international community were losing patience with the slow progress in Bosnia, and international attention was shifting to other areas."

60 http://web.amnesty.org/library/print/ENGEUR63014196 visited on September 1, 2006.

61 Srebrenica: Een "Veilig" Gebied: Reconstructie, Achtergronden, Gevolgen en Analyses van de Val van een Safe Area, Amsterdam: Nederlands Instituut voor Oorlogsdocumentatie, 2002 [henceforth cited as NIOD Report; an English version of the report is accessible on the internet: www.niod.nl: J.C.H. Blom and P. Romijn, Srebrenica, a Safe Area: Reconstruction, Background, Consequences and Analyses of the Fall of a Safe Area, (Amsterdam, 2002)]. 1727, 1753, and 1778.

62 NIOD Report, 3130. See also: David Rieff, *A Bed for the Night: Humanitarianism in Crisis* (London: Vintage 2002), 8: "(...) [W]hat thinking

person can take seriously the idea that there is such a thing as the international community?"

63 See: Bruno Simma and Andreas L. Paulus, "The 'International Community': Facing the Challenges of Globalization," *European Journal of International Law*, vol. 9 (1998), 266–77 at 277.

Chapter 5   The Promotion of Human Rights: Standard-Setting

1 William Korey, *NGOs and the Universal Declaration of Human Rights: "A Curious Grapevine"*, New York: St. Martin's Press, 1998, 2. Se also: Felice D. Gaer, "Reality Check: Human Rights NGOs Confront Governments at the UN," in: Thomas Weiss and Leon Gordenker (eds), *NGOs, the UN and Global Governance*, Boulder/London: Lynne Rienner, 1996, 51–66 at 51–52.

2 John P. Humphrey, *Human Rights & the United Nations: A Great Adventure*, Dobbs Ferry, N.Y.: Transnational Publishers Inc., 1984, 13.

3 Korey, *supra*, note 1. See also: Johannes Morsink, *The Universal Declaration of Human Rights*, Philadelphia: University of Pennsylvania Press, 1999, 2. At each of the sessions of the Commission on Human Rights that prepared the text of the Universal Declaration, numerous NGOs were present, some of which submitted their own drafts to the Commission. Morsink mentions the following: American Federation of Labor, International Federation of Christian Trade Unions, Interparliamentary Union, Catholic International Union for Social Service, International Union of Catholic Women's Leagues, Commission of the Churches on International Affairs, Coordinating Board of Jewish Organizations, International Abolitionist Federation, International Committee of the Red Cross, International Council of Women, Women's International Democratic Federation, International Federation of Business and Professional Women, World Federation of United Nations Associations, and the World Jewish Congress (Morsink, 9).

4 *Statute of Amnesty International* as amended by the 28th International Council, meeting in Morelos, Mexico, 11 to 17 August 2007, article 1. Johannes Morsink in his standard work on the Universal Declaration of Human Rights calls it "the moral anchor of the worldwide movement [of human rights]" (Morsink, *supra*, note 3, xii).

5 Korey, *supra*, note 1, 4.

6 Kerstin Martens, "An Appraisal of Amnesty International's Work at the United Nations: Established Areas of Activities and Shifting Priorities since the 1990s," *Human Rights Quarterly*, vol. 26 (2004), 1050–1070 at 1065.

7 Helena Cook, "Amnesty International at the United Nations," in: Peter Willetts (ed.), *"The Conscience of the World": The Influence of Non-Governmental Organisations in the UN System*, London: Hurst and Company, 1996, 181–213 at 189.

8 For example, in the city of Amsterdam tourists can visit a museum that displays all kinds of machinery and other mechanisms that were used to practice torture in the historic past.

9 Nigel Rodley, "Torture, Freedom from-" in: Rhona K.M. Smith and Christien van den Anker (eds), *Human Rights*, London: Hodder Arnold, 2005, 332–336 at 332.

10 Amnesty International, *Report on Torture*, (1973); *Torture in the Eighties* (1984) and *Take a Step to Stamp Out Torture* (2000).

11 It was originally to be held at the headquarters of UNESCO, but the fact that the names of member-states of UNESCO had been mentioned in the original Amnesty report created a problem for that intergovernmental organization, that in the end refused the use of its premises. "But UNESCO's refusal of its facilities for the conference served only to embarrass itself. Front-page stories in *Le Monde* and *Le Figaro* stirred public sympathy for Amnesty even as they challenged the integrity of UNESCO." (Korey, *supra*, note 1, 172).

12 Cf. Alfred Heijder and Herman van Geuns, *Professional Codes of Ethics*, London: Amnesty International, 1976. For a more recent account of the subject see: Peter Baehr and Menno Kamminga, , "Een Gedragscode voor Mensenrechten-NGOs?"["A Code of Behaviour for Human Rights NGOs?"] in: C. Flinterman and W. van Genugten (eds), *Niet-statelijke Actoren en de Rechten van de Mens: Gevestigde Waarden, Nieuwe Wegen*, Den Haag: Boom Juridische Uitgevers, 2003, 67–80.

13 UNGA resolution 3452 (XXX), 9 December 1975.

14 Cf. J. Herman Burgers and Hans Danelius, *The United Nations Convention against Torture: A Handbook on the Convention against Torture and Other Cruel, Inhuman or Degrading Treatment or Punishment*, Dordrecht/Boston/London: Martinus Nijhoff Publishers, 1988, 19.

15 UNGA Resolution 34/169, 17 December 1979; see Burgers and Danelius, *supra*, note 14, 20. Reiding reports that Amnesty International "(...) was to a large extent responsible for the Netherlands' first adaptations in its stand on universal jurisdiction in the UN Convention against Torture." (Hilde Reiding, *The Netherlands and the Development of International Human Rights Instruments*, Antwerp: Intersentia, 2007, 420).

16 UNGA Resolution 39/46. 10 December 1984.

17 Cook, *supra*, note 7, 191.

18 Burgers and Danelius, *supra*, note 14, 24.

19 UNGA Resolution, 57/199, 18 December 2002.

20 Reed Brody and Felipe Gonzáles, "Nunca Más: An Analysis of International Instruments on 'Disappearances", *Human Rights Quarterly*, vol. 19 (1997), 365–405 at 366. This practice, named "Nacht und Nebel" ("Night and Fog") was based on a directive of Adolf Hitler in 1941 resulting in the kidnapping and disappearance of political activists and resistance helpers throughout Germany's occupied territories.

21 In later years the phenomenon spread to countries outside Latin America, e.g. Iraq, Uganda, the Philippines, Sri Lanka, and Turkey. The most recent report of the UN Working Group on Disappearances dealt with

cases in 81 countries, 16 of which in Latin America and 65 elsewhere. (*Report of the Working Group on Enforced or Involuntary Disappearances*, A/HRC 7/2, 10 January 2008.

22   See: Iain Guest, *Behind the Disappearances: Argentina's Dirty War against Human Rights and the United Nations*, Philadelphia: University of Pennsylvania Press, 1990, 49 ff.

23   Amnesty International consistently puts the term between quotation marks in order to indicate that the person in question has not really disappeared, but has most probably been abducted by the security forces.

24   Brody and Gonzáles, *supra*, note 20, 369.

25   UNGA Resolution 47/133 (18 December 1992).

26   Cook, *supra*, note 7, 193.

27   UNGA Resolution 61/177, 20 December 2006.

28   www.icaed.org/global-action; accessed 28 August 2008.

29   Universal Declaration of Human Rights, Preamble, par. 5. According to Johannes Morsink, "the absence of sexism in the Universal Declaration is primarily due to the aggressive lobbying of Mrs. Begtrup [the Danish chairperson of what was then the sub-commission on the status of women] and the steady pressure of the Soviet delegation."[Johannes Morsink, "Women's Rights in the Universal Declaration," *Human Rights Quarterly*, vol. 13 (1991), 229–256 at 231.] He also mentions that it came as a surprise that Mrs. Eleanor Roosevelt, the chairperson of the Commission on Human Rights, was not more sympathetic to the goals of the women's lobby. He calls that a "blind spot", shared by many other less powerful delegates (Morsink, 255–256).

30   Arvonne S. Fraser, "Becoming Human: The Origins and Development of Women's Human Rights," *Human Rights Quarterly*, vol. 21 (1999), 853–906 at 857.

31   UNGA Resolution, 54/4, 15 October 1999. Mona Rishmawi, director of the Centre for the Independence of Judges and Lawyers, affiliated with the International Commission of Jurists, has called the Convention "a landmark treaty in the struggle to end discrimination based on sex" [Mona Rishmawi, "Working on Women's Human Rights: The Developing Approach of the International Commission of Jurists," in: J.A. Smith and L.F. Zwaak (eds), *International Protection of Human Rights*, SIM Special no. 15 (Utrecht, 1995), 65–76 at 66.]

32   OAS/Ser.L.V./II.92/doc.31 rev. 3 (1994).

33   Mara R. Bustelo, "The Committee on the Elimination of Discrimination against Women at the Crossroads," in: Philip Alston and James Crawford (eds), *The Future of UN Human Rights Treaty Monitoring*, Cambridge: Cambridge University Press, 2000, 79–111 at 105.

34   *Ibid.*, 106.

35   See: Shanti Dairiam, "From Global to Local: the Involvement of NGOs," in: Hanna Beate Schöpp-Schilling and Cees Flinterman (eds), *The Circle of Empowerment: Twenty-five Years of the UN Committee on the Elimination of Discrimination against Women*, New York: The Feminist Press at the City University of New York, 2007, 313–325.

36 O'Hare mentions especially the Global Tribunal on Violations of Women's Human Rights, organized by the Women's Global Leadership Group as being instrumental in placing the question of violence against women on the agenda of the World Conference. (Ursula A. O'Hare, "Realizing Human Rights for Women," *Human Rights Quarterly*, vol. 21 (1999), 364–402 at 373 note 51.)

37 *Vienna Declaration and Programme of Action*, U.N. Doc. A/CONF. 157/23 (1993), pt. 1, par. 18.

38 Anne Gallagher, "Ending the Marginalization: Strategies for Incorporating Women into the United Nations Rights System," *Human Rights Quarterly*, vol. 19 (1997), 283–333 at 284. She explains the term "mainstream" to refer to the various instruments, committees, programs, and procedures serviced by the Office of the UN High Commissioner for Human Rights.

39 Fleur van Leeuwen, "A Woman's Right to Decide? The United Nations Human Rights Committee, Human Rights of Women, and Matters of Human Reproduction," *Netherlands Quarterly of Human Rights*, vol. 25 (2007), 97–116 at 98.

40 Rachael Lorna Johnstone, "Feminist Influences on the United Nations Human Rights Treaty Bodies," *Human Rights Quarterly*, vol. 28 (2006), 148–185 at 150.

41 *Ibid.*, 154.

42 Jane Connors, "NGOs and the Human Rights of Women at the United Nations," in: Peter Willetts (ed.), *"The Conscience of the World": The Influence of Non-Governmental Organisations in the UN System*, London: Hurst and Company, 1996, 147–180 at 167.

43 www.amnesty.org/en/campaigns/stop-violence-against-women, accessed 21 July 2008.

44 Ineke Boerefijn, *De Blinddoek Opzij: Een Mensenrechtenbenadering van Geweld tegen Vrouwen* ["The Blindfold Away: A Human Rights Approach of Violence against Women"]. Inaugural lecture Maastricht University, 8 December 2006, 10; translated from the original Dutch.

45 Cynthia Price Cohen, "The Role of Nongovernmental Organizations in the Drafting of the Convention on the Rights of the Child," *Human Rights Quarterly*, vol. 12 (1990), 137–147 at 138.

46 UNGA, Resolution, 1386 (XIV), 20 November 1959.

47 UNGA Resolution 31/169 (1976), 21 December 1976.

48 Price Cohen, *supra*, note 45, and Price Cohen, "The United Nations Convention on the Rights of the Child: Involvement of NGOs," in: Theo C. van Boven, Cees Flinterman, Fred Grünfeld and Rita Hut (eds), *The Legitimacy of the United Nations: Towards an Enhanced Legal Status of Non-State Actors*, Utrecht: SIM Special no. 19, 1997, 169–184.

49 On the drafting process see: Jacqueline Smith, "The Rights of the Child," in: Monique Castermans-Holleman, Fried van Hoof and Jacqueline Smith (eds), *The Role of the Nation-State in the 21st Century: Human Rights, International Organisations and Foreign Policy. Essays in Honour of Peter Baehr*, The Hague/Boston/London: Kluwer Law International, 1998, 163–173 at 166–169.

50 Price Cohen in Van Boven *et al.*, *supra*, note 48, 170–171.

51   The following NGOs took part in the early sessions of the Working Group: International Federation of Women Lawyers, the Women's Democratic International Federation, International Union for Child Welfare, World Jewish Congress, International Humanist and Ethical Union, International Union of Judges, International Association of Youth Magistrates, Society for Comparative Legislation. (Price Cohen in Van Boven *et al.*, *supra*, note 48, 171).

52   *Ibid.*, See also: Lawrence L. LeBlanc, *The Convention on the Rights of the Child*, Lincoln and London: Nebraska University Press, 1995, 42–45.

53   Between 1983 and 1990 the following organizations participated: International Catholic Child Bureau, International Commission of Jurists, Zonta International, Human Rights Internet, Friends World Committee for Consultation, Rädda Barnen International, Amnesty International, Associated Country Women of the World, Baha'i International Community, International Council of Jewish Women, ATD Fourth World, International Social Service, Minority Rights Group, Anti-Slavery Society for the Protection of Human Rights, World Association for the School as Instrument of Peace, World Organization for Early Childhood Education, International Committee of the Red Cross, International Association of Juvenile and Family Court Magistrates and International Federation of Women in Legal Careers (Price Cohen in Van Boven *et al.*, *supra*, note 44, 173).

54   Price Cohen in Van Boven *et al.*, *supra*, note 45, 175. See also: Reiding, *supra*, note 15, 274 who refers to "mutual cooperation based on an equal standing".

55   Reiding, *supra*, note 15, 275.

56   Price Cohen in Van Boven *et al.*, *supra*, note 45, 179.

57   N. Cantwell, Non-Governmental Organisations and the United Nations Convention on the Rights of the Child," *Bulletin of Human Rights*, vol. 91 (1992), 16–24 at 19.

58   Italics supplied.

59   www.crin.org/ngogroupforcrc, accessed 21 July 2008.

60   Claire Breen, "The Role of NGOs in the Formulation of and Compliance with the Optional Protocol to the Convention on the Rights of the Child on Involvement of Children in Armed Conflict," *Human Rights Quarterly*, vol. 25 (2003), 453–481.

61   *Ibid.*, 461–462.

62   United Nations General Assembly, Resolution 54/263, 25 May 2000.

63   This section is based on: Peter R. Baehr, "Amnesty International and its Self-Imposed Limited Mandate," *Netherlands Quarterly of Human Rights*, vol. 12 (1994), 5–22 at 18–19.

64   When this author discussed the matter at the 1987 International Council, he was told by a colleague from Zimbabwe that in that country there were no homosexuals. I retorted that in the Netherlands we did have homosexuals and that I did not understand why he was opposed to the issue, if, as he claimed, there were no homosexuals in Zimbabwe. He was neither amused nor persuaded by this argument.

65 Amnesty's International Statute then read: "(...) to oppose by all appropriate means irrespective of political considerations: a) the imprisonment, detention or other physical restrictions imposed on any person by reason of his or her political, religious, or other conscientiously held beliefs or by reason of his or her ethnic origin, *sex*, colour, language, national or social origin, economic status, birth or other status, provided that he or she has not used physical violence (hereinafter referred to as 'prisoners of conscience'"); italics supplied. The text has since then been changed.

66 The same is roughly true at the regional level. In 2007, the member-governments of ASEAN signed a charter of human rights that included the creation of an Asean human rights body, but had no provisions for enforcing compliance with any human rights standard. See: "Historic Asean Charter Reveals Divisions," *International Herald Tribune* (Paris), 20 November 2007.

67 Bendell emphasizes that the likelihood that NGOs representatives are listened to in the political process include *the personality of advocates*, their skills in the English language and the notoriety of their organization in the mass media. (Jem Bendell, *Debating NGO Accountability*, NGLS Development Dossier, New York and Geneva: United Nations, 2006, 43); italics supplied.

68 Lindblom reports that "[a]n NGO representative explained that when you are involved in a process like the Statute of the International Criminal Court for a period of several years, you get to know each other and become friends." (Anna-Karin Lindblom, *Non-governmental Organisations in International Law*, Cambridge etc.: Cambridge University Press, 2005, 474.

69 See *supra* Chapter 3.

70 Berkovitch speaks even of "global sisterhood" (Nina Berkovitch, "The Emergence and Transformation of the International Women's Movement," in: John Boli and George M. Thomas (eds.), *Constructing World Culture: International Nongovernmental Organizations since 1875*," Stanford: Stanford University Press, 1999, 100–126 at 123. She also observes, however: "The Mid-Decade Meeting in Copenhagen [1980] was the most conflict-ridden with Western women pillorying clitoridectomy and similar practices as violations of human rights while women from Africa and the Middle East, where these practices are common, resisted this characterization and the uses made of it." (*ibid.*, 123).

Chapter 6 The Protection of Human Rights

1 *Statute of Amnesty International* as amended by the 22nd International Council meeting in Ljubljana, Slovenia, 12–20 August 1995. The wording of the International Statute has since been changed and does not mention the term "prisoners of conscience" any more. The term is retained in the "Prisoners of Conscience Appeal Fund".

2 "Prisoners of conscience, torture victims, these are Amnesty's moral bedrock." (Stephen Hopgood, *Keepers of the Flame: Understanding Amnesty International*, Ithaca and London: Cornell University Press, 2006, 73.)

3 It is not a coincidence that the piece that led to the founding of
Amnesty International, an article in the British Sunday paper, *The
Observer* (28 May 1961), written by the British lawyer Peter Benenson,
carried the title "The Forgotten Prisoners". It is curious to know that the
names of the detained Portuguese students, mentioned in the article,
who had protested against the regime of the dictator Salazar, are not to
be found in the files of prisoners of conscience. See: Hopgood, *supra*,
note 2, 55.

4 When as a member of the International Executive Committee of AI,
I visited an Egyptian government official in the late eighties, he asked
me whether I could put an end to the great number of letters he received
from Amnesty members. These took a great deal of his time to read and
answer them! Knowing fully well that this was part of an ongoing international campaign, I informed him that the letters would stop as soon
as the human rights violations in his country had ended.

5 Hopgood, *supra*, note 2, 83.

6 Christian Tomuschat, *Human Rights: Between Idealism and Realism*, Oxford:
Oxford University Press, 2003, 234.

7 On 24 January 2008, when she was awarded the Annetje Fels-
Kupferschmidt medal.

8 "Groups of no less than five members may, on payment of an annual fee
determined by the International Council, become affiliated to AMNESTY
INTERNATIONAL or a section thereof. (...) An affiliated adoption group
shall accept for adoption such prisoners as may from time to time be
allotted to it by the International Secretariat, and shall adopt no others
as long as it remains affiliated to AMNESTY INTERNATIONAL. No group
shall be allotted a prisoner of conscience detained in its own country."
(*Statute of Amnesty International*, as amended by the 28th International
Council meeting in Morelos, Mexico, 11 to 17 August 2007, article 14.).
It is rather likely that this article will be changed by a future meeting of
the Council.

9 This section is based on: Peter R. Baehr, "Human Rights: Far better or Far
Worse?" in: Fons Coomans, Fred Grünfeld, Ingrid Westendorp and Jan
Willems (eds), *Rendering Justice to the Vulnerable: Liber Amicorum in Honour
of Theo van Boven*, The Hague/London/Boston: Kluwer Law International,
2000, 41–55.

10 Manfred Nowak, *U.N. Covenant on Civil and Political Rights, CCPR Commentary*, Kehl/Strasbourg/Arlington: N.P. Engel, n.d. 585.

11 See for example: Amnesty International, *Chinese Authorities' Broken Promises
Threaten Olympic Legacy*, AI Index ASA 17/089/2008, 28 July 2008.

12 See for example the entries in the Amnesty International 2007 Report on
Australia, Austria, Belgium, Canada, Denmark, Finland, France, Germany,
Greece, Ireland, Israel, Italy, Japan, Malta, Netherlands, New Zealand,
Portugal, Spain, Sweden, Switzerland, the United Kingdom, and the
United States.

13 Amnesty International always carries on its website a number of "good
news stories". Some recent examples: SYRIAN PRISONER OF CONSCIENCE

FREED (8 August 2008); TUNISIAN JOURNALIST FREED (22 July 2008); UK MINISTRY OF DEFENCE AGREES TO COMPENSATE IRAQI TORTURE VICTIMS (14 July 2008); ACTIVIST RELEASED IN UZBEKISTAN (8 June 2008); ROYAL PARDON FOR MOROCCAN DEMONSTRATORS (11 April 2008); IRANIAN TRADE UNIONIST FREED (11 April 2008). www.amnesty. org/en/news-and-updates/good-news; accessed 9 August 2008.

14 Personal interview with death penalty expert Bart Stapert.

15 See: John Gerard Ruggie, "American Exceptionalism, Exemptionalism and Global Governance," in: Michael Ignatieff (ed.) *American Exceptionalism and Human Rights,* Princeton and Oxford: Princeton University Press, 2005, 304–338 at 306.

16 Priscilla B. Hayner, *Unspeakable Truths: Confronting State Terror and Atrocity,* New York and London: Routledge, 2001. See also: Michelle Parlevliet, "Considering Truth. Dealing with a Legacy of Gross Human Rights Violations," *Netherlands Quarterly of Human Rights,* vol. 16 (1998), 141–174.

17 Cf. Daan Bronkhorst, *Truth and Reconciliation: Obstacles and Opportunities for Human Rights,* Amsterdam: Amnesty International, 1995, 26–27; Daan Bronkhorst, "Naming Names: Identity and Identification in Human Rights Work," *Netherlands Quarterly of Human Rights,* vol. 16 (1998), 457–474.

18 www.ictj.org; accessed 10 August 2008; italics supplied.

19 Raphael Lemkin, *Axis Rule in Occupied Europe,* Washington D.C.: Carnegie Endowment for International Peace, 1944. For a review of Lemkin's work, see: Lawrence J. LeBlanc, *The United States and the Genocide Convention,* Durham and London: Duke University Press, 1991, 17–22.

20 Convention on the Prevention and Punishment of the Crime of Genocide, UNGA resolution 260 A (III), 9 December 1948.

21 International Court of Justice, *Application of the Convention on the Prevention and Punishment of the Crime of Genocide (Bosnia and Herzegovina v. Yugoslavia),* 11 July 1996.

22 UN Security Council, *Report of the Secretary-General Pursuant to Paragraph 2 of Security Council Resolution 808 (1993),* S/25704, 3 May 1993, 4.

23 David Rohde, *A Safe Area. Srebrenica: Europe's Worst Massacre since the Second World War,* London etc.: Pocket Books, 1997. See also: Jan Willem Honig and Norbert Both, *Srebrenica: Record of a War Crime,* London: Penguin Books, 1996. See also: Peter R. Baehr, "Accountability of the United Nations: The Case of Srebrenica," (in print).

24 See: Fred Grünfeld and Anke Huijboom, *The Failure to Prevent Genocide in Rwanda: The Role of Bystanders,* Leiden/Boston: Martinus Nijhoff Publishers, 2007.

25 Cecilia Medina Quiroga, *The Battle of Human Rights: Gross, Systematic Violations and the Inter-American System,* Dordrecht/Boston/London: Martinus Nijhoff Publishers, 1988, 16.

26 UNDP Annual Report 2008, www.undp.org; accessed 10 August 2008.

27 Ineke Boerefijn, Alex van Gans and Rolanda Oostland, "De Rol van Niet-gouvernementele Organisaties in de Toezichtprocedures op Basis van

VN-Mensenrechten-Verdragen," ["The Role of Non-Governmental Organizations in the Supervision Procedures of UN Human Rights Treaties"] in: C. Flinterman and W. Van Genugten (eds.), *Niet-statelijke Actoren en de Rechten van de Mens: Gevestigde Waarden, Nieuwe Wegen*, The Hague: Boom Juridische Uitgevers, 2003, 121–133 at 131.

28 This section is based on: Peter R. Baehr, "The Netherlands: A Walhalla of Economic and Social Rights?" in: Rhoda E. Howard-Hassmann and Claude E. Welch Jr. (eds), *Economic Rights in Canada and the United States*, Philadelphia: University of Pennsylvania Press, 2006, 189–202.

29 NJCM has, however, criticized the Netherlands report to the ESC Committee for lacking information on the progress made in achieving the observance of the rights: "In general, the report is of a rather descriptive nature and does not contain an analysis or opinion of the government on the state of affairs concerning the implementation of economic, social and cultural rights, nor on the developments since the last report. (...) The Dutch report makes very few references to the problems and obstacles encountered in the process of (progressively) realizing the rights laid down in the Covenant. "[Dutch Section of the International Commission of Jurists *Commentary on the Second Periodic Report of the Netherlands Submitted in Accordance with Article 16 of the International Covenant on Economic, Social and Cultural Rights*, December 8, 1997 (hereafter NJCM), 3].

30 *Ibid.*

31 See Baehr, *supra*, note 28, 191–193.

32 NJCM, *supra*, note 29, 23.

33 *Ibid.*, 5. It also expressed its concern about the lack of protection against disability discrimination and about the scattered initiatives to promote the employment opportunities of *young* disabled persons. See further: Aart Hendriks, *Gelijke Toegang tot de Arbeid voor Gehandicapten: Een Grondrechtelijke en Rechtsvergelijkende Analyse* ["Equal Access to Employment for People with Disabilities: An Analysis from a Human Rights and Comparative Law Perspective"], Deventer: Kluwer, 2000.

34 NJCM, *supra*, note 29, 26–27.

35 Economic and Social Council, *Implementation of the International Covenant on Economic, Social and Cultural Rights, Second Periodic Report: Netherlands, 05/08/96* (E/1990/6/Add. 11), par. 48.

36 NJCM, *supra*, note 29, 6.

37 *Ibid.*, 11.

38 Economic and Social Council, *Implementation of the International Covenant on Economic, Social and Cultural Rights, Second Periodic Report: Netherlands, 05/08/96* (E/1990/6/Add. 11), par. 247 (e).

39 NJCM, *supra*, note 29, 17 and 26.

40 NJCM, *supra*, note 29, 21.

41 See: Fried van Hoof, "De Praktische Betekenis van Economisch, Sociale en Culturele Rechten in Nederland?"["The Practical Significance of Economic Social and Cultural Rights in the Netherlands?"], in: M.K.C. Arambulo, A.P.M. Coomans and B.C.A. Toebes (eds), *De Betekenis*

van Economische, Sociale en Culturele Rechten in de Nederlandse Rechtsorde: Vrijblijvend of Verplichtend?, Leiden: Stichting NJCM-Boekerij, 1998, 10.

42 UNGA Resolution 60/251, 15 March 2006.

43 Marianne Lilliebjerg, "The Universal Periodic Review of the UN Human Rights Council – An NGO Perspective on Opportunities and Shortcomings," *Netherlands Quarterly of Human Rights*, vol. 26 (2008), 311–314 at 311.

44 www.ohchr.org/EN/HRBodies/UPR/Pages/UPRMain.aspx, accessed 27 July 2008; italics supplied.

45 *Dutch NGOs Contribution to the First Universal Periodic Review of the Netherlands by the UN Human Rights Council*, November 2007.The report was submitted on behalf of the following NGOs: Dutch section of the International Commission of Jurists (NJCM), Art. 1, Netwerk VN-Vrouwenverdrag, Dutch CEDAW-Network, Johannes Wier Stichting, Aim for Human Rights, E-Quality, Movisie, International Information Centre and Archives for the Women's Movement, Justice and Peace Netherlands, Defence for Children International Nederland, Stichting Buitenlandse Partner, Vereniging voor Vrouw en Recht Clara Wichmann, Stichting Landelijk Ongedocumenteerden Steunpunt, Stichting LOS.

46 Amnesty International, the International Federation of Action by Christians for the Abolition of Torture and Action by Christians for the Abolition of Torture in the Netherlands, and the Global Initiative to End All Corporal Punishment of Children. See: *Summary Prepared by the Office of the High Commissioner for Human Rights In Accordance with Paragraph 15 © of the Annex to Human Rights Council Resolution 5/1: the Netherlands*, UNGA A/HRC/WG.6/1/NLD/3, 13 March 2008. See also: Amnesty International, *The Netherlands: Submission to the UN Universal Periodic Review*, First Session of the HRC UPR Working Group, AI Index: EUR 35/001/2007, November 2007.

47 See: Tessa Dopheide, "Universal Periodic Review: Het Grote Mensenrechtenexamen van de VN,"["Universal Periodic Review: the Great Human Rights Examination of the UN,"] *NJCM Bulletin*, vol. 33 (2008), 891–901 at 900.

48 The International Commission of Jurists together with its Dutch section (NJCM).

49 See Dopheide, *supra*, note 47.

50 Martha Meijer, "Weblog vanuit Genève," ["Weblog from Geneva"], www.aimforhumanrights.nl/home/weblog-geneve, acccessed 19 June 2008.

51 *Amnesty International Public Statement*, AI Index: IOR 41/009/2008 (Public), 7 April 2008.

52 J. Smith *et al.*, "Globalizing Human Rights: The World of Transnational Human Rights NGOs in the 1990s," *Human Rights Quarterly*, vol. 20 (1998), 379–412 at 389.

53 *Ibid.*, 391.

54 "Nevertheless, more than one-third of all NGOs reported at least some contact with the World Bank and about one-fifth reported contact with the IMF." *Ibid.*, 397.

55 Brigitte Hamm, "FoodFirst Information and Action Network," in: Claude E. Welch, Jr. (ed.), *NGOs and Human Rights: Promise and Performance*, Philadelphia: University of Pennsylvania Press, 2001, 167–181 at 175.

56 *Ibid.*, 176.
57 Nathalie Prouvez and Nicolas M.L. Bovay, "The Role of the International Commission of Jurists," in: Welch, *supra*, note 55, 119–140 at 135.
58 Human Rights Watch World Report 2001, 2; italics supplied.
59 http://hrw.org/wiz2k7/essays/globalization; accessed 10 August 2008.
60 P.R. Baehr, "Amnesty International and its Self-Imposed Limited Mandate," *Netherlands Quarterly of Human Rights*, vol. 12 (1994) 5–21 at 20. See also Hopgood, *supra*, note 2, 210.
61 Morton E. Winston, "Assessing the Effectiveness of International Human Rights NGOs," in: Welch, *supra*, note 55, 25–54 at 47.
62 *Ibid.*
63 Amnesty International, Report 2002, London 2002, 8. This had been preceded the year before, when then Secretary-General Pierre Sané wrote in the foreword to the report for 2001: "Globalisation – the spread to the free market economy, multi-party political systems and technological change – has been accompanied by growing wealth for some, but destitution and despair for many. (...) The new human rights challenges arising from globalisation have stimulated AI to take on new areas of work, namely socio-economic rights and economic actors."
64 *Statute of Amnesty International*, as amended by the 22nd International Council meeting in Ljubljana, Slovenia, 12–29 August 1995.
65 Vienna Declaration and Programme of Action, adopted by the World Conference on Human Rights, on 25 June 1993, UN Doc. A/CONF.157/23. It said also: "All human rights are universal, indivisible and interdependent and interrelated" (par. 5).
66 *Statute of Amnesty International*, as amended by the 27th International Council Meeting, in Morelos, Mexico, 11–17 August 2007, article 1; italics supplied.
67 www.amnesty international.org; accessed 9 August 2008.
68 Cf N.M.C.P. Jägers, *Corporate Human Rights Obligations: In Search of Accountability*, Antwerp: Intersentia, 2002, 9 refers to the "highly publicized cases in the 1990s (...) of *Shell* in Nigeria, *British Petroleum* in Colombia, and *Nike* in, *inter alia*, Indonesia."
69 For a discussion of the term "global civil society", see: Helmut Anheier, Marlies Glasius and Mary Kaldor, *Global Civil Society 2001*, New York: Oxford University Press, 2001, 11 calling it "a fuzzy and contested concept". See also: *Panel of Eminent Persons on United Nations Civil Society Relations ("The Cardozo Report")* (A/58/817), 13 who define "civil society" as follows: "Refers to the associations of citizens (...) entered into voluntarily to advance their interests and ideologies."

Chapter 7 Non-Governmental Entities

1 In a recent article Todd Howland has argued that the resistance movement in El Salvador, FMLN [Farabundo Martin National Liberation Front], that held territory and conducted "foreign relations", could be

considered to have the requisite characteristics to enter into a binding treaty: "What is interesting is that the FMLN was treated as having treaty making powers when they entered into the Peace Accords, but thereafter did not have the same resources available to it as a traditional State when the treaty was violated." (Todd Howland, "How El Rescate, a Small Nongovernmental Organization, Contributed to the Transformation of the Human Rights Situation in El Salvador," *Human Rights Quarterly*, 30 (2008), 703–757 at 710 note 19).

2 Amnesty International, *Somalia: Routinely Targeted: Attacks on Civilians in Somalia*; www.amnesty.org/en/library/asset/AFR52/2008/en; accessed 13 August 2008, 4 ; hereafter "Amnesty Somalia".

3 www.state.gov/g/drl/rls/hrrpt/2007/100504.htm; accessed 13 August 2008; hereafter "State Department 2007".

4 Amnesty Somalia, 6.

5 *Ibid.*, 8; italics supplied.

6 *Ibid.*, 15.

7 *Ibid.*, 24.

8 *Ibid.*, 26.

9 Amnesty Somalia 27; italics supplied.

10 Amnesty Somalia, 31.

11 Human Rights Watch, *The Human Rights Crisis in Somalia: Statement prepared by Human Rights Watch for the "Arria formula" meeting on Somalia*, UN Security Council, 31 March 2008, http://hrw.org/english/docs/2008/03/31/somali18408.htm; accessed 14 August 2008; hereafter "HRW Somalia".

12 HRW Somalia, 2.

13 *Ibid.*, 4.

14 Amnesty International, *Colombia: Submission to the UN Universal Periodic Review: Third Session of the UPR: Working Group of the UN Human Rights Council: 1–15 December 2008*. www.amnesty.org/en/library/asset/AMR23/026/2008/en/f4c5f; hereafter Amnesty Colombia.

15 State Department 2007.

16 Amnesty International Colombia, 14.

17 Human Rights Watch, *Colombia: Events of 2007*, http//:hrw.org/english-wr2k8/docs/2008/01/31/colomb17754.htm; hereafter HRW Colombia.

18 HRW Colombia, 2.

19 Amnesty International, *DR Congo*, 1; www.amnesty.org/en/region/africa/central-africa/dr-congo; accessed 15 August 2008.

20 State Department 2007.

21 Amnesty International, *DR Congo*, 3.

22 Human Rights Watch, *Democratic Republic of Congo. Events of 2007*, 1; http://hrw.org/englishwr2k8/docs/01/31/congo17824.htm; accessed 15 August 2008.

23 Amnesty International, *Annual Report 2008 Spain* 1; italics supplied; http://thereport.amnesty/org/eng/regional/europe-and-central-asia/spain; accessed 15 August 2008.

24 State Department 2007.

25 Amnesty International, *Annual Report, 2008 Spain*, 3.
26 Amnesty International, *Annual Report 2008, Afghanistan*; italics supplied; http://thereport.amnesty.org/eng/region/asia-pacific/afghanistan; accessed 15 August 2008.
27 State Department, 2007.
28 Amnesty International, *Annual Report, Afghanistan*.
29 Amnesty uses this spelling rather than the more common Taliban.
30 www.amnesty.org/en/library/asset/ASA11/001/2007/en/dom; accessed 15 August 2008.
31 *Ibid.*, 31–32.
32 Human Rights Watch, *World Report: Afghanistan Events of 2007*, http://hrw.org/englishwr2k8/docs/2008/01/31/afghani7600.htm; accessed 15 August 2008.
33 http://hrw.org/english/docs/2007/08/01/afghanistan16550_txt.htm; accessed 15 August 2008.
34 http://hrw.org/english/docs/2007/04/16/afghan15688_txt.htm; accessed 15 August 2008.
35 http://hrw.org/campaigns/afghanistan/2006/education/; accessed 15 August 2008.

Chapter 8   Conclusions

1 Peter R. Baehr, *Human Rights: Universality in Practice*, Houndmills, Basingstoke Hampshire: Palgrave, 2001, 131–133.
2 See: William R. Pace, "The Relationship between the International Criminal Court and Non-Governmental Organizations," in: Herman A.M. von Hebel, Johan G. Lammers, Jolien Schukking (eds) *Reflections on the International Criminal Court: Essays in Honour of Adriaan Bos*, The Hague: T.M.C. Asser Press, 1999, 189–211.
3 Sophie C. van Bijsterveld, "Tussen Burger en Internationale Organisatie: NGO's als Vehikel voor Veranderende Internationale Constitutionele Verhoudingen," ["Between the Citizen and International Organisations: NGOs as Vehicles for Changing International Constitutional Relations"] in: C. Flinterman and W. van Genugten (eds), *Niet-statelijke Actoren en de Rechten van de Mens; Gevestigde Waarden, Nieuwe Wegen*, Den Haag: Boom Juridische Uitgevers, 2003, 81–92 at 90.
4 Though, at least within Amnesty International, a claim has recently been made for "measurable change" from and within the organization; see its Integrated Strategic Plan for the period 2004 to 2010. A great deal of attention is currently paid to what is called "impact assessment".
5 "Claude E. Welch Jr., (ed.), *NGOs and Human Rights: Promise and Performance*, Philadelphia: University of Pennsylvania Press, 2001, 2.
6 Menno Kamminga, "What Makes an NGO 'Legitimate' in the Eyes of States?" in Anton Vedder (ed.), *NGO Involvement in International Governance and Policy: Sources of Legitimacy*, Leiden/Boston: Martinus Nijhoff, 2007, 175–195 at 193.

7 "The dropping of rain hollows out a stone."

8 Interview with Bart Stapert, 20 August 2008.

9 According to reliable estimates, in China more legal executions took place than in any other country in the world; at least 5000 according to the Italian human rights organization "Hands Off Cain"; www.handsoff-cain.info/bancadati/index.php?tipotema=arg&i...; accessed 21 August 2008.

10 Personal interview.

List of Interviewed Persons

Kees Bleichrodt , Director University Assistance Fund, 11 August 2008;

Reed Brody, Counsel and Spokesperson Human Rights Watch, 4 September 2008; 24 July 2008;

Cees Flinterman, honorary professor of human rights; member Committee for the Elimination of Discrimination against Women, 4 August 2008;

Lilian Gonçalves, former chair of the Dutch section of Amnesty International, member of its International Executive Committee, 16 September 2008;

Thomas Hammerberg, Commissioner for Human Rights of the Council of Europe and former Secretary-General of Amnesty International, 22 September 2008;

Farah Karimi, General Director Oxfam NOVIB, 8 October 2008;

Gerd Leipold, Executive Director Greenpeace International, 7 October 2008;

Eduard Nazarski, Director Dutch Section Amnesty International, 3 September 2008;

Dick Oosting, Europe Director International Center for Transitional Justice; former director European Office Amnesty International, 25 July 2008;

Bart Stapert, Former chair of the governing board Dutch Section of Amnesty International, 20 August 2008;

Dirk Steen, staff member Dutch section of Amnesty International, 9 September 2008.

Bibliography

Anheier, Helmut, Marlies Glasius and Mary Kaldor, *Global Civil Society 2001*, New York: Oxford University Press, 2001.

Arts, Bas, Math Noortman and Bob Reinalda, *Non-State Actors in International Relations*, Aldershot: Ashgate, 2001.

Aston, Jurij Daniel, "The United Nations Committee on Non-governmental Organizations: Guarding the Entrance to a Politically Divided House," *European Journal of International Law*, vol. 12 (2001), 943–962.

Baehr, Peter R., "Human Rights NGOs and Globalization," in: Karin Arts and Paschal Mihyo (eds), *Responding to the Human Rights Deficit: Essays in Honour of Bas de Gaay Fortman*, The Hague/London/New York: Kluwer Law International, 2003, 31–48.

Baehr, Peter R., "Human Rights Organizations and the United Nations: A Tale of Two Worlds", in: Dimitris Bourantonis and Jarrod Wiener (eds), *The United Nations in the New World Order: The World Organization at Fifty*, Houndmills, Basingstoke: Macmillan, 1995, 170–189.

Baehr, Peter R., "Mobilization of the Conscience of Mankind: Conditions of Effectiveness of Human Rights NGOs," in: Erik Denters and Nico Schrijver (eds), *Reflections on International Law from the Low Countries in Honour of Paul de Waart*, The Hague/Boston/London: Martinus Nijhoff Publishers, 1998, 135–155.

Bell, Christine and Johanna Keenan, "Human Rights Nongovernmental Organizations and the Problems of Transition," *Human Rights Quarterly*, vol. 26 (2004), 330–374.

Bell, Daniel A. and Jean-Marc Coicaud (eds), *Ethics in Action: The Ethical Challenges of International Human Rights Nongovernmental Organizations*, Cambridge: Cambridge University Press, 2007.

Bendell, Jem, *Debating NGO Accountability*, New York and Geneva: United Nations, 2006.

Berg, Esther van den, *The Influence of Domestic NGOs on Dutch Human Rights Policy: Case Studies on South Africa, Namibia, Indonesia and East Timor*, Antwerp/Groningen/Oxford: Intersentia, 2001.

Boven, Theo van, "The Role of Non-Governmental Organisations in International Human Rights Standard-Setting: A Prerequisite of Democracy," in: Fons Coomans, Cees Flinterman, Fred Grünfeld, Ingrid Westendorp and Jan Willems (eds), *Human Rights from Exclusion to Inclusion: Principles and Practices: An Anthology from the Work of Theo van Boven*, The Hague/London/Boston: Kluwer Law International, 2000, 347–361.

Breen, Claire, "The Role of NGOs in the Formulation of and Compliance with the Optional Protocol to the Convention on the Rights of the Child on Involvement of Children in Armed Conflict," *Human Rights Quarterly*, vol. 25 (2003), 453–481.

Brett, Rachel, "Non-Governmental Actors in the Field of Human Rights," in: Raija Hanski and Markku Suski (eds), *An Introduction to the International Protection of Human Rights. A Textbook*, Turku/Åbo: Institute for Human Rights, Åbo Akademi University, 2d. rev. ed., 1999, 399–413.

Brett, Rachel, "The Role and Limits of Human Rights NGOs at the United Nations," *Political Studies*, vol. XLIII (1995), 96–110.

Carey, Henry F. and Oliver P. Richmond (eds), *Mitigating Conflict: The Role of NGOs*, London: Frank Cass, 2003.

Christenson, Gordon A., "World Civil Society and the International Rule of Law," *Human Rights Quarterly*, vol. 19 (1997), 724–737.

Clark, Ann Marie, *Diplomacy of Conscience: Amnesty International and Changing Human Rights Norms*, Princeton: Princeton University Press, 2001.

Clark, Ann Marie, "Non-Governmental Organizations and their Influence on International Society," *Journal of International Affairs*, vol. 48 (1995), 507–525.

Clark, Ann Marie, Elisabeth J. Friedman, and Kathryn Hochstetler, "The Sovereign Limits of Global Civil Society: A Comparison of NGO Participation in UN World Conferences on the Environment, Human Rights and Women," *World Politics*, vol. 51 (1998), 1–35.

Cohen, J.L. and A. Aarato, *Civil Society and Political Theory*, Cambridge Mass.: MIT Press, 1992.

Collingwood, Vivien and Louis Logister, "State of the Art: Addressing the 'NGO Legitimacy Deficit,'" *Political Studies Review*, vol. 3 (2005), 175–192.

Cook, Helena, "Amnesty International at the United Nations," in: Peter Willetts (ed.), *The Conscience of the World: The Influence of Non-Governmental Organisations in the UN System*, Washington D.C.: The Brookings Institution, 1996, 181–213.

Dairiam, Shanthi, "From Global to Local: The Involvement of NGOs," in: Hanna Beate Schöpp-Schilling and Cees Flinterman (eds), *The Circle of Empowerment: Twenty-five Years of the UN Committee on the Elimination of Discrimination Against Women*, New York: The Feminist Press at the City University of New York, 2007, 313–325.

Edwards, M., *NGO Rights and Responsibilities: A New deal for Global Governance*, London: Foreign Policy Centre, 2000.

Glasius, Marlies, *The International Criminal Court: A Global Civil Society Achievement*, London: Routledge, 2006.

Gordenker, Leon, "NGOs and Democratic Process in International Organisations," in: Monique Castermans-Holleman, Fried van Hoof & Jacqueline Smith (eds), *The Role of the Nation-State in the 21st Century, Human Rights, International Organisations and Foreign Policy, Essays in Honour of Peter Baehr*, The Hague/Boston/London: Kluwer Law International, 1998, 277–289.

Grant, Stefanie, "The NGO Role: Implementation, Expanding Protection and Monitoring the Monitors," in: Anne Bayevsky (ed.), *The UN Human Rights Treaty System in the 21st Century*, The Hague: Kluwer Law International, 2000, 209–217.

Hopgood, Stephen, *Keepers of the Flame: Understanding Amnesty International*, Ithaca and London: Cornell University Press, 2006.

Hudock, Ann C., *NGOs and Civil Society: Democracy by Proxy?* Cambridge: Polity Press, 1999.

Joachim, Jutta M., *Agenda Setting, the UN, and NGOs: Gender Violence and Reproductive Rights*, Washington D.C.: Georgetown University Press, 2007.

Josselin, Daphne and William Wallance (eds), *Non-State Actors in World Politics*, Basingstoke: Palgrave, 2001.

Kamminga, Menno T., "The Evolving Status of NGOs under International Law: A Threat to the Inter-State System?" in: Philip Alston (ed.), *Non-State Actors and Human Rights*, Oxford: Oxford University Press, 2005, 93–111.

Keck, Margaret E. and Kathryn Sikkink, *Activists Beyond Borders: Advocacy Networks in International Politics*, Ithaca and London: Cornell University Press, 1998.

Korey, William, *NGOs and the Universal Declaration of Human Rights: "A Curious Grapevine,"* New York: St. Martin's Press, 1998.

Landman, Todd and Meghna Abaraham, *Evaluation of Nine Non-Governmental Human Rights Organisations*, The Hague: IOB, 2004.

Lindblom, Anna-Karin, *Non-governmental Organizations in International Law*, Cambridge etc.: Cambridge University Press, 2005.

Løvald, Johan and Rezlan Ishar Jenie, *United Nations: The Relationship between Member-States and Civil Society, Including Non-Governmental Organizations*, Report to the President of the 60th General Assembly, 5 July 2006.

Martens, Kerstin, "An Appraisal of Amnesty International's Work at the United Nations: Established Areas of Activities and Shifting Priorities since the 1990s," *Human Rights Quarterly*, vol. 26 (November 2004), 1050–1070.

Martens, Kerstin, "NGO Participation at International Conferences: Assessing Theoretical Accounts," *Transnational Associations*, vol. 3 (2000), 115–126.

Mutua, Makau, "Standard Setting in Human Rights: Critique and Prognosis," *Human Rights Quarterly*, vol. 29 (2007), 547–630.

Nader, Lucia, "The Role of NGOs in the UN Human Rights Council," *SUR International Journal on Human Rights*, vol. 4 (2007), 7–27.

Nowak, Manfred (ed.), *World Conference on Human Rights, Vienna, June 1993: The Contribution of NGOs Reports and Documents*, Wien: Manzsche Verlags- und Universitätsbuchhandlung, 1994.

Otto, Dianne, "Nongovernmental Organizations in the United Nations System: The Emerging Role of International Civil Society," *Human Rights Quarterly*, vol. 18 (1996), 107–141.

Pace, William R., "The Relationship between the International Criminal Court and Non-governmental Organizations," in: Herman A.M. von Hebel, Johan G. Lammers and Jolien Schukking (eds), *Reflections on the International Criminal Court: Essays in Honour of Adriaan Bos*, The Hague: T.M.C. Asser Press, 1999, 189–211.

Pace, William R. and Mark Thieroff, "Participation of Non-Governmental Organizations," in: Roy S. Lee (ed.), *The International Criminal Court: The Making of the Rome Statute*, The Hague: Kluwer Law International, 1999, 391–398.

Risse, Transnational Actors and World Politics, in: W. Carlsnaes, T. Risse and B.A. Simmons (eds), *Handbook of International Relations*, London: Sage 2002, 255–274.

Roth, Kenneth, "Defending Economic, Social and Cultural Rights: Practical Issues Faced by an International Human Rights Organization," *Human Rights Quarterly*, vol. 26 (2004), 63–73.

Scholte, Jan Aart, "Civil Society and Democracy in Global Governance," *CSGR Working Paper* No. 65/01 (January 2001).

Scholte, Jan Aart, "Civil Society and Democratically Accountable Global Governance," *Government and Opposition*, vol. 39 (2004), 211–233.

Slim, Hugo, "By What Authority? The Legitimacy and Accountability of Non-Governmental Organisations," The International Council on Human Rights Policy, International Meeting on Global Trends and Human Rights, Before and After September 11th, Geneva, January 10–12, 2002.

Smith, Jackie and Ron Pagnucco with George A. Lopez, "Globalizing Human Rights: The Work of Transnational Human Rights NGOs in the 1990s," *Human Rights Quarterly*, vol. 20 (1998), 379–412.

Steiner, Henry J. and Philip Alston, *International Human Rights in Context: Law, Politics, Morals*, Oxford: Oxford University Press, 2nd ed., 2000.

Tolley, Howard B. Jr., *The International Commission of Jurists: Global Advocates for Human Rights*, Philadelphia: University of Pennsylvania Press, 1994.

Vedder, Anton (ed.), *NGO Involvement in International Governance and Policy: Sources of Legitimacy*, Leiden/Boston: Martinus Nijhoff, 2007.

Warkentin, Craig, *Reshaping World Politics: NGOs, the Internet and Global Civil Society*, Oxford: Rowman and Littlefield, 2001.

Weiss, Thomas and Leon Gordenker (eds), *NGOs, the UN and Global Governance*, Boulder/London: Lynne Rienner, 1996.

Welch, Claude E. Jr. (ed.), *NGOs and Human Rights: Promise and Performance*, Philadelphia: University of Pennsylvania Press, 2001.

We the Peoples: Civil Society, the United Nations and Global Governance. Report of the Panel of Eminent Persons on United Nations-Civil Society Relations ["Cardozo Report"] UNGA, United Nations General Assembly, A/58/817, 11 June 2004.

Willetts, Peter (ed.), *"The Conscience of the World": The Influence of Non-Governmental Organisations in the UN System*, London: Hurst and Company, 1996.

Willetts, Peter, "From 'Consultative Arrangements' to 'Partnership': The Changing Status of NGOs in Diplomacy at the UN," *Global Governance*, vol. 6 (2000), 191–213.

Willetts, Peter, "What Is Non-Governmental Organization?", *UNESCO Encyclopaedia Of Life Support Systems*, 2002.

Wiseberg, Laurie S., "Protecting Human Rights Activists and NGOs: What More Can Be Done?", *Human Rights Quarterly*, vol. 13 (1991), 525–544.

Zafarullah, Habib and Mohammad Habibur Rahman, "Human Rights, Civil Society and Nongovernmental Organizations: The Nexus in Bangladesh," *Human Rights Quarterly*, vol. 24 (2002), 1011–1034.

Index